MACMILLAN HISTORY OF LITERATURE

General Editor: A. NORMAN JEFFARES

MACMILLAN HISTORY OF LITERATURE

EIGHTEENTH-CENTURY ENGLISH LITERATURE

Maximillian E. Novak

M

First published 1983 by
THE MACMILLAN PRESS LTD
Companies and representatives
throughout the world

ISBN 0 333 26913 6 (hc)
ISBN 0 333 26914 4 (pbk)

Typeset by
Wessex Typesetters Ltd
Frome, Somerset
Printed in Hong Kong

Contents

List of Plates

17. St. Martins in the Fields, London. Built by James Gibbs between 1722 and 1726, who was strongly influenced by Sir Christopher Wren and by Italian architects. This church is widely regarded as Gibbs' masterpiece. Courtesy: British Tourist Authority.

18. The Royal Crescent, Bath, built by John Wood between 1761 and 1765. Wood invented the concave row of houses.

19. Lloyd's Coffee House, 1798. Courtesy: The Mansell Collection.

Editor's Preface

THE study of literature requires knowledge of contexts as well as texts. What kind of person wrote the poem, the play, the novel, the essay? What forces acted upon them as they wrote? What was the historical, the political, the philosophical, the economic, the cultural background? Was the writer accepting or rejecting the literary conventions of the time, or developing them or creating entirely new kinds of literary expression? Are there interactions between literature and the art, music or architecture of its period? Was the writer affected by contemporaries or isolated?

Such questions stress the need for students to go beyond the reading of set texts, to extend their knowledge by developing a sense of chronology, or action and reaction, and of the varying relationships between writers and society.

Histories of literature can encourage students to make comparisons, can aid in understanding the purposes of individual authors and in assessing the totality of their achievements. Their development can be better understood and appreciated with some knowledge of the background of their time. And histories of literature, apart from their valuable function as reference books, can demonstrate the great wealth of writing in English that is there to be enjoyed. They can guide the reader who wishes to explore it more fully and to gain in the process deeper insights into the rich diversity not only of literature but of human life itself.

A. NORMAN JEFFARES

1
Transitions

MANY historians prefer to ignore the existence of centuries in order to focus on other periods of time that seem neater or more amenable to some particular theory of history. One art historian, treating the period from the beginning of the eighteenth century to the French Revolution, argues that the age began in a muddle and ended in a revolution. But from the standpoint of British history, literary as well as social and political, a picture of the entire century has its attractions. By 1700, the general political and economic configurations of the revolution of 1688 looked as if they would hold. And hold they did through two genuine invasions that attempted to restore the family of James II to the throne and a fairly surprising number of abortive plots and plans for invasions that never came off. Sir Walter Scott (1771–1832) is the best literary source for these events, and in *The Antiquary,* the action of which takes place at the end of the century, he presents a picture of almost everyone in the novel, rich and poor, Whig and Tory, together on the beach as a united people, waiting to repel an expected invasion of Bonaparte's French army. If this is part of Scott's historical myth, it is nevertheless a myth that has much to commend it as an image of reality.

From a literary standpoint, the most fascinating aspect of these hundred years is that almost everything that was to emerge at the end of the century was present at the beginning. It is a wonderful period to examine from the standpoint of literary ideals in conflict, and rather than examining it with hindsight, as a period culminating in the nineteenth century (a view highly endorsed by the nineteenth century), I want to see it in dialectical terms. During this century literary forms once regarded as crude, like the novel, came into the highest fashion, while genres such as the epic and tragedy tended to take second place. It was an age of contradictions. Taught by Dryden during the Restoration to appreciate literary periods and changes, it was an age intensely aware of those contradictions.

I Unresolved Issues

The first year of the new century presents a good example of these forces in conflict as well as some clear endings of the old century. Dryden died in 1700 but not before writing *The Secular Masque* in which he wrote the obituary for the Restoration. Lamenting the prevailing self-interest and deception that were both a philosophic stance and a mode of life during those years, Dryden wrote:

> All, all of a piece throughout;
> Thy chase had a beast in view;
> Thy wars brought nothing about;
> Thy lovers were all untrue.
> 'Tis well an old age is out
> And time to begin a new.

Dryden was also to bring out his *Fables* in that year. Written in heroic couplets, this seemingly miscellaneous collection of translations from Chaucer, Boccaccio, Ovid and Homer mixed in with an original dedicatory poem, the brilliant poetic essay on the life of the ideal English country gentleman, 'To My Honor'd Kinsman, John Dryden of Chesterton', and prefaced by one of Dryden's best critical essays, gave new directions to the coming century. Dryden's translations were actually closer to 'imitations', in the sense of that time, that is, the poet felt at liberty to interpret the original in such a manner as to leave great freedom for inventiveness and the writing of what was often a separate poem. (Although Geoffrey Chaucer (c. 1340–1400) was commonly regarded as the father of English poetry, his language was considered too archaic for the comprehension of most readers. Dryden thought he was as much in need of 'translation' for the audience of 1700 as Italian, Roman and Greek writers. Chaucer's verse was considered rough and primitive and not until the edition of Thomas Tyrwhit (1730–86), published between 1775 and 1778, was his poetic skill argued with some force.)

Dryden belongs properly to the previous century, but his

stance in these poems was extremely significant. By 1700 he might be described as a Tory whose Jacobite leanings had already moved into the realm of nostalgia rather than hope of political actions. No longer Laureate and living under a King whom he regarded as a usurper, Dryden used his translations in such a way as to convey his political message, not as he had done earlier when writing in support of the government in power in 'The Medal', by direct attack, but in a subtle fashion through innuendo in given lines and through clever narrative parallels with the present political situation. Dryden did not wish to bring down the vengeance of the government on himself but he did want to make his point as he had been doing since James II fled the country, throwing the seal of England into the Thames and leaving the country to be governed by William III, whom many English called with contempt, Hogen Mogen, a popular corruption of a Dutch word meaning high and mighty. 'To My Honor'd Kinsman' is a direct glorification of the Parliament man who draws his strength from the English soil and supports the English law. But the other poetry exists in a form of disguise – on the surface a translation, underneath, a libellous attack on the government. The philosopher Shaftesbury, (1671–1713) who was writing at this time, was to argue that the spirit of repression was responsible for the rise of wit and irony, because it forced the writer to conceal his arguments by indirection. Dryden's method, as practised in *The Fables,* was to become the major poetical method of the first decade of the century.

Another significant event of 1700 was the performance of Congreve's (1670–1729) *The Way of the World*. It was Congreve's last comedy and the last of the truly brilliant, witty plays that made the Restoration England's great age of comedy. Other writers continued writing in the mode that Vanbrugh, Southerne and Congreve brought to perfection during the 1690s, but in the chilly atmosphere that had settled on the stage since Jeremy Collier's attack, 'A Short View of the Immorality, and Profaneness of the English Stage' (1698), this type of comedy could not flourish. Collier's attack coincided with the rise of the Societies for Reformation of Manners which actually published black lists of offenders against public decency. They had official sanction from the court; magistrates actually harassed actors into cleaning up the old comedies. The great ideal of the Restoration had been wit. But wit had gradually become associated with licence, and it seemed impossible to create a witty character who was not in some way a purveyor of obscene ideas and sexual innuendoes. Richard Blackmore's (1655–1729) *Satyr Against Wit,* published in 1700, was typical of the new movement that placed morality above cleverness and argued that the wit typical of the Restoration was essentially anti-social.

Congreve's heroine, Millamant, has lived in the city and read 'filthy plays' that have taught her much about the ways of the world. On the other hand, Mrs Fainall, whose mother, Lady Wishfort, is an ardent reader of moral tracts like those of Collier's, has been brought up away from men and in total ignorance. She has found some happiness in an affair with the protagonist Mirabell, but she is married to the villainous Fainall, who almost destroys the happiness of everyone by threatening to expose his wife's affair before the law courts. In the end, Mirabell and Millamant, after much dispute over the possibility of happiness in marriage, agree to marry, and Fainall is defeated. But if Congreve attempted to vindicate the role of sophisticated literature in teaching people about the way of the world and if he still presented a protagonist whose moral standards were not very different from those of earlier Restoration wits, it was done with a distinct sense of a parting shot. *The Way of the World* was one of those plays of Congreve in which the wit was so complex that the audience often had delayed reactions, laughing long after the lines had been spoken. No one was to attempt that kind of complex wit on the stage during the rest of the century.

The Way of the World was Congreve's first comedy in four years, and during that time comedy had begun to change. In 1696, Colley Cibber (1671–1757) had writen *Love's Last Shift,* a comedy in which the heroine, Amanda, is a woman of perfect fidelity who reforms her long-strayed husband by her virtue. In the following year, Vanbrugh (1664–1726) showed the ambiguity of Cibber's moral stance in *The Relapse,* but it was the rather clumsy and inartistic Cibber who was the playwright of the future. Congreve complained that the lines delivered by Cibber's comic characters only 'seemed' like wit. The entire style of the language had changed. It had become simple and direct. And even a relatively witty playwright like George

Farquhar, (1678–1707) whose *Recruiting Officer* (1706) and *Beaux' Stratagem* (1707) preserve that close analysis of human motivation that was the province of Restoration Comedy, wrote in a comic style that was far removed from the complexities of an Etherege or Wycherley.

II The new sensibility

By 1705 the triumph of the new comic style was almost complete. In that year, Cibber produced *The Careless Husband,* and a new writer, Sir Richard Steele, (1672–1729) *The Tender Husband.* Cibber's play was 'sentimental' in the sense that it presented unexamined emotions for the approbation of the audience. The husband of Cibber's play uses his maid as his mistress and is so struck by the tact of his wife in communicating her knowledge of the situation that he reforms entirely. Steele, as in his earlier comedy, *The Funeral* (1702), mingled low comedy with his moral scenes, but all his comedies had scenes of weeping well suited to the new mode of reform. In *The Tender Husband,* the wife, Mrs Clerimont, kneels before her husband in tears and begs his forgiveness after he has shown her the danger of what an affair might bring. He raises her:

> Then kneel, and weep no more – my Fairest – my
> Reconcil'd! – Be so in a Moment, for know I cannot
> (without wringing my own Heart) give you the least
> Compunction – Be in Humour – it shall be your own Fault,
> if ever there's a serious Word more in this Subject.
> MRS CLERIMONT: I must correct every Idea that rises
> in my mind, and learn every Gesture of my Body a-new – I
> detest the thing I was.

More will be said about sentimental literature when we come to Steele's other comedies and to Sterne; there is a strong sentimental vein in the literature of sensibility that came over to England in French romances and novels. In the much-read romances, this kind of sensibility involved love between heroic princes and princesses. But as the romances were replaced by 'novels' concerned with members of the nobility and occasionally with people who in England would have been called the gentry, the emotions of such works broadened as well. With Cibber and Steele, the tender emotions are exploited for members of the middle class, and there is a deliberate use of scenes that will raise tears, including those between father and sons. A heroine in the romances might not go to bed without a satisfying 'diet of tears', and this was to become more and more true of ordinary heroines in English literature.

Poetry too was going through a period of sensibility. Poems such as William Congreve's 'To Cynthia Weeping and Not Speaking' and Matthew Prior's (1664–1721) 'To Cloe Weeping' belong to a body of poetry that combined sensuality and sensibility into a mode that, as it developed during the century, became identifiable as Rococo art. Congreve specialised in such poetry, his reputation as a poet was high in the first two decades of the eighteenth century, and the kind of poetry he wrote was significant. His brief and cynical poems on women were the last flowering of the Restoration lyric that had been raised to perfection by the Earl of Rochester (1647–80). That was a dead end, but his translations of Horace's *Odes* were widely admired and were part of a general effort at doing the *Odes* into English. Congreve also wrote in a form that was soon to be rejected by the age as awkward and artificial – the irregular pindaric ode. The best known were those addressed to the King and Queen, particularly his *Ode* on William III's victory at Namur. Such a poem was essentially political in nature, and belonged to the extraordinarily popular type of poetry – that on 'state affairs' – to be considered in the next section.

III   Politics and art

The series of *Poems on Affairs of State* that first appeared around 1697 brought together the political poetry of the reigns of Charles II and James II. Much of this poetry had existed only in manuscript before this publication, and the sudden appearance of a mass of extremely clever, satirical verse had an enormous impact on the poetry of the coming century. Volumes continued to appear in the first decade of the century as poets inspired by the political poetry of a newly discovered past began to try their hand at this genre during the brief period after the lapse of the licensing act, when there was a general freedom of the press. The early masters of political satire, Andrew Marvell (1621–78) and Dryden, were dead, but poets like Daniel Defoe (1660–1731), inspired by the wits of the Restoration, were quick to write their own imitation of this verse for their age.

Most of these poems were in pentameter couplets. The odes that had been so popular during the Restoration were to be satirised as an attempt at false sublimity, but the solid couplets of the majority of the *Poems on Affairs of State* seemed the proper vehicle for the type of statement about society that the new century wanted. Defoe's 'True-born Englishman' (1701) drew upon this tradition in attacking the xenophobia that had raised attacks on William and on those Dutchmen on whom he had attempted to bestow favours. Though occasionally awkward in the technical aspects of poetry, this popular poem achieved one of the ideals of poetry of this type. It could be witty, and even adept at times, but its object was that of all good political poetry – to persuade. It was a weapon of propaganda. Defoe depicted the reign of Charles II and his followers with an irony that had its subtleties while being available to anyone in the audience who could read or be read to:

> The Civil Wars, the common Purgative,
> Which always use to make the Nation thrive,
> Made way for all that Strolling Congregation,
> Which throng'd in Pious *Charles's* Restoration.
> The *Royal Refugee* our Breed restores,
> With *Foreign Courtiers,* and with *Foreign Whores:*
> And carefully repeopled us again,
> Throughout his Lazy, Long, Lascivious Reign.

Although the last line might be selected as an example of good alliteration and metrical effects that attempt to capture the sense of how excruciatingly long it took to get rid of him, the best effects come from the irony. At a time when the High Church still regarded the civil wars as an era when the terrible act of regicide – an act against God – was committed, Defoe dismisses them as typical of the way nations struggle toward better government. And since that period was one of religious conflict, Charles's court is depicted as a 'Congregation',

though history has preserved the image of their loose sexual
morals. 'Pious' is an epithet seldom applied to Charles II, but
then, no one ever used the term 'Refugee' to describe the
person who was considered to have assumed the throne after
the beheading of his father. The juxtaposition of *'Foreign
Courtiers'* and *'Foreign Whores'* suggests their similarity, not
merely in their sexual lives but in their willingness to do
anything for money.

The *Poems on Affairs of State* also gave to the poets of the age
of Queen Anne a medium that was capable of moving large
segments of the population to action. A ballad such as *Lilli-
Burlero* inspired contempt in the forces of William III for the
Irish they were to fight and defeat, and works like 'The True-
born Englishman' or Jonathan Swift's (1667–1745) political
ballads could cast the careers of individuals into doubt and
weaken entire ministries. It was a time when writers could feel
the pulse of the mob and send them out into the streets. Seldom
has poetry had such an effect or poets so much power. And
seldom have poets been so politically and socially involved.
Samuel Garth's (1661–1719) 'The Dispensary', published a
year before the century's end, used the model of the mock epic
established by Boileau (1636–1711) in *Le Lutrin* (1679), to
satirise the war between the doctors and apothecaries over
dispensing medicines. Garth's poem with its gently mocking
tone set the pattern of polite satire during the first half of the
century. Even more questionable as a subject of epic treatment
would be the starving poet of John Philips's (1676–1709) 'The
Splendid Shilling' (1701). With his eye on Virgil and Milton,
Philips parodied the epic conventions of inversion and the
attempt at the sublime by picturing a common event of an
ordinary day. In such a poem, a realistic technique and
accurate description is allowed to lower the raised tone of the
poetic rhetoric appropriate to the epic. The result is not
burlesque but a peculiarly Augustan balance between the
absurd and the serious.

IV   Building retreats and cultivating gardens

'All the world are running Mad after Building', wrote Sir John
Vanbrugh at the beginning of the eighteenth century, and that

statement would have been true enough at the century's end when the estate owner who had ruined himself and his family through his 'improvements' was a common figure in the novels of the time. Vanbrugh was reflecting on an interest that involved both social and artistic ideals. Building the ideal city was a concern that produced the remarkable geometrical designs of Claude-Nicholas Ledoux (1736–1806) and Étienne-Louis Boullée (1728–99) in France, and in England the ideals of eighteenth-century urban building may be seen in the plan of its most popular scene of amusement – Bath. There John Wood (1704–54) conceived of an entire city constructed along lines of beauty and utility. He was responsible for the Royal Forum and the general effect of turning a series of town houses into a unified structure that presented the visual effect of a single palace. His son, John Wood the younger (1728–82), added to the designs of his father with the magnificent Royal Crescent, and the great British architect of the close of the century, Robert Adam (1728–92), designed the graceful Pulteney Bridge. Although John Wood never managed to have his entire plan followed, Bath still remains a wonderful example of what the eighteenth century wanted in architecture – a blend of grace and beauty and an odd combination of exuberance and restraint, and even that streak of vulgarity in present-day Bath had its counterpart in our period.

Bath had its amusements then as now, but visitors often reported their relief at returning to the pleasures of their private homes. It was the retreat to the country estate that inspired much of the art of the period, and the thought and feeling about such a move is encapsulated in a poem published in 1700, one of the most popular poems of the century, 'The Choice' by John Pomfret (1667–1702). To explain that popularity it is necessary to look beyond any aesthetic value in the poem. Samuel Johnson (1709–84), in his 'Life of Pomfret', resigned himself to the judgement that 'he who pleases many must have some species of merit'.

Although the eighteenth century was an age of political turmoil, there was a substantial body of people who opted out of politics. They included people from the entire political spectrum – Jacobites who felt no loyalty to a government sprung from an unlawful line, as well as Whiggish idealists who believed that any contact with government would result in contamination. Although the Whigs were hardly an organised political party in the modern sense and although the idea of political parties had few defenders before 1715, those who opposed the power of the court, believed in religious toleration, and held that Englishmen had inalienable rights under the law may be classified as Whigs. After the Tories had accepted most of the ideals of the Revolution of 1688, they shared many ideas with the Whigs, especially since they were not sympathetic toward the Hanoverian monarchy, but they tended to distrust commerce, to be sceptical about notions of 'liberty' and to be ardent supporters of the Church of England. The metaphorical garden that Candide decided to cultivate as he let the world go by, was started many years before by the English country gentlemen. (In *Candide* (1759), a satirical work of fiction by Francois-Marie Arouet de Voltaire (1694–1778), the hero and his friends, after a series of remarkable and often disastrous adventures, find themselves in possession of a small estate where they arrive at a degree of contentment by avoiding the passionate involvements of the world.) Pomfret's uncomplicated picture of isolation in a country house with books and a few choice friends seemed the best kind of life to many of his readers:

> Near some fair town, I'd have a private seat,
> Built uniform, not little, nor too great:
> Better, if on a rising ground it stood;
> Fields on this side, on that a neighbouring wood.
> It should within no other things contain,
> But what were useful, necessary, plain.

The ideal of the country estate as the centre of the truly happy life occupied the entire century. Pomfret's challenge at the end of his poem, 'All Men wou'd wish to Live, and Dye like me', found an echo in many a breast, and there were few nature poems that did not have their section dealing with the retirement of the good man in the country. It was often to the Roman poet Horace (65–8 B.C.) that British poets appealed as their model, but Pomfret's version of the 'happy man' theme was never far from their thoughts.

This attempt to build an ideal retreat left what are some of the most visible aspects of the eighteenth century to modern eyes and to some extent the most vivid. The visual experience was prized above all others by contemporary thinkers, and the pleasure they experienced in their buildings and gardens is still available to us. A trip to Hampstead's Kenwood House, where exhibitions of eighteenth-century painting have been held in recent years, or to Chiswick House in Middlesex, built between 1715 and 1725 by Richard Boyle, third Earl of Burlington (1694–1753) may supply a better sense of some of the aesthetic ideals of the period than reading the poetry. A visit to Blenheim Palace in Woodstock, just outside Oxford, with its buildings started in the first decade of the century by John Vanbrugh and its landscaping done by Lancelot ('Capability') Brown (1715–73) after the middle of the century may provide a better lesson in the history of taste than any number of books on this subject. And since many of the great estates of the time were made possible by enclosure acts that consolidated large estates for the wealthy and drove the rural poor to the cities and to emigration, no other area of artistic creation makes the relationship between politics and art so apparent.

Vanbrugh's decision to abandon the use of language in the theatre for the mastery of architectural mass and space must seem regrettable to any admirer of Restoration comedy, but it was a significant gesture. The rewards of patronage for the builder seemed more secure than anything that could be gained from the theatre after the 'Collier Controversy'. Vanbrugh's best work as an architect came with the plans for Castle Howard in Yorkshire starting in 1700 and with the work on Blenheim Palace, the gift of a grateful nation to John Churchill, Duke of Marlborough (1650–1722), after his victory over the forces of Louis XIV on the banks of the Danube in 1704. It might have been expected that Vanbrugh would have followed what was the great architectural ideal of the time, that established by Andrea Palladio (1518–80), who claimed to be following the rules set forth by the Roman Architect, Vitruvius (*fl.* first century B.C.). Vanbrugh was thoroughly familiar with Pallidio's work, but he and his assistant, Nicholas Hawksmoor (1661–1736), followed a different path. Both Castle Howard and Blenheim are remote enough from the classical forms advocated by Palladio; they are rather examples of what has been called English Baroque. Both are magnificent, domed buildings, better for viewing than for comfortable living. To that extent they represent the theatrical ideals of the baroque which had its association with a political state that was omnipotent and seemingly permanent.

Such buildings gave way to a number of styles, but the ideal of the villa, a house that was more modest, private and practical, gradually won over the grand palace. And it was Palladio's concepts that formed the basis for most of these buildings. When Colin Campbell (1676–1729) published his *Vitruvius Britannicus* (1715–25), he proclaimed that Palladio ought to be followed because he had 'arrived at a *Ne plus ultra* of his Art'. What was most desirable, he argued, was 'Antique Simplicity', grace and symmetry. In the hands of the best architects of the times the villa became a building of simple but symmetrical exteriors with interiors that reflected classical taste. And surrounding these buildings were no longer the formal Dutch-French gardens of the seventeenth century with their geometric patterns and trees in pots but a landscape which reflected an ordered yet natural scene. Even before the beginning of the eighteenth century, Sir William Temple (1628–99) had written in praise of the 'Sharawadgi' in Chinese gardens, a form that aimed at irregularity, and as the century progressed there was a gradual movement toward a concept of nature that included a sense of randomness. Gardeners began putting more and more stress on winding paths and irregular patches of trees. The entire effect was known as the 'English Garden' and its influence spread to the continent. Eventually gardening came to be considered a major art form.

Even before 'Capability' Brown began changing the landscapes of estates throughout Great Britain, garden architects such as Stephen Switzer (1682–1745) and Charles Bridgeman (d. 1738) had gained major reputations through their work, and Pope's garden at Twickenham, the gardens at Stowe and the Leasowes became the subjects of essays and books. One principle that revolutionised gardening after it was employed by Bridgeman was that of the ha-ha, the method of placing fences in broad ditches, thereby opening out the view from the house to extend to the entire countryside. Without a fence to impede the view, a more natural and expansive scene was open to the eye, but the gardens themselves were filled with human artefacts – temples, ruins and even an occasional Chinese pagoda. Even Brown's more 'natural' landscapes had a standard hermit's cell as well as Gothic and Roman ruins. As in the paintings of landscape that the age most admired, there was always a sign of human activity or human figures. Not until the end of the century when writers like Sir Uvedale Price (1747–1829), Richard Payne Knight (1750–1824) and William Gilpin (1724–1804) advanced a theory of the 'picturesque' landscape did the natural tend to overwhelm the human, but even then, Brown's ideals had a strong defender in Humphrey Repton (1752–1818), who kept the human habitation at the heart of the landscape. Pride in these estates led to a popular form of architectural painting, and Arthur Devis (1711–87) posed his family portraits as garden conversation pieces with the family estate placed firmly in the background as vivid and human as any of the living figures.

V   The Georgic tradition

If Promfret's 'The Choice' was to be symptomatic of one aspect of the century's art, so was another work published in 1700, Nahum Tate's (1652–1715) 'Panacea; A Poem upon Tea'. Though neither famous nor terribly interesting in itself, its title and to some extent its subject matter were typical of the rash of poems produced throughout the century on similar subjects: John Philips's 'Cyder' (1709), John Gay's (1685–1732) 'Rural Sports' (1713) and 'The Fan' (1714), and James Grainger's (c. 1721–66) 'Sugar Cane' (1764). Such poems were, loosely speaking, in the tradition of Virgil's *Georgics* and attempt to inform the reader about some aspect of contemporary life while entertaining him. The subjects chosen were often, like the furnishings of Pomfret's house, 'Useful, Necessary, plain'. It would be unfair to group all these poems together without suggesting that Tate's poem gives very little information about kinds of tea or its growing and that Gay deliberately selects aspects of life that have elements of play. But there was a strong ingredient of utilitarianism in the century, and poems that could at once please and teach were greatly admired.

In some ways Tate's poem is not in this tradition at all. With its fiction of the origin of tea in China, it is rather a typical example of rococo art. Tea appears as a plant and beverage after a period of great luxury and disorder is ended with a revolution. The revolution does not solve the nation's problems, since the people are still plagued by the diseases brought on by luxury. When they go to consult Confucius, they find tea plants growing outside his cell, and by those plants and their delicious liquid, everyone is cured. Tate's poem brings us around to the image of the end of the last century and the start of the new. The political allegory hints at the return of energy and the retreat from sexual licence – a prediction that was true enough of the early eighteenth century. Certainly there was not to be the peace in politics that Tate foresaw, but there was something to be said for the new Whig vision of progress that is suggested. Then the use of a Chinese fable suggests something about the new cosmopolitanism of England. The attempt to imitate the 'Refin'd and Civiliz'd *Chinese*' in their tea drinking was part of a larger effort to round off the edges of English society and replace the dissent of the seventeenth century with a period of culture and politeness. If the aim of the Societies for Reformation of Manners was essentially directed at external behaviour, behind their actions there was some thought that external manners might eventually reform the inner person. Finally, a society involved in drinking tea, whatever the medicinal virtues of that drink, was oriented toward the company of cultivated men and women, and if the old Restoration comedy that depicted the predatory rake chasing the wenches was no more a true picture of that time than the image of the ladies drinking tea and gossiping was true of the eighteenth century, still the relative refinement of the latter image was not so far from some of the aims of the time.

In the second canto of Tate's poem, the Olympian goddesses compete to be the patroness of tea. Minerva claims it is the inspiration of poems, heroes and men of learning. Venus claims it for beauty in a passage that clearly foreshadows some of Alexander Pope's (1688–1744) methods in 'The Rape of the Lock':

> See there how grateful *Tea,* their choice Delight,
> Its gen'rous Patronesses does requite!
> Sublimes their Native Charmes; and makes 'em shine
> As bright, almost, as lasting too as mine.
> Who then but Beauty's Goddess, can pretend
> A Title to the Plant that's Beauty's Friend?

Diana claims it as the drink that preserves virtue, Thetis daughter of Neptune, claims it for commerce while Health and the goddess of sleep and dreams put in their claims. It is kept separate from all, yet it embodies all the virtues of that age, including its fantasies and dreams.

One final comment on transitions should include the histories, memoirs and collections of pamphlets from the seventeenth century that appeared during the eighteenth. The great *History of the Rebellion* by Edward Hyde, Earl of Clarendon (1609–74) was not published until 1702–04; Gilbert Burnet's (1643–1715) *History of My Own Times,* containing a wealth of information about the reigns of Charles II and James II, was not published until 1723–34; and the impressive *Character of Charles II* by George Savile, Marquis of Halifax (1633–95) did not appear until 1750. And in 1744 the great collection of seventeenth- and eighteenth-century tracts, *The Harleian Miscellany,* provided a vivid record of the controversies that created the two great revolutions of the seventeenth century. The result was a consciousness of historical connections. Writers of the eighteenth century felt a sense of continuity with the past from 1642 until their own time. If they rejected many of the ideals of the Restoration they knew or thought they knew what they were rejecting.

2
The age of disguise

'IT is very hard, under all these Masks to see the true Countenance of any Man', Defoe complained in one of his pamphlets. The age of Queen Anne and the decades that followed were distinguished not merely by a mass of anonymous pamphlets, newspapers and lampoons but by works in which the writer assumed a personality or mask and wrote through that stated point of view. It is hardly surprising that the period that began with a women's and men's fashion of masking and disguise became fascinated with the public masquerade at which, for an evening, any ticket purchaser could assume what identity he or she pleased. Few controversial works were published with the name of the writer on the title page, and in an age of lampoon and satire, controversy was everywhere. We are fairly accustomed to reading newspapers with unsigned editorials and accounts of the day's events, but the early modern form of newspaper was a relatively new literary phenomenon at this time.

I The new satire

Part of the cause for this interest in anonymous material may go back to the 1690s and the free publication and republication of so many poems and pamphlets that had been written anonymously for protection. A more complex reason may be found in Locke's investigation of identity and his conclusion that, aside from our bodily appearance, we only know who we are by remembering our identity moment by moment. The possibilities inherent in the exploitation of an unusual persona were grasped by a number of writers. From about 1696 to perhaps as late as 1699, Jonathan Swift (1667–1745) worked on his *Tale of a Tub,* which, along with *The Battle of the Books* and

A Discourse on the Mechanical Operation of the Spirit, were published without Swift's knowledge in 1704. The narrator of *Tale of a Tub* is a writer recently released from the mad-house and suffering from the perils of unsuccessful authorship in the form of biting poverty. His madness seems enhanced by the materials he has to treat – an account of modern writing and criticism and a fable about three brothers that has an obvious application to the history of the Christian Churches, subjects that in their display of man's irrational behaviour might well drive anyone insane.

The narrator is a product of his time. Indeed he has an insane cheerfulness about the products of his contemporaries and feels that greatness is only a momentary thing achieved by the most recent work which, in its turn, will be consigned to oblivion. Novelty and an originality purchased at any cost is what makes for excellence in his eyes, and he declares his book to be the best ever until it too will be swallowed in the gulf of time. Like modern man, he lives in the present without any real sense of the continuity of human life or the importance of its past achievements. He has been reared in an age of system builders such as Descartes, Hobbes and Locke. René Descartes (1596–1650), working from doubts about how we know anything with certainty, began from the proposition of the thinker's awareness of his act of cogitation, and from the statement 'I think, therefore I am', built a system of knowledge. Thomas Hobbes (1588–1679) argued that the world, as we know it, operates by material, not spiritual, causes. John Locke (1632–1704) maintained that there were no innate ideas and that everything we know exists as 'Ideas' in the mind. Although Locke affirmed a real world, he acknowledged that the senses through which that world is perceived do not give us a very clear or accurate notion of that reality. Such writers did not begin with the knowledge of Christian life and Christian society. Instead, they built out from the self and its perceptions of the world. So the narrator is going to build his system out of his unstable self after exploring the general state of the modern world. The method selected is an alternation of digressive chapters on modern thought and a fable about Peter (Catholic), Jack (Calvinist) and Martin (Church of England). The fable seems relatively simple and has a fairy tale beginning. It tells that three brothers each received a sturdy, unadorned coat from their dying father. In attempting to live according to the latest fashion Peter and his brothers violate the will of their father and decorate their coats with all kinds of ribbons and laces in keeping with the worship of a tailor God. Eventually Lord Peter goes mad with Pride and insists that he be obeyed in all things. Jack finally realises the seriousness of the deviations from his father's original will and tears up the decorations on his coat until, ironically enough, it appears not very different from Peter's. Only Martin attempts to reduce the coat gradually to its original state.

This obvious religious parable with its attack on religious enthusiasm is mingled with an account of madness among modern critics and thinkers which leads to a confusion between the importance of ordinary life and the attempt either to penetrate to the very depth of meaning or else to live entirely on the surface of ideas. In the brilliant ninth section everything is brought together, as the narrator in a burst of narcissism recommends employing the insane, now at Bedlam, for useful tasks in the commonwealth. He removes the thin line between sanity and insanity, suggesting that since everyone is, to a degree, possessed by unreason, 'use' might be made of the insane. The preoccupation is that of the projector who wants to employ people for the sake of the commonwealth, but the irony turns in many directions at once, sometimes being very specific parodies of writers such as Roger L'Estrange (1616–1704) and Dryden, sometimes opening out to generalisations about humanity. Through it all, Swift preserves the mask of his still slightly mad narrator, and the chaos of the ninth section is a reflection of the chaos within the mind of the speaker.

Swift's convoluted method of irony – an irony that often traps the reader and then turns on him to reveal his own gullibility – is well illustrated in Swift's brilliant delineation of the religion of the mythical country in which Peter, Jack and Martin live:

> For, about this time it happened a sect arose, whose tenets obtained and spread very far, especially in the *grand monde,* and among every Body of good fashion. They worshipped a sort of Idol, who, as their doctrine delivered, did daily create men, by a kind of manufactury operation. This Idol they placed in the highest parts of the house, on an altar erected about three foot: He was shewn in the posture of a Persian Emperor, sitting on a superficies, with his legs interwoven under him. This god had a goose for

his ensign; whence it is, that some learned men pretend to deduce his original from *Jupiter Capitolinus*. At his left Hand, beneath the altar, *hell* seemed to open, and catch at the animals the Idol was creating; to prevent which, certain of his priests hourly flung in pieces of the uninformed mass, or substance, and sometimes whole limbs already enlivened, which that horrid gulph insatiably swallowed, terrible to behold. The goose was also held a subaltern divinity, or *deus minorum gentium,* before whose shrine was sacrificed that creature, whose hourly food is human gore, and who is in so great renown abroad, for being the delight and favourite of the Egyptian Cercopithecus. Millions of these Animals were cruelly slaughtered every day, to appease the hunger of that consuming deity. The chief Idol was also worshipped as the inventor of the yard and the needle, whether as the god of seamen, or on account of certain other mystical attributes, hath not been sufficiently cleared.

Swift's image of a tailor god whose power to make human beings by creating, not their whole body but their exterior garments, is a brilliant and witty stroke in which the pattern of language seems to make connections never grasped before. The prose of the tailor with his legs bent under him is compared to that of a Persian emperor, but it might just as well be compared to a statue of Buddha. The tailor's 'hell' into which the left-over cuttings of his trade were thrown becomes within this scheme a real hell, since the only important part of man in this scheme are his clothes. The very scene of these offerings is convincingly depicted as 'terrible to behold'. And the image of human sacrifice is further amplified in the picture of the lice sacrificed to the goose. The entire picture closes with that connection between clothes and sexuality (semen and 'seamen') in the punning allusion to the tailor god as the god of sailors.

All of this is enormously clever, inventive, imaginative and witty, and the picture ties in with the entire discussion of the relationship between insides and outsides that attempts to bridge the dualism of body and mind, a central concern of seventeenth- and eighteenth-century philosophy. Clothing, that exterior of man by which he creates an artificial self, may easily be taken for the real man, and this is what has happened in the creation of the tailor god. But even as we are attracted by Swift's brilliance in creating what seems like a self-sufficient system of language and reference, we are being twitted on our admiration for religious metaphor and verbal constructs. The way in which language seems to create its own system of relationships in the religion of the tailor god is similar to the way sects read into the Bible the kinds of references that they wanted to see. How easily the mind is entranced by such imaginative pyrotechnics and how absurd the images really are! That Thomas Carlyle (1795–1881) could find inspiration in such a system for his *Sartor Resartus* (1833) suggests some of the power of Swift's creation. But we are supposed to laugh at it and to be puzzled by its odd attraction for us. It is a system in which imagination has overpowered the reason, verbal relationships the real meaning of words, and innovation the historical facts of faith. In short, it is a kind of trap for the reader.

The two other pieces in this volume are, in a sense, a reflection of *Tale of a Tub*. *The Battle of the Books* (1704) is specifically about the contemporary quarrel between those who argued for the ancients as the best source of wisdom and a very active group of thinkers who saw their age as surpassing anything the ancient world could offer. The battle was not merely literary but concerned science, philosophy and national pride. In France, where such quarrels are often more bitter than in England, it raised the question of the greatness of the age of Louis XIV and hence involved political matters. In England, it involved a particular quarrel between Swift's patron, Sir William Temple (1628–99) and a group of scholars, particularly the great classical scholar, Richard Bentley (1662–1742). When Swift revised the text of *Tale of a Tub* in 1710, he incorporated the remarks of one of his and Temple's opponents, William Wotton, into notes, thereby giving the work a mock scholarly appearance.

In spite of its wit and the fascinating discourse between the Bee and the Spider at the beginning, *The Battle of the Books* is a less original work than the *Tale*. *The Discourse concerning the Mechanical Operation of the Spirit* (1704) makes explicit the theory offered in the *Tale* that the impulse behind religious enthusiasm is libido and that the wild emotions raised at the prayer meetings of various religious cults are little more than surrogates for sexual energy. That such meetings often turn into scenes of debauchery was in his view hardly surprising. Swift's distrust of the imagination and other faculties that in any way impinge on the operation of the reason is partly an inheritance of attacks on Presbyterians and Quakers that may be found throughout the Restoration and partly a persuasive and original view of irrationality that had a profound effect on English thought throughout the eighteenth century.

Even before the publication of Swift's early masterpiece, Defoe was experimenting in using various masks in his pamphlets, but he brought to such writing his particular gifts for fiction when, in 1703, he parodied the writings of a number of extremists among the High Churchmen, particularly, Henry Sacheverell (c. 1674–1724). *The Shortest Way with the Dissenters* captured many of the stylistic quirks of Sacheverell who, in his sermons, had been threatening the religious Dissenters from the Church of England with some kind of terrible fate. He never said what he meant to do, but phrases in which he threatened to hang out the 'bloody banner' of persecution against the Dissenters were too much for Defoe. *The Shortest Way* is written in the style of the High Church, but what was before a series of hints became a direct call to start the persecution now and to let a little blood flow among the leading Dissenters. It was a risky piece of irony, particularly because Defoe did not break the fictional pose at the end but rather let his High Churchman conclude with the difficult image of the High Church like Christ crucified between the Catholics and the Dissenters, the call 'Now *let us Crucifie the Thieves*' and a plea for the Church to establish its foundation 'upon the Destruction of Her Enemies'. The argument reduced the threats against the Dissenters to the kind of pogrom that no one ever suggested, no matter how extreme a defender of the Church of England. Toleration of different religious beliefs was the law of the land. Who could be happy at reading such a piece? High Churchmen had to feel themselves ridiculed, except for those few, perhaps mythical, readers who liked the idea so well that they missed the exaggeration of their sentiments. And the Dissenters could hardly be amused by a work that raised the possibility of their persecution. Doubtless there were many who appreciated Defoe's ironic fiction, but it has some of the earmarks of a work written for the author's own amusement. Defoe was identified as the author and arrested for writing a seditious libel.

II   The new journalism

Defoe made the mistake of pleading guilty and was ordered to
stand in the pillory, a fate that was to result in the death of his
fellow journalist, John Tutchin (c.1661–1707), in 1707. But
Defoe turned the event into a triumph by writing his 'Hymn to
the Pillory' in which he denounced those who sentenced him to
this punishment:

> And thus he's an example made.
> To make men of their honesty afraid,
> That for the time to come they may
> More willingly their friends betray;
> Tell 'em the M— that placed him here,
> Are Sc—ls to the times,
> Are at a loss to find his guilt,
> And can't commit his crimes.

Defoe was supposed to remain silent for seven years, but his
talents were so obvious that the ministry decided to hire him to
defend their position by a newspaper. The *Review* which Defoe
published single-handedly from 1704 until 1713 was not the
first newspaper, but compared to the official news reports of
the *London Gazette* and the question-answer format of *The
Athenian Mercury* that was so popular during the 1690s, or the
dialogue form of John Tutchin's *Observator*, Defoe's paper was
a major improvement. As Mr Review, Defoe often answered
letters, and he even established a mock society, The
Scandalous Club, to take care of such material, but for the
most part, he wrote essays on politics and trade. They were
often controversial, occasionally witty, and always written
with that particularly lively style that made Defoe the most
popular as well as the most prolific journalist of his day. The
Review shifted with the wind of politics once too often and
became less useful to the government for that reason, but
before that time, it had popularised Whig theories of politics
and trade and engaged with some formidable opponents.
When it ended, there were other journals, such as Swift's
Examiner (1710) that had added to the excellent level of political
journalism during the reign of Queen Anne.

But as we shall see, the real success of the period in
journalism was the work of Richard Steele and Joseph Addison

(1672–1719) and their most masterful creations: *The Tatler* (1709–11) and *The Spectator* (1711–12). Both periodicals were collected and published in volume form, and the critic who argued that their influence in England, particularly *The Spectator,* fell only slightly short of the Bible was exaggerating but slightly. To understand the reasons for their success at the time and their continued popularity is to understand the direction of English art, thought and life in this period, for while writers like Defoe and Swift drew much on their experiences in coming of age in the previous century, Addison and Steele were products of a new age of polished manners, and reformed morals.

III   Art and society

Addison announced that the intention of the Spectator was to temper wit with morality and enliven morality with wit. London, the centre of English culture, was now a city offering frequent concerts as well as operas. Henry Purcell (1659–95) had died, but the interest in opera that he inspired continued; and in 1711, George Friedrich Handel (1685–1759) put on his *Rinaldo* in London to the delight of audiences. During the Restoration, the critic Thomas Rymer (1641–1713) was to find Shakespeare's plays ludicrous and hold up an ideal of art governed entirely by the rules, but between 1709 and 1710 Nicholas Rowe (1674–1718) brought out the first modern edition of Shakespeare's works. Shakespeare was considered a writer inspired by nature rather than art, but for an age that saw in the beauty of nature the clearest indication of God's plan, what could be better? Queen Anne gave tacit approval to a reformed type of drama by appointing Congreve and Vanbrugh to oversee the morality of the stage. Defoe was outraged, but what better way of affirming the importance of the drama in national life than to appoint the greatest living writers of comedy as the guardians of the theatre?

Significant developments were also taking place outside London. At the turn of the century, Bath was still primarily a health spa with enough company for an occasional country dance on the bowling green. There was also some gambling, and the opportunity of making easy money attracted the attention of Richard Nash (1674–1774), a man of no means, some education, a love of pleasure and considerable talent as a gambler. In his *Life of Richard Nash* (1762), Oliver Goldsmith (1728–74) stresses the lack of refinement of manners in the life of Bath: 'General society among people of rank or fortune was by no means established. The nobility still preserved a tincture of Gothic haughtiness, and refused to keep company with the gentry at any of the public entertainments of the place'. Little attention was paid to dress. Men wore boots and women aprons. In 1706, shortly after being appointed as Master of Ceremonies, Nash published a list of eleven 'RULES TO BE OBSERVED AT BATH'. They were offered in a manner that was somewhat playful, but the serious intent behind them was clear.For example, the seventh rule, 'That no gentleman or lady take it ill that another dances before them; – except such as have no pretence to dance at all', was intended to stress the social occasion of the balls. Feelings like jealousy and anger were not to be displayed in public, and every man was ordered to dance with more than one woman during the minuet.

The eleventh rule warns against those who spread lies and ends by jesting about such people belonging to the 'sect of Levellers'. However such a comment may have been intended, Bath was a place in which all kinds of people mingled, united by illness or the desire for society. Defoe pictured the Cross Bath where the visitors descended into the hot spring to the accompaniment of music and where men and women conversed freely. Thus Bath became the place where the nobility, gentry and middle ranks came together in an atmosphere ruled, at least ideally, by politeness. Nash succeeded in getting a prohibition against wearing swords after one particularly violent duel, and while swords continued to be displayed elsewhere as a sign of gentility, they came to be less common. Foreign travellers commented on the absence of swords in places of pleasure such as Bath and Newmarket, and by the 1780s, they had all but disappeared. Unfortunately, despite condemnation by the age's moralists from Defoe and Steele onward, duelling itself did not disappear. 'Progress' consisted in the use of pistols rather than swords, as in the famous duel between two leading politicians, Charles James Fox (1749–1806) and William Adam (1751–1839) in 1779. During the reign of George III for all the obvious improvement in manners, sixty-five men were to die as a result of duels.

Nash insisted that visitors dress in what he considered a civilised fashion. Women were not allowed to wear aprons and men had to leave their boots at home. Through his labours, Bath gradually became, in Goldsmith's words, 'the theatre of summer amusements for all people of fashion'. A playhouse was erected in 1705, which, if it was never to rival the productions in London, gradually became thoroughly professional. A number of booksellers sprang up in Bath, and one of the amusements of the city was to drop by one of these establishments to examine the latest publications. What may have been the earliest official lending library was established there in the middle of the century. Even more than London, then, Bath may have helped to establish the social tone of English life throughout the century. And Nash's accomplishment was fully recognised by his contemporaries. Dr William Oliver (1695–1764), in an obituary of 13 February 1761 set them down at considerable length, but the key passage was:

> His fundamental law was, that of good breeding.
> Hold sacred decency and decorum,
> His constant maxim:
> Nobody, howsoever exalted,
> By beauty, blood, titles, or riches,
> Could be guilty of a breach of it, unpunished.

Through the practical efforts of Nash and the advice of Addison and Steele, the century came to cultivate the social arts as well as the fine arts.

On the level of national pride, there was a new feeling of strength with the union of England and Scotland in 1707 and the victories of Marlborough in the war against France that ended in 1712. Poets such as Defoe wrote a new poem for each defeat of the French forces, and Addison wrote a long poem 'The Campaign' (1704) to give permanent literary fame to the victory at Blenheim in that year. The war abroad had its reflection in the political turmoil of this time, but if the bitterness between the two parties led to occasional gestures at impeachments of previous ministers, for the most part the system of elections seemed to be working well enough. The attempt to try Sacheverell in 1710 for sedition could raise a mob to riot and burn the meeting houses of the Dissenters, but such acts of violence did not destroy the effort at living well and pursuing what happiness might be found on earth. In 1690 Nicholas Barbon had argued that changing fashions and luxury were not evils, as many thought, but economic goods. They kept money and products circulating and stimulated trade. Barbon practised his own preaching and proceeded to organise building projects on a mass scale throughout an expanding London. Citizens were prospering, and for all the complaints about them, the servants of the upper and middle ranks prospered too. The ideal of social mobility that came in with the revolution of 1688 was under considerable attack, but writers like Addison, Steele and Defoe lost no opportunity for praising the merchants of Great Britain as an energetic group that had enriched the country.

And if Great Britain could boast of its accomplishments in war, in its institutions of government and in its cultural life, it also could boast of having championed scientific investigation in the continuing work of the Royal Society and its most illustrious member, Sir Isaac Newton (1642–1727). If Newton's discoveries had been the pride of the seventeenth century, the dissemination of his ideas was the job of the eighteenth century. Abridgements of the *Principia* (1687) and *Optics* (1704) in newspapers circulated simplified notions of his ideas, and the suggestion at the end of the *Principia* that a God was necessary to ensure the operations of gravity and other laws of physics provided the model for numerous theologians to expatiate on the rational structure of the universe and the wisdom of God in creating it. He ruled over a very large universe, but the greatest scientist of the age had assured everyone that He was still there as the lord of nature.

IV   Philosophic attitudes

Perhaps nothing was so symptomatic of the beginning of the eighteenth century as the appearance of two philosophers, Anthony Ashley Cooper, 3rd Earl of Shaftesbury (1671–1713) and Bernard Mandeville (1670–1733), representing opposing views of man and society. Both drew upon past ideas;

both were original in their approach to these ideas; and both spoke to the new century in forceful terms. Shaftesbury's tutor had been John Locke (1632–1704), whose *Essay concerning Human Understanding* (1690) was to form the basis of empirical thinking about matter and sense experience just as his *Two Treatises concerning Government,* published in the same year, was to form the basic view of the relationship between government and society for the age. In the *Essay,* Locke had argued that there were no innate ideas. Man was born with a mind that was a blank slate and received his impressions of the world through his senses. These senses were not very reliable, but man had to act on these impressions ('ideas') to form his approach to life. In such a scheme, man's idea of God was as clear as any of his other ideas. In the *Two Treatises*, Locke posited the existence of a social contract between individuals to form a community before a second contract was signed to establish a government. Government, whatever its form, might safely be dissolved or changed for a period of time without fear of anarchy. It was in relation to the apparent stability of such ideas that both Mandeville and Shaftesbury were to build their systems.

Shaftesbury rejected much that his tutor put forward. He came to believe that Locke was wrong about innate ideas. For Shaftesbury, man was born with a 'moral sense' which was closely associated with his sense of aesthetic form. The order and beauty of the universe might easily be perceived by the man of taste, and that same understanding of order informed his moral sense. John Keats's (1795–1821) later dictum at the end of the 'Ode on a Grecian Urn' (1819): 'Beauty is truth, truth beauty' was first stated by Shaftesbury. And just as he believed in Platonic forms of beauty that were eternal in the mind and in the world, so he transformed Plato's allegories into an enthusiastic response to the beauty and order of the universe. The influence of the great Greek Philosopher, Plato (c. 427–347 B.C.), was never entirely diminished. Shaftesbury may be seen as an heir of the 'Cambridge Platonists' who were active in the middle and late seventeenth century, and Thomas Taylor, the Platonist (1758–1835) was active at the end of the eighteenth century.

One of the sections of his collection, *Characteristics of Men, Manners, Opinions Times,* which first appeared in 1711, bore the

subtitle, 'a Philosophical Rhapsody', and in this dialogue,
Theocles would fall into ecstasy over the beauty and order of
nature. Whereas during the Restoration 'enthusiasm' had
been a word that evoked the excesses of the religious sects, now
a new kind of enthusiasm is espoused, an enthusiasm for
disinterested virtue and the beauty of God's creation. Theocles
wins over his friend to the new spirit:

> If there be any seeming extravagance in the case, I must
> comfort myself the best I can, and consider that all sound
> *love* and *admiration is* ENTHUSIASM: 'The transports of
> *poets,* the sublime of *orators*, the rapture of *musicians,* the
> high strains of the *virtuosi;* all mere ENTHUSIASM! Even
> learning it-self, the love of *Arts* and *Curiositys,* the
> spirit of *travellers* and *adventurers; gallantry, war,*
> *heroism;* All, all ENTHUSIASM!'–'Tis enough: I am content to
> be this *new Enthusiast*, in a way unknown to me before'

In so far as Shaftesbury's doctrines were without particular
Christian dogma, they differed greatly from the ideas of the
Cambridge Platonists and were generally held to be examples
of deistic thought, the belief in a distant if generally benevolent
God who seldom if ever interfered in the life of mankind. This
universalism was well suited to Enlightenment ideas in England
and the continent. Shaftesbury preached an ideal of tolerance,
virtue and taste. To fall under his influence was to aim at a
moral and civilised life above the cares of politics and free from
most of the annoyances of ordinary life. Ideas of poverty and
violence seem far away, and he preferred to believe that some
of the tales about Cannibalism among the savages that Locke
found in the accounts of explorers were simply lies. Under
such circumstances, he was often attacked as preaching a
philosophy that was beyond mortal man to realise and as out of
touch with the realities of life as the teachings of some of the
Stoic philosophers of ancient Rome.

No one pointed this out more forcefully than Mandeville.
The Fable of the Bees was first published as a relatively brief
poem, *The Grumbling Hive,* in tetrameter couplets in 1705 but
Mandeville added a series of prose 'Remarks' to it in 1714,
and in 1723, after a controversy in which he attacked the need
for Charity Schools to educate the poor, he published an
expanded version with *A Search into the Nature of Society.*

Originally a native of Holland, Mandeville drew many of his ideas from the scepticism of Pierre Bayle (1647–1706) who wrote from the tolerant city of Amsterdam and from the ideas on self-interest that underlay the writings of the mercantile economists at the end of the century. Such economists were fond of quoting Machiavelli on the necessity of speaking of the way the world really *was* rather than of speaking about the way it *ought* to be. During the eighteenth century, Nicholas Machiavelli (1469–1527), who advocated studying man not as he should be but as he actually was, lost much of the reputation for villainy that he had on the Elizabethan stage and emerged as a philosopher with an understanding of human nature. In treating moral and social issues within the same frame of reference, Mandeville attempted to show that self-interest governed society in spite of a hypocritical veneer of high morality. His argument was that once we can see clearly, we can realise our self interest and act upon it. Without such realisation, we are likely to operate on false assumptions.

The major moral of *The Grumbling Hive* was that society worked very well when men (or bees) were allowed to follow their natural instincts. Society was like a great bowl of punch; its individual ingredients were not necessarily very good but everything worked very well together. Only when the hive decided to tamper with the workings of society did trouble start. If such a view seems to be a version of *Laissez faire* economics, it should not be surprising. But whereas Adam Smith (1723–90) (see below: p. 170) postulated a guiding hand above that kept the mechanisms running properly, Mandeville saw only a kind of mechanical balance that appears to be natural to man as an animal. He regards the institutions of society as conventions created by the clever to control the very weak and very strong. Religion is useful to keep the poor in line. Marriage seems to work well enough, but it is merely a control over the sexual impulse. Modesty is not a virtue; it is merely a matter of training. In reality, the sweetest girl has thoughts that would shock the most experienced male if they were ever stated. It is the business of those on top of society to see that there is no revolution from below. Thus the poor ought to be kept ignorant and constantly at labour. Occasionally a poor man will struggle to the top and the prodigal son of a rich man spend everything and fall to the bottom. Such events, provided they do not upset the smooth working of the entire society are healthy enough.

As for Shaftesbury's ideas of virtue, Mandeville said, with heavy irony, that they were noble and said much for Shaftesbury's idealism. Unfortunately they were not true. In the prose 'Remarks' Mandeville undertook to demonstrate that motives like pity and benevolence were merely aspects of self-love under a different guise. In one vivid passage, Mandeville gives an example of a large sow that gets loose and devours a charming little child. The emotion we feel is not what would later be called 'sympathy' so much as a simple and rather painful kind of identification. We identify for a moment with the child and the pain it is undergoing and feel for ourselves, not for the child. In a similar scene of devouring, Mandeville gives the example of a lion confronting an unarmed merchant. Not being very hungry, the lion allows the merchant to plead his case. The merchant speaks of the special virtues of his species but the lion is not impressed. The aspiring being presented by Shaftesbury is, for Mandeville, merely another kind of animal, somewhat more intelligent, perhaps somewhat greedier. That is all Mandeville will grant him. Enthusiasts are the kind of people who blind themselves to the reality of themselves and society.

Writers like Defoe shook their heads over Mandeville's bluntness while tending to agree with him. His method, however, belonged more to the previous century, to writers like Hobbes and Rochester. It should hardly be surprising that Addison and Steele preferred Shaftesbury. In that part of the *Characteristics* called 'An Essay on the Freedom of Wit and Humour', Shaftesbury noted that direct revelation of ideas along with an intolerance of opposing notions would not win over an eighteenth-century audience no matter how right the argument:

> The temper of the pedagogue sutes not with the age. And the world, however it may be *taught*, will not be tutor'd. . . . In a gentlemen we allow of pleasantry and raillery, as being managed always with good Breeding, and never gross or clownish. But if a mere scholastick, intrenching upon all these characters, and writing as it were by starts and rebounds from one of these to another, appears upon the whole as little able to keep the temper of christianity, as to use the reason of a philosopher, or the raillery of a man of breeding; what wonder is it, if the monstrous product of such a jumbled brain be ridiculous to the world.

V 'Tatler' and 'Spectator'

It was precisely with the raillery of a Man of Breeding that the *Tatler* and particularly *The Spectator* attempted to teach the age. They also accepted the idea of a standard of good taste that Shaftesbury considered part of every cultivated person in praising what seemed to them obviously good and obviously bad. As might have been expected, they did not strike many original poses, but occasionally they set out to teach their audience how to appreciate good art, good morals and good ideas in the face of some prevailing notions. They were not afraid to take risks.

The *Tatler* was begun on 12 April 1709 by Steele, writing under the mask of Isaac Bickerstaff. Like so many literary ideas of this period, the name was suggested by Jonathan Swift. In 1708, Swift used the name of Bickerstaff to write a series of predictions of the future by way of parodying the work of the astrologer, John Partridge. Among the many predictions was one forecasting the death of Partridge. A number of the wits joined Swift in this clever series of pamphlets which included an account of Partridge's actual death as predicted. When Partridge claimed, with great indignation, that he was not dead, they retorted that he had been dead for some time without knowing it. Steele's Bickerstaff eventually takes on much more weight as a character than the supposed figure of this literary hoax. He speaks sometimes in his roles as 'astrologer, civilian, and physician' with mock authority. He appears as a person of broad tastes with a wide knowledge of London coffee houses and somewhat positive in his opinions. From the coffee house he draws information about foreign affairs, scandal, trade, and matters concerning literature and the stage.

The *Tatler* was Steele's inspiration but he was soon joined in it by Joseph Addison with whom he had been a close friend both at Charterhouse School and at Oxford. In its orientation toward reform, particularly reform of the theatre, *The Tatler* continued to bear the imprint of Steele throughout its history. Although Addison was to become a Secretary of State under the Whig government of 1717, it was Steele who was the more partisan of the two. He launched an attack on the morality of Restoration comedy, especially on William Wycherley's

(1640–1716) *The Country Wife* (1675) and George Etherege's (c. 1635–91) *Man of Mode* (1676). Speaking as Isaac Bickerstaff, he claimed to be a member of the Society for Reformation of Manners, and while he could not condemn all plays like some members of that Society, he felt that comedies of this kind should not be shown. He also served the purposes of that Society in singling out a nobleman who entered the boxes 'flustered': 'The women sat in terror of hearing something that should shock their modesty, and all the gentlemen in as much pain, out of compassion to the ladies, and perhaps resentment for the indignity which was offered in coming into their presence in so disrespectful a manner'. Although Steele does not mention the man's name, he obviously assumes that all will know who is meant. In the manner of the Societies, he is out to reveal vice where he encounters it.

But the *Tatler* did many other things besides. The issue for 7 May 1709 printed Philips' fine poem, 'A Winter piece to the Earl of Dorset'. The character of Jenny Distaff, the fictional sister of Isaac Bickerstaff is developed into a full character within a series of essays. And a debate over the nature of satire, whether it should be specific or general, was caried forward in a number of papers. Addison added to the publication his interest in fanciful visions with direct morals and a more philosophical turn of mind. If Steele was bent on reforming the morals of his readers through light commentary and raillery, Addison was more interested in educating his audience and lifting the general level of taste. Shaftesbury's equation between taste and morality was also a principle in Addison's programme.

The Spectator first appeared on Thursday, 1 March 1711 and ran until 6 December 1712. It appeared at a time when political feelings were at a high pitch. The Tories under Harley and St. John had taken over the government from the Whigs and were engaged in making a peace with France in spite of objections from the still vociferous Whigs. The Duke of Marlborough (1650–1722), who had led the victorious English forces for eight years, was to be forced to resign, and the war was finally brought to a close with little gained. The pamphlet and newspaper war carried on during this time were verbal counterparts to the most violent battles in the field, but through it all, *The Spectator*, written by two Whigs, succeeded in treating the life of the town, its literature and social events, as if the fierce political broils were no part of the considerations of gentlemen and ladies of taste.

This is not to say that *The Spectator* was not political. The club to which the supposed author belonged had as one of its members Sir Andrew Freeport, a merchant. And when Sir Andrew spoke for the ideals of commerce, he was greeted with applause by all. On the other hand, the old landed interest was represented by Sir Roger de Coverley, a lovable old Tory who, through the affection that those around his property felt for him, still reigned in his area like a benevolent monarch. We learn much of Sir Roger – his old loves, his relations with his family and tenants, his ideas. It is impossible not to like him, but no one would take anything he had to say seriously. He belonged to a quaint, dying world, as moribund as that of Sir Andrew Freeport was full of movement and energy. No more direct statement of political opinion could be made, but it was not made directly. Instead, it was given by way of the impression these fictional characters make on the reader.

There is one picture of the battles between the two political parties. The beginning of *Spectator* No. 81 is a good indication of the tone struck by Addison on this matter:

About the middle of last winter I went to see an *opera* at the theatre in the *Hay-Market*, where I could not but take notice of two Parties of very fine women, that had placed themselves in the opposite side-boxes, and seemed drawn up in a kind of battle array one against another. After a short survey of them, I found they were *patched* differently; the faces on one hand, being spotted on the right side of the forehead, and those upon the other on the left. I quickly perceived that they cast hostile glances upon one another; and that their patches were placed in those different situations, as party signals to distinguish friends from foes. In the middle-boxes, between those two opposite bodies, were several ladies who patched indifferently on both sides of their faces, and seemed to sit there with no other intention but to see the *opera*. Upon enquiry I found that the body of *Amazons* on my right hand were Whigs, and those on my left, Tories; and that those who had placed themselves in the middle-boxes were a neutral party, whose faces had not yet declared themselves. These last, however, as I afterwards found, diminished daily, and took their party with one side or the other, insomuch that I observed in several of them, the patches which were before dispersed equally, are now all gone over to the Whig or Tory side of the face. The censorious say, that the men whose hearts are aimed at are very often the occasions that one part of the face is thus dishonoured, and lyes under a kind of disgrace, while the other is so much set off and adorned by the owner; and that the patches turn to the right or to the left, according to the principles of the man who is most in favour. But whatever may be the motives of a few fantastical coquets, who do not patch for the public good, so much as for their own private advantage, it is certain that there are several women of honour who patch out of principle, and with an eye to the interest of their country. Nay, I am informed, that some of them adhere so steadfastly to their party, and are so far from sacrificing their zeal for the public to their passion for any particular person, that in a late draught of marriage articles a Lady has stipulated with her husband, that, whatever his opinions are, she shall be at liberty to patch on which side she pleases.

Addison's achievement here should be obvious. He reduces party strife to the level of cosmetics and the trivialities of young women seeking to attract men. That women were being brought into the arena of politics is a sign of its absurdity as well as an indication of the degree to which it is dividing the entire fabric of society and intruding on the private affairs of family. If the passage suggests some condescension for the role of women in society, with doubt being cast on the number of them genuinely interested in the 'Public Good' compared to those trying to please their admirers, that should not blind us to their use simply as examples. Those aimed at are the men genuinely engaged in politics who have allowed the spirit of party to triumph over their interest in the good of the country. By reducing that spirit to the nature of which side to patch on, Addison does much what Swift was later to do in *Gulliver's Travels* (1726) in the depiction of political disputes in the land of Lilliput where the matters at issue involved the height of heels and the best end of the egg to be broken.

Later on in the publication of *The Spectator,* in the issue for 31 July 1712, Addison lashed out at those 'Party Zealots on both sides' who insist on seeing party reflections in his journal. And if, as has been suggested, politics is a major factor in *The Spectator,* party politics, of a specific kind was not. Many numbers of *The Spectator* were written on matters of art and society. He gave over eighteen papers to a thorough analysis of Milton's genius in *Paradise Lost*, claiming for it the status formerly granted only to the epics of Homer and Virgil. In a series of eleven papers dealing with perception, art and taste, he adapted many of Locke's ideas to the ways in which both nature and art are perceived. This presentation of the

'Pleasures of the Imagination' brought to a wide audience ideas on the sublime (*Greatness*) that had been developing through the Restoration and treated it in relationship with the novelty and beauty. In so doing, he placed an emphasis on fanciful and imaginative writing and found Shakespeare the true master at this. Although Addison drew heavily on French critics, particulary René Rapin (1621–87), for many of his ideas, he was not afraid to praise ballads for their imaginative power and to raise the long ballad on the border battle between England and Scotland, 'Chevy Chase', to the level of great, polished literature.

In these efforts, Addison was amazingly successful in shaping the taste of British readers throughout this period. Dryden had admired Shakespeare, but that admiration had seldom been without some feeling that Shakespeare's genius was all the result of natural force rather than artistry. Addison does not worry about such matters. He quotes Hamlet's vision of the ghost as a great example of terror in the drama and dismisses French critics who might want no blood on the stage. Such judgements remained the standard judgements throughout the century. And why should they not?

Before the tax on newspapers passed in 1712, the circulation of *The Spectator* was as much as four thousand. Through the coffee-houses, where copies were available to customers, it reached thousands more. And it went to British colonies and trading outposts around the world. One correspondent sent a letter from Sumatra. In the American Colonies, Cotton Mather (1663–1728) mentions reading a copy, and within Britain, copies went as far as the Highlands of Scotland. The subscription list of a collected edition of 1712–13 included thirty-six women, well-known politicians, and a large number of men engaged in business. Collected editions of this kind were popular throughout the century. The French scholar, Alexandre Beljame (1842–1906) even suggested that *The Spectator* was responsible for the spread of literacy throughout the nation. 'People who would otherwise not have read at all', he commented 'unconsciously acquired the habit, and the taste for reading thus became widespread'. Collections of various sections, such as the essays on Sir Roger de Coverley, were still common reading during the early part of the twentieth century but that popularity has faded along with the popularity of the periodical essay. Years after Addison and Steele gave it shape, Defoe and Swift added their own particular manner to it, and Dr Johnson at the end of the century brought it to a higher level of moral seriousness than that achieved by Addison and Steele. Johnson thought highly of the form and admired *The Spectator* accordingly. Modern readers are likely to approach Addison and Steele after reading Johnson's powerful essays in *The Rambler* and *The Idler*. Compared to Johnson's, their essays may seem thin, but there is much to say for that deliberate attempt at light literature and ability to turn profound ideas into something that seems not quite so serious. If we miss that part of the eighteenth century, we miss an essential way in which writers and audience wanted to approach life.

3

The young Alexander Pope and the poetic art

POPE claimed in his 'Epistle to Dr. Arbuthnot' (1735) that he could not help becoming a poet:

> Why did I write? What sin to me unknown
> Dipp'd me in ink, my parents', or my own?
> As yet a child, nor yet a fool to fame,
> I lisp'd in numbers, for the numbers came.

Born on 21 May 1688, Pope dedicated himself to poetry at an early age. His family belonged to England's Roman Catholic minority, and many of his friendships were among old Catholic families. His father was a merchant who made enough to retire in 1688. Pope grew up at Binfield and around the age of twelve contracted that tuberculosis of the spine that left him dwarfed (4′ 6″), twisted and hunchbacked. Joseph Spence (1699–1768), a minor writer, critic and compiler of a series of 'Anecdotes' about Pope and some of his friends, reports that he taught himself Latin and Greek at the age of twelve and went up to London to study French and Italian. While there is some doubt about the details of this precocity, there is no question of his early ability. His first poems date from as early as 1700.

Pope began imitating the traditional English poets very early. If Dryden had given English poetry a sense of its history and development, Pope was the first poet to go beyond Dryden's nostalgic view of himself, cast between two ages of literature, to a sense of the continuity of English poetry and of his part in it. His favourite poet was Edmund Spenser, (c. 1552–99), the author of the allegorical and richly descriptive epic romance, *The Faerie Queen* (1590–96), and Pope wrote imitations of that poet ('The Alley') as well as of Chaucer, Edmund Waller (1606–87), Abraham Cowley (1618–67), the Earl of Rochester and Charles Sackville, sixth Earl of Dorset

(1638–1706). These are exercises, of course, but they show his interest in mastering the poetic styles of his predecessors. Pope is sometimes mistakenly thought of as the poet of the 'Age of Reason' or the prosaic writer in verse of an 'age of Prose'. Anyone reading Pope with an open mind would have difficulty explaining such an image. Pope told Spence that at the age of twelve he wrote part of an epic which opened under water in a scene at the court of Neptune. If the later Pope considered himself as an impassioned writer on moral subjects, we should not mistake the young Pope for anything but a poet writing on emotional subjects in a verse that was capable of powerful lyrical effects.

I   Early writings

He made friends with older literary figures such as the Restoration playwright William Wycherley (c. 1640–1716) and the friend of Dryden's later years, the poet and critic, William Walsh (1663–1708). In 1705, Walsh introduced Pope to Will's, the coffee-house of the poets, and a year later, the publisher, Jacob Tonson (c. 1656–1736), noted that he had been shown one of the 'Pastorals' by William Congreve as well as Walsh and was eager to publish it. The 'Pastorals' were not published until 1709, but they were the kind of beginning that was traditional for budding Virgils. As might have been expected, they were very much in the pastoral tradition and imitative, but Pope showed a wonderful control of the sound of English poetry:

> Where'er you walk, cool gales shall fan the glade;
> Trees, where you sit, shall crowd into a shade;
> Where'er you tread, the blushing flowers shall rise,
> And all things flourish where you turn your eyes.

Pastoral had not yet come under the attack that Samuel Johnson was to level at it throughout his career as insincere and artificial, but French critics such as Bernard le Bovier Fontenelle (1657-1757) and Jean Le Clerc (1657–1736) had already questioned its relevance to contemporary life. Pope wrote a 'Discourse on Pastoral Poetry', which he published with the 'Pastorals' in 1717 that defends pastoral as the picture of an ideal state of life, a defence that Johnson would hardly have found sufficient.

Pope's next effort, published in 1711, was his 'Essay on Criticism', a work which led to considerable praise from Addison in *Spectator* No. 253. Pope already knew Steele and soon became acquainted with Britain's arbitor of literary taste, though by then, Pope's reputation was established. The 'Essay on Criticism' is filled with wonderful turns of wit and should be read not so much as an original work of critical theory as a poetic statement about the sacredness of art and the poet's calling. The true artist is really above many of the rules laid down for critics, but since critics are often so irresponsible and ignorant, they need some guidelines. The example of Aristotle shows that there may be genius in criticism as well as poetry, but it is rare. *The Poetics* of the Greek philosopher Aristotle (384–322 B.C.) had been a major influence on Renaissance criticism, but Pope would probably have read him through the interpretations of the French critic, Rapin, who published a treatise on The *Poetics* in 1674. Pope thought that the true critic must be a cautious and moral man and in one of his most brilliant passages, he showed how critics tend to favour one particular kind of poetry believing they have found the key to all great poems:

> Some to conceit alone their taste confine,
> And glitt'ring thoughts struck out at every line;
> Pleas'd with a work where nothing's just or fit,
> One glaring chaos and wild heap of wit.
> Poets, like painters, thus unskill'd to trace
> The naked nature and the living grace,
> With gold and jewels cover every part,
> And hide with ornaments their want of art.
> True wit is nature to advantage dress'd,
> What oft was thought, but ne'er so well express'd;
> Something whose truth convinced at sight we find,
> That gives us back the image of our mind.
> As shades more sweetly recommend the light,
> So modest plainness sets off sprightly wit:
> For works may have more wit than does them good,
> As bodies perish thro' excess of blood.

Pope continues his visual analogies throughout this remarkable passage culminating in the final dress image:

> Expression is the dress of thought, and still
> Appears more decent as more suitable.
> A vile conceit in pompous words express'd
> Is like a clown in regal purple dress'd

and he concludes this section with an analysis of archaic words in poetry and the advice to use caution in employing or eliminating either old or new words. At the beginning of this passage, Pope was probably thinking of the poetry of William Wycherley, which he had helped to edit, and which fits Pope's description of a type of poetry that strives too hard to be witty. The real poetry lies deeper than the 'ornaments', deeper in fact than the words in which it is written. Pope adapts Rapin's notion of the separation between words and thoughts and suggests a kind of poetic essence that is separate from the form ('dress') in which it is cast. At the same time, we should not take the notion of 'What oft was thought, but ne'er so well express'd' as a call for imitation of old ideas with a mere veneer of originality. Behind much theorising about art at this time was the belief in some essential quality of beauty. In the paintings, sacred art was female figure naked while profane art was represented by a clothed female form. Pope recommends plainness in one of the most elaborately developed images in English poetry; on the other hand, it is not an image with which we have difficulty. Witty it certainly is, but Pope's clothes image deepens at the same time that it clarifies his position.

Pope published 'The Rape of the Lock' in its early version in 1712, but since he did not make it into the masterpiece we read today until 1714, it would be well to discuss his 'Windsor Forest' first. Pope had actually written this poem at the same time as the 'Pastorals', but revised it in 1713 to include a praise of the Tory Peace of Utrecht and dedicated it to Lord Lansdowne, one of the twelve new Peers created by Queen Anne to force the peace treaty through the House of Lords. As such, it was clearly a Tory poem, and in many ways, as has been shown recently, a poem replete with veiled Jacobite sentiment. Pope had by now fallen into close friendship with Swift, John Gay (1685–1732), and Dr John Arbuthnot (1667–1735), all Tories. And while he kept up his friendships with writers of Whiggish sympathies in an effort to remain free of party quarrels, the very bitterness of factional feeling at the time forced him in the direction of his Tory inclinations. Pope was yet to contribute a prologue to Addison's tragedy, *Cato,* performed on 14 April 1713 and a dedicatory poem to Addison's *Dialogues on Medals*, but he was gradually moving away from the Addison group.

'Windsor Forest' is modelled on Sir John Denham's (1615–69) 'Coopers Hill' (1642), a poem that used the occasion of a panoramic description of the area around London to make a statement about English politics during the civil wars. There is much less resolution in Denham's poem and much more in the way of political statement as the threat of insurrection seems about to upset the order of nature. Pope's poem not only praises the poem of 'Majestick *Denham*', but in the passage:

> No Seas so rich, so gay no Banks appear,
> No Lake so gentle, and no Spring so clear,

imitates Denham's most famous lines. But Pope's poem is about the Peace of Utrecht, signed in October 1711, not about a threatening insurrection, and about a utopian future that such an era without war will bring. It is also a praise of Queen Anne who has brought an end to war, and by implication a criticism of William III, the monarch whose invasion of England brought an end to the reign of another Stuart, James II. In referring to the harsh laws against the kind of poaching that those who lived near Windsor Forest regarded as a rightful use of common land, Pope was emphasising a problem that involved an area of England in which Jacobite sympathies ran high, and in stressing the loyalty to Queen Anne of those dwelling around the forest, Pope was suggesting a connection between the sympathies of the Queen and the government of Harley and St. John and the feelings of the foresters. It would be a mistake to read too much into such references, but Pope's political sympathies seem clear enough in the poem.

Pope followed Denham in keeping as his central image the paradox of *discordia concors* by which unity arises out of apparent lack of harmony:

> Here Hills and Vales, the Woodland and the Plain,
> Here Earth and Water seem to strive again,
> Not *Chaos*-like together crush'd and bruis'd,
> But as the World, harmoniously confus'd:

> Where Order in Variety we see,
> And where, tho' all things differ, all agree.

Such a statement might stand as a description of Pope's theory of art itself and more particularly as the way he had used the couplet to achieve effects of tension and unity. The ambivalence in the poem is particularly evident in the hunting sequences. Nature itself is so beautiful that the role of the hunter or the fisherman seems cruel:

> See! from the Brake the whirring Pheasant springs,
> And mounts exulting on triumphant Wings;
> Short is his Joy! he feels the fiery Wound,
> Flutters in Blood, and panting beats the Ground.
> Ah! what avail his glossie, varying Dyes,
> His purple Crest, and Scarlet-circled Eyes,
> The vivid Green his shining Plumes unfold;
> His painted Wings, and Breast that flames with Gold?

And the image of the hunter extends from the allegory of the river Lodona pursued by Pan and turned into a stream to the taking of a town on the continent by British troops who 'seize th'amaz'd, defenceless Prize' in the same way the hunter seizes the partridge. Yet there is a kind of glory in the 'Sylvan War' of hunting, in the picture of the 'bold Youth' rushing after the deer and in the glory of Queen Anne's appearance as a hunter. If Pope reserves his most sympathetic verse for the sufferers from war and the hunt, he is not without admiration for the hunter.

Although poems of this kind have been called loco-descriptive, and although Pope himself concludes,

> My humble Muse, in unambitious Strains,
> Paints the green Forests and the flow'ry Plains,

the element of history and political statement looms large behind the descriptions. The image of the future that Pope presents stresses freedom and the end to tyranny. He sees slaves freed, and in a nice reversal envisages Indians sailing up the Thames to wonder at the oddity of Englishmen. Though the final verse paragraph brings the reader back to contemporary Britain, the poem has a majestic sweep in its movement backward and forward in time and in a space that extends from England to Peru. Pope gives many of his lines an almost epic dignity, and he is trying to maintain a level of dignified seriousness in keeping with his larger subject, but we should not miss the very personal, lyrical force of the poem. If the youth bounding after the deer is not exactly Wordsworth bounding through the woods, we feel Pope's emotional love of the area where he grew up. If there are many conventions in the treatment of personifications, there are also direct statements of his love for a nature whose beauty he makes come alive as we read.

II   Pope and rococo art

Addison warned Pope against tampering with the earlier version of 'The Rape of the Lock', and Pope may well have felt that such advice proceeded from a degree of envy. The poem of 1714 is one of the great masterpieces of English poetry. It is also Pope's first effort at a large and mature theme. When it appeared in print the critic John Dennis (1657–1734), still smarting from a slighting reference Pope made to him in the 'Essay on Criticism', wrote a long essay in which he treated it not in terms of mock-epic, but as a brief, comic epic. On these grounds, he protested that the airy beings who surround Belinda, the forces of Ariel, unlike Zeus in the *Iliad,* have no real power at all. This was a cogent point, whatever use Dennis was to make of it. Pope's poem is about the social world of England in his time. So far from making that world seem silly or tawdry, Pope ends by making it a society of some importance. It is a world in which the serious concerns of life are confused with the trivial, but the little artefacts of vanity in that world take on cosmic significance. There is no lack of satirical undercutting in Pope's picture of this very feminine world, but there is never any doubt that it is a world worth satirising.

Pope was more than a poet interested in creating vivid images with words; he was also a lover of painting and even an amateur practitioner of that art. Just a year after the publication of 'The Rape of the Lock' he wrote his 'Epistle to Mr. Jervas' in praise of the master who gave him lessons. It is useful to consider Pope's poetry in relation to rococo painting, to which it bears a strong resemblance. The leaders of this school in France were Antoine Watteau (1684–1721), Francois

Boucher (1703–70), and Jean-Honoré Fragonard (1732–1806). Their art was sensual and playful. Watteau liked to depict groups of figures, like travelling actors or picnickers, in moments of relaxation or love making. Boucher painted female nudes in lighter tones than Watteau, while Fragonard, a student of Boucher, continued painting his scenes of lovers' meetings in ornate gardens long after most serious artists had turned to what they considered more profound themes. There was often a sense of danger amid the playfulness of the figures, but it was an art dedicated to a certain overt charm. Congreve's Millamant acts at being a figure out of the rococo world of artifical feeling and constant play, and some of the sensuousness of his and Prior's lyrics belong to this form as well. But in poetry only Pope raised it to the highest art.

'The Rape of the Lock' is about sex in a world of social forms. Surrounded by the luxuries of the life of the wealthy in England during the eighteenth century, the beverages brought from the other side of the earth, the elegant china, the cosmetics brought from equally exotic places, and partaking in the rounds of social life – reading delightful novels, playing cards, going to balls – Belinda has lost her sense of the serious and essential parts of a woman's life in her time. She must marry, have children, raise them, arrange the economy of her household, suffer the usual griefs of family life, grow old and die. If we, by chance, lose sight of these matters in reading the poem, Clarissa tells Belinda just that in Canto V. But it would be a mistake to think that Pope was doing anything in Clarissa's speech but reminding us of what lies (except for a few lines) outside the body of the poem. For the most part, the reader experiences the poem as a delightful comedy about the war between the sexes, a war in which many wounds are given but no one actually dies.

The opening of the poem belongs to Belinda's world and the guardian *Sylph,* Ariel, who keeps guard over all women who are beautiful, chaste and too concerned with their own beauty to pay much attention to men. The light coming into the bedroom sets the scene in a mixture of satiric and realistic strokes:

> Sol thro' white curtains shot a tim'rous ray,
> And op'd those eyes that must eclipse the day;

> Now lap-dogs give themselves the rousing shake,
> And sleepless lovers, just at twelve, awake:
> Thrice rung the bell, the slipper knock'd the ground,
> And the press'd watch return'd a silver sound.

The exaggeration about Belinda's beauty raises her to epic proportions, and the absurdity of the compliment does not remove its positive effect. Next we have the kind of irony by juxtaposition that Pope practises throughout the poem. Lap-dogs were affected by wealthy young ladies, and their value is equated with the importance of the lovers who, playing their roles in romance, must be without sleep from the torment of their passion. In fact, of course, they manage to sleep until noon. This is followed by the image of a call for the servant, first with the bell cord and then by rapping the floor with a slipper, and pressing the watch to sound the time with a 'silver sound'. Belinda is doing all this, but she is oddly absent from these actions as if they were the product of some supernatural power.

Ariel then steps forward to take credit for preserving the chastity of Belinda and those like her. He is the leader of 'unnumber'd Spirits' who were once women like Belinda, coquettes whose spirit survive after death. The light triviality of this narrative takes on a significant sexual and even sinister quality in the picture of the passionate contacts underlying social forms:

> What guards the Purity of melting Maids,
> In Courtly Balls, and Midnight Masquerades,
> Safe from the treach'rous Friend, the daring Spark,
> The Glance by Day, the Whisper in the Dark;
> When kind Occasion prompts their warm Desires,
> When Music softens, and when Dancing fires?

The answer to these questions is actually complex, but Ariel's claim is not. The Sylphs keep maids chaste. Neither virtue or common sense have anything to do with it.

The first canto ends with Belinda at her toilet engaging in the narcissistic veneration of her own beauty, as she puts on various cosmetics with the aid of her maid and the attending Sylphs. There are all kinds of ironies in this passage, and since cosmetics were not generally condoned, it might be thought that Pope was satirising the unnaturalness of Belinda's 'Rites of Pride'. Pride is certainly a sin, but the degree to which we are asked to condemn Belinda is hardly measurable. The thrust of the passage suggests the dressing of a Cleopatra, one whose beauty makes everything excusable. If part of her beauty is the result of art, so much the better for a society that treasured art and artefacts:

> Unnumber'd treasures ope at once, and here
> The various Off'rings of the world appear;
> From each she nicely culls with curious toil,
> And decks the goddess with the glitt'ring spoil.
> This casket India's glowing gems unlocks,
> And all Arabia breathes from yonder box.
> The tortoise here and elephant unite,
> Transform'd to combs, the speckled and the white.
> Here files of pins extend their shining rows,
> Puffs, powders, patches, bibles, billet-doux.

The presence of the 'bibles' among such bric-a-brac suggests that this is a world in which religion is an afterthought, something to be put aside and not thought of seriously until old age. Such matters undercut but do not destroy an image of the transcendent beauty of women in this world.

The passage echoes the arming of the hero in epic, and we might pause to consider the use of epic conventions in the poem. Belinda is not the traditional hero in one particular point. She is a woman. Virgil had his Camilla to fight alongside the men, but Belinda is not going out to do battle. Her world is dominated by women and women's games and within her world she may indeed be regarded as the leading power. Pope deliberately echoes the *Aeneid* and *Paradise Lost* in his devices. Belinda's progress to the court is like Aeneas's voyage up the river; the locks that threaten the 'destruction of mankind' are like the fruit offered to Adam by Eve in Milton's epic. The card-playing is portrayed as an example of heroic games; there is a voyage to the Cave of Spleen in the manner of a voyage to hell. Belinda, who sees herself undone by love, echoes Virgil's Dido. And the cosmic view at the end echoes Milton, though Pope's picture of a world of unreal items, harlot's smiles and the tears of heirs has, in some ways, greater power.

We might ask how important this epic machinery is. For Pope's contemporaries, it had the power of allusion. The readers were brought back to epic situations with which they were familiar and could see how Pope played with them. But any reader should be able to detect the tone of epic dignity when it appears, and in Ariel's speech, in which he threatens those Sylphs who fail at their tasks with such punishments as being hung over the fumes of a cup of hot chocolate, we gain a sense of the smallness of Ariel's world, which in turn gives a different sense to the position of Belinda's world. And while a learned reader may gain some pleasure from recognising in Clarissa's monitory speech an echo of Sarpedon's speech to Glaucus on the rationale underlying heroic deeds, from the twelfth book of the *Iliad,* a translation of which Pope published in 1709, any careful analysis of Clarissa's argument would have to include some consideration of the duty of the upper ranks to justify their position in society:

> How vain are all these glories, all our pains,
> Unless good sense preserve what beauty gains:
> That men may say, when we the front-box grace,
> Behold the first in virtue, as in face!
> Oh! if to dance all night, and dress all day,
> Charm'd the small-pox or chas'd old age away;
> Who would not scorn what huswife's cares produce,
> Or who would learn one earthly thing of use?

The action of 'The Rape of the Lock' has much in common with the comedy of manners. The Baron has laid his plans, and after losing to Belinda at the card game, ombre, cuts the lock. Belinda shrieks in horror. The rape of the hair serves Pope as a symbolic rape that shows off the folly of society in valuing external image and reputation above the realities of life. The public disgrace is too much for Belinda who suggests that an actual rape in private might have been preferable:

> O hadst thou, cruel! been content to seize
> Hairs less in sight, or any hairs but these!

And Thalestris, her friend, reinforces this sentiment by suggesting that Belinda has lost her honour and that it will be difficult to defend her without the stain rubbing off. But in some sense the rape is indeed a genuine rape, not only because Belinda regards it as such but because Pope evokes the symbols of rape so vividly in his references to the hair and to the scissor

('The little Engine on his Fingers' Ends') that we are forced to translate the symbols into reality. The inevitability of this process of association and imagination was later to be exploited by Laurence Sterne in much the same context. And just as virginity is not to be restored, so the lock is not to be returned for all the furious battle between the men and women at the end.

Rape has always been regarded as a serious crime and seldom more so than today, but Pope prevents us from viewing it too soberly. In Umbriel's descent to the Cave of Spleen, he encounters a fantastic world of the human unconscious, which in good Lockean psychology puts together significant images out of ideas that may not seem to fit together except through the power of suggestion. It is a cross between images evoked by Hieronymous Bosch and Lewis Carroll; both the Dutch painter Bosch (c. 1450–1516) and the English mathematician and writer Carroll (1832–98) were creators of fantastic worlds. If Bosch's creations are closer to nightmare, it would be a mistake to ignore that element in Carroll's Alice books (1865, 1872). Of the Cave of Spleen Pope writes:

> Here living *teapots* stand, one arm held out,
> One bent; the handle this, and that the spout:
> A pipkin there like *Homer's* tripod walks;
> Here sighs a jar, and there a goose-pye talks;
> Men prove with child, as pow'rful fancy works,
> And maids turn'd bottles, call aloud for corks.

Behind all the pretension of society and even behind the sober morality of Clarissa's speech lies the physical animal with its sexual needs. In Pope's image of the *id*, everything is jumbled together, and feelings, common sense, and the most profound thoughts are heaped into a series of nonsensical images. From this standpoint, the Baron's action was neither despicable nor clever. It was merely human.

Pope added to this profoundly comic vision a skill that was truly amazing. To stress the artistry of the verse is hardly necessary. Numerous critics have commented on the brilliant use of zeugma. The application of two shifting meanings in a single verb, had never before been managed to achieve such concise and poignant satirical effects:

Whether the Nymph shall break *Diana's* law
Or some frail *China* Jar receive a flaw,
Or stain her honour, or her new brocade,
Forget her pray'rs, or miss a masquerade,
Or lose her heart, or necklace at a ball

Pope's virtuosity as a poet is so remarkable, that one hesitates to stress it lest we forget the lyrical genius and inspiration that lie behind this poem.

The Pope of 'The Rape of the Lock' was still a very young poet and very much a poet of sensibility: he was still working in the mode that dominated the verse of Congreve and Prior. His interests were still directed toward depicting scenes of sexual comedy or sensual feeling. It was the latter impulse that dominated his writing of 'Eloisa to Abelard' (1717), a monologue in which Eloisa, speaking from her nunnery, expresses her continuing passion for her former lover, Abelard. Fulfilment is impossible, for Abelard has been castrated by Eliosa's uncle, Fulbert. Having turned entirely to his religious studies, Abelard became abbot of Saint-Gildas. The correspondence between them began in 1132 and involved a series of letters in which Abelard sought to cool the passion of Eliosa and recommend her to have faith in God. The historical Héloise was a woman of great learning and energy, and as abbess of the Paraclete, originally a church founded by Abelard, she remained a powerful figure in the ecclesiastical establishment. Her love for Abelard was real enough, but spurious letters were added to the collection to make it resemble a popular fictional form of the time, the collection of passionate letters between two lovers.

Although Pope owed much to Ovid's *Heroic Epistles,* composed in the form of fictional verse letters, most of which are from the wives or mistresses of various heroes, complaining of the inconstancy of their husbands or former lovers, 'Eloisa to Abelard' owes even more to the French novel of sensibility and its treatment of love. Also significant is the choice of a subject from the Middle Ages with its evocative Gothic gloom. Pope drew on the translation from the French done by John Hughes (1677–1720), and the common interest of Hughes and Pope in this material says much about Pope's literary interests at the time. Hughes was a contributor to *The Spectator* and had many of the same social and literary interests as Addison. An admirer of Shakespeare, Hughes, in an essay on *Othello*, wrote one of the earliest sympathetic treatments of a Shakespearean tragedy. He also wrote an essay on allegory that appeared before an edition of Spenser and was an enthusiastic writer on music. Many of the tendencies in criticism and taste that can be discovered in Hughes were typical of the main line of literary appreciation during the first two decades of the century.

'Eloisa to Abelard' is often thought to give unsympathetic treatment to Eloisa. Critics have pointed out that her sexual longings for Abelard are out of keeping with her role as nun, and some have seen in her wish that Abelard take her last breath a kind of blasphemy:

> See my lips tremble, and my eye-balls roll,
> Suck my last breath, and catch my flying soul!

Certainly, her last breath ought to have been that of a pious soul thinking only of heaven, and Pope was clearly playing with the paradox of hot passion and cold religion fighting a battle in the soul of a passionate woman. But surely Pope was interested in the situation itself – the illustration of emotion in action. And certainly the poem closes on a sympathetic image of the modern poet as a man of sensibility and sympathy able to grasp the struggles through which both lovers have passed:

> And sure if fate some future bard shall join
> In sad similitude of griefs to mine,
> Condemn'd whole years in absence to deplore,
> And image charms he must behold no more,
> Such if there be, who loves so long, so well;
> Let him our sad, our tender story tell;
> The well-sung woes will sooth my pensive ghost;
> He best can paint 'em, who shall feel 'em most.

The appeal at the end is to the poet of deep enough sensibility to grasp the situation of the two, long-dead lovers, and there is a hint that the writer of the poem is just such a person. If some modern readers have felt a lack of sympathy in Pope's treatment of Eloisa, we should still recognise his achievement. Eloisa's torments, her burning love in an atmosphere in which all should be ritual and piety, create a contrast that is constantly interesting and poetically effective. What is lacking is that which we have come to expect from the dramatic monologue since Robert Browning (1812–94) the development of complexities of character. We see Eloisa close to sexual climax as she thinks of her absent lover, but we do not know her in any kind of depth. Pope sets the mood magnificently, and the 'actress' is splendid. We know that there was an historical Eloisa, but Pope gives us little reality beyond the passionate struggle. In this sense, Pope's achievement is a limited one.

In the same 1717 volume as 'Eloisa to Abelard', Pope printed his 'Elegy to the Memory of an Unfortunate Lady'. So much print has been spent on the identification of the lady that the poem itself has often been neglected. Pope attempted a picture of passion in 'Eloisa to Abelard' somewhat like a cross between Racine's *Phèdre* (1677) and Mlle de Lafayette's *Princess de Cleves* (1678). Both Jean Racine (1639–99) and the Comtesse de Lafayette (1634–93) portrayed the passions as uncontrollable and overwhelming, but Lafayette's treatment of passion as an aspect of sensibility was more in tune with the eighteenth century. In the 'Elegy', however, Pope tried to create an even more woeful situation. If Eloisa projected herself into the future to imagine lovers coming to the tomb she was to share with her former lover, now Pope gives us a genuine ghost, the ghost of a young woman who has committed suicide and is forced to wander the earth. Now the poet called upon by Eloisa is directly in the poem as the person of deep feeling and sensibility capable of understanding and sympathising with her plight. The story of the lady is told obliquely. Like Eloisa, she was betrayed by the uncle who was supposed to be her guardian. After cursing him and his family for their cruelty, the poet tells of her death among strangers. He broods over the oblivion that awaits her without a stone in her memory and with the inevitable forgetfulness that time must bring. Pope ends on an ambiguous note. The closure resembles that of 'Eloisa to Abelard', but this time it turns directly on the feeling of the poet and his own fate:

> Poets themselves must fall, like those they sung;
> Deaf the prais'd ear, and mute the tuneful tongue.
> Ev'n he, whose soul now melts in mournful lays,
> Shall shortly want the gen'rous tear he pays;

> Then from his closing eyes thy form shall part,
> And the last pang shall tear thee from his heart,
> Life's idle business at one gasp be o'er,
> The Muse forgot, and thou belov'd no more!

Pope's poet is a historian of sensibility, the repository of a remembered life of torment. Having placed himself at the centre of the poem, Pope withdraws himself from it by generalising on death itself and, by implication, on the pain of life.

Compared to 'Eloisa' the 'Elegy' suffers from an excess of very specific emotion produced by a person and a series of events which remain vague and abstract. There is no historical event to give a sense of reality, and the treatment of the poet's feelings creates a desire to know more. The poem has something in common with the deliberate writing of fragmentary poems later in the century. Part of our pleasure in the poem arises from a desire to fill in the areas of the story that remain undeveloped. In terms of literary history, it shows Pope exploiting that area of terror that Addison found so admirable in *Hamlet* and its ghost. But Pope's ghost with her 'bleeding bosom' evokes immediate sympathy, and the curse that the poet levels at the guardian seems tame compared to the elder Hamlet's comments on his brother. The 'Elegy' suffers from having the air of a set poetic piece in which the emotion is drawn from the subject matter rather than proceeding out from the poem itself.

III   Translations

Perhaps Pope's most distinguished productions of these early years, at least in the eyes of his contemporaries, were his translations of Homer. The *Iliad* appeared from 1715 to 1720 and the *Odyssey* from 1725 to 1726. Although Pope's extensive use of Elijah Fenton (1683–1730) and William Broome (1689–1745) as assistants for translating the *Odyssey* took some of the lustre off his accomplishment, everyone recognised that Pope had turned Homer into a poet for the eighteenth century and had done it brilliantly. In his preface to the *Iliad,* Pope praised Homer for his inventiveness, for his daring use of metaphor, and for his poetic 'Fire'. 'Homer', he wrote, 'opened a new and boundless Walk for his imagination'. What Homer possessed as a poet may be found in Shakespeare and Milton among the English poets: 'In Milton it glows like a furnace kept up to an uncommon Fierceness by the Force of art: In Shakespeare it strikes before we are aware'.

This is hardly the Pope whom Matthew Arnold (1822–88) considered the kind of poet produced by an 'age of prose'. But it is also hardly surprising that by the end of the eighteenth century, it was the young Pope whom everyone admired. By the time he came to edit Shakespeare in 1725 and to write the Postscript to his translation of the *Odyssey* a year later, Pope was moving in the direction of the satirist and moralist of the last two decades of his life. He saw in the writer of the *Odyssey* an older and, perhaps, wiser poet, who did not aim so constantly after sublime effects. He still admired Milton but felt that he failed to imitate Homer's 'plainness and perspicuity in the dramatic parts'. And in writing on Shakespeare, he found much to blame in the barbarism of Shakespeare's time that led him astray. Clearly Pope was beginning to change some of his views on the nature of poetry and the role of a poet. In some sense, the early Pope may be regarded as a genius who was shaped by the taste of his time and produced poetry that surpassed anything written by his contemporaries. The later Pope chose his own road and did much to carry poetry with him even after it was not entirely clear that his direction was the natural one for his age.

4

Sublime nature and corrupt civilisation: the emergence of 'new' literary ideals

IN April 1719 Defoe published what has sometimes been considered the first modern novel, *Robinson Crusoe*, or, to give its full title: *The Life and Strange Surprizing Adventures of Robinson Crusoe, Of York, Mariner: Who lived Eight and Twenty Years, all alone in an un-inhabited Island on the Coast of America, near the Mouth of The Great River Oroonoque; Having been cast on Shore by Shipwreck, wherein all the Men perished but himself. With An Account how he was at last as strangely deliver'd by Pyrates. Written by Himself.* It was an instant success, not only in Great Britain but on the continent. In fact, it was one of the first universally applauded works of literature to come out of England. At a time when few Germans and Frenchmen would have heard of Shakespeare, Chaucer and Dryden, within a few years of its publication everyone who could read was likely to be familiar with *Robinson Crusoe*. In England it spawned a number of imitations – romances which somehow or other managed to get their characters onto an island – but in the German-speaking areas of Europe it produced a vast number of *Robinsonaden,* of which the *Swiss Family Robinson* (1813) by Johann Wyss (1781–1830) is the best known. Jules Verne (1828–1905) found inspiration in it for his science fiction, and in addition to stage versions and the films of Luis Bunuel (b. 1900) and others, a science fiction film version, *Robinson Crusoe on Mars*, say, will now and then make a comeback. And modern novelists will occasionally find in Defoe's masterpiece some crucial point that they want to adapt to their own purposes. The idea – the myth – of *Robinson Crusoe* is still very much with us.

I   Sublimity and realism in Defoe

As a continuing modern myth it lends itself to the work of economists, political scientists, sociologists, theologians and philosophers. And so it did in the eighteenth century. Although most English readers regarded it as an adventure story, others considered it a kind of moral romance. Jean-Jacques Rousseau (1712–78), the great French philosopher, treated it as a treatise on education in his *Emile* (1762) and as an occasion for solitary meditation in his *Confessions* (1780, 1788). Karl Marx (1818–83) treated it as an illustration of the labour theory of value. In fact, Defoe built into his seemingly straightforward sailor's yarn the interests of his life, and these were precisely the elements that later writers have discovered while often thinking that they were imposing their own systems on a simple fable. Defoe wrote full-length books on economics, economic geography, politics, social projects, education, moral philosophy, cataclysmic events, history, and social manners. He had also experimented with fictional memoirs and other fictive forms for nearly three decades before writing *Robinson Crusoe* and was regarded by many as the liveliest prose writer in Great Britain. By 1719, Defoe had mastered many of the mannerisms of Addison's *Spectator* essays and was writing his own pieces for several newspapers – *Mist's, Applebee's, Mercurius Politicus,* among others. *Robinson Crusoe* was the product of a lifetime of writing.

Many modern critics have tended to read *Robinson Crusoe* entirely in religious terms. Certainly all the materials are there for such a reading – the references to Providence, the discovery of Crusoe's Christian faith, and his sense that his entire life was ruled by God's will. But it is notable that there is no reference to Providence on the title page, and that every event that Crusoe credits to Providence is also given a natural or scientific explanation. Crusoe's interpretation is his own. The reader may draw other conclusions. And the religious interpretation excludes much in the book that involves Crusoe's character and interests as well as the important sections devoted to Crusoe's development of his island into a mini-paradise with plantations and a country house. What Defoe did was create a new myth from the old myths. It is possible to see the island as an allegory of Eden, with Crusoe as its Adam, but on the plainest level, he is only 'Poor Robin', as his parrot calls him, trying to survive his own loneliness and the possible attack of cannibals. As such, he is very much the isolated modern man, beset by anxieties and problems. When Defoe attempted to justify his work by an allegorical interpretation that made the work his autobiography, this was what he meant.

The sense of isolation that pervades *Robinson Crusoe*, the terrors of the storms, the wild beasts and the cannibals, evoke a sense of the sublime power of natural forces. No doubt the sense of power is enhanced by the seeming purpose behind nature. Having ventured foolishly from Brazil to encounter near-death and a 'terrible' salvation, he finds when he ventures offshore in the boat of his own making that he is almost destroyed once more. After witnessing another shipwreck from which there are no survivors, he stands on the shore shaking involuntarily and muttering, in despair, against his fate. After the arrival of Friday, the novel has an almost comic tone as he dwells on the nature of his kingdom, but before returning to safety, he trades the dangers of his island for the terrifying charge of the wolves in the white snow of the Pyrenees.

In exploiting sublime effects, Defoe was at the very beginning of what was one of the major artistic movements of the period. The poets writing during the 1720s were proclaiming an interest in nature and the sublime as the true end of poetry, and by the middle of the century, artists such as Philip James Loutherbourg (1740–1812) were making their reputations by painting scenes of flood, fire and storms. But what disturbed the critic Charles Gildon (1665–1724) was not Defoe's use of the sublime, but his realism, which Gildon associated with bourgeois values. In *The Life and Strange Surprising Adventures of Mr. D----- De F--* Gildon, whose critical standards were rigidly oriented toward the 'rules' laid down by French critics, objected to Crusoe's beliefs, to his method of making beer, to remarks on God's way of ruling the world through natural causes, and, most of all, to the enormous success of the work. 'There is not an old Woman that can go to the Price of it, but buys thy Life and Adventures, and leaves it as a Legacy, with the *Pilgrims Progress,* the *Practice of Piety,* and *God's Revenge against Murther* to her Posterity', Gildon lamented.

Defoe literally invented realistic prose fiction. He used his realistic method in more conventional ways in his novels about crime, for in that genre, the picaresque novels of Spanish literature had used a similar technique; but in a work that might easily have collapsed into allegory or romance, Defoe keeps his island real, names objects, defines the processes by which things are made and counts the items found in the pocket of a drowned boy. When Crusoe sees the print of a single foot in the sand, he wants to assure himself of its reality. He looks about for other prints, measures it against his own foot, and names 'the very print of a foot, toes, heel, and every part of a foot'. Rousseau was right. *Robinson Crusoe* is very much about the solidity of things and the world we experience. Crusoe, who is given to wild schemes, has to learn how objects feel and what they are made of. Without such knowledge he cannot survive.

There was another reason for Gildon's outrage. Because he admired the great, established genres of literature – epic, tragedy, odes – he hardly recognised prose fiction as an acceptable mode of writing. And in this he would have found little disagreement among established critics. The continental critic, Jean le Clerc, in his review of *Serious Reflections of Robinson Crusoe* (1720), remarked that before Defoe prose fiction was mainly the province of women writing romances for other women. And this was true enough. In the same year as *Robinson Crusoe,* Mrs Eliza Haywood (1693–1756) published her very successful novel, *Love in Excess,* an adaptation of contemporary French novels in its emphasis on passion and its deliberate eroticism. A few years before, in 1714, Mrs Mary de la Riviere Manley (1663–1724) published the last of her many novels of scandal, *The Adventures of Rivella.* A more moral type of novel, but with the same emphasis on romantic adventure, was soon to be written by Mrs Penelope Aubin (c. 1685–1731), but it is questionable that Defoe would have thought any of these writers acceptable in his terms. Le Clerc argued that Defoe had introduced a new kind of vivid moral romance that was not to be confused with the novels of the time.

In three of his other works of fiction, Defoe continued to explore the significant themes involving human beings under stress and faced with terrible dangers. In *The Farther Adventures of Robinson Crusoe* (1719) he explored another aspect of deprivation in an encounter with a ship on which the passengers were dying of hunger and thirst. In a vivid passage one of the maids tells how she bit her arm to suck the blood in order to ease her terrible thirst. A section in which Defoe develops his notion of the way a state may develop, with his island as an example, is followed by more voyaging, including some dramatic scenes of violence and horror. In *Memoirs of a Cavalier* (1720), Defoe improved on the methods of his earlier military memoirs to show both the glories and the horrors of war. And in *A Journal of the Plague Year* (1722) he chose the history of the Plague of 1665 to reflect on the possibility of a plague in 1722. As in *Robinson Crusoe,* Defoe's account of the plague was the beginning of a number of motifs in fiction. Since one of the problems for the state in a plague of these dimensions was the possible breakdown in order, Defoe's treatment of the plague had ramifications for historical novels which liked to focus on such moments. Good examples are Allesandro Manzoni's (1785–1873) *The Bethrothed* (1825–26) and William Harrison Ainsworth's (1805–82) *Old Saint Paul's* (1841). The idea of a society destroyed by plague has had a significant part in novels dealing with the future of life on other planets, from Mary Shelley's (1709–1851) *The Last Man* (1826) to Ray Bradbury's (b. 1920) *Martian Chronicles* (1950).

The excellence, however, of *A Journal of the Plague Year* lies in the remarkable vividness of its description of London during the Plague – the sounds of shutters flapping in the wind in streets emptied of their inhabitants, the horror of the pits prepared for the dead into which the bodies were thrown without ceremony, the horrible screams of the victims. Moments of this kind contrast with careful statistics on the number of the dead, essays on the problem of quarantining families, and the narrative accounts of the three artisans who crossed London seeking the better air of the country and of 'H.F.', Defoe's memoirist. Defoe achieves a sense of the drama amid the absurdity of the events. He tells a story of an infected man who takes a garret room for one night at the Pied Bull after breaking out of a house that had been closed by the authorities. He orders a pint of warm ale from the maid, who completely forgets about it in the hurry of business:

The next morning, seeing no appearance of the gentleman, somebody in the house asked the servant that had showed him upstairs what was become of him. She started. 'Alas!' says she, 'I never thought more of him. He bade me carry him some warm ale, but I forgot'. Upon which, not the maid, but some other person was sent up to see after him, who, coming into the room found him stark dead and almost cold, stretched out across the bed. His clothes were pulled off, his jaw fallen, his eyes open in a most frightful posture, the rug of the bed being grasped hard in one of his hands, so that it was plain he died in a few minutes after he sat down upon the bed.

The overall effect of a great catastrophe is never diminished by the details. Rather there is an odd intermixture of sublime and groteque. The touch of half-comedy in the negligence of the maid, played against the horrible posture of the dead man, is pure Defoe. The style is deceptively artless, and the best of critics have found themselves speaking of Defoe's 'homely' prose. In fact, Defoe could write at times like Jeremy Taylor (1613–67) with a highly ornate style when the occasion warranted. (Defoe had read Taylor's *Rule and Exercise of Holy Living* (1650) and *Rule and Exercise of Holy Dying* (1651) before 1682, and imitated Taylor's style in parts of 'Conjugal Lewdness' (1727).) He also had no difficulty in producing the plain but balanced style that came to be associated with Augustan prose. But more often than not, he preferred to follow the ideal of clarity and what he called 'Energy'.

Although Defoe depicted man's struggle against a terrifying nature in some of his other novels, *Captain Singleton* (1720), with its brilliantly-described trek across an imaginary Africa filled with monstrous creatures, is essentially a novel about crime. True enough, the crime described is piracy and the novel is therefore somewhat different from other novels depicting crime and punishment in England and Europe. But a pirate ship was a social unit, and Defoe's protagonist functions in a community of a sort. Defoe's best work about crime, however, is firmly set in cities like London and Paris or in the plantations of America. In *Moll Flanders* (1722), Defoe showed the career of a clever woman, from her birth in Newgate prison to her successful end as a plantation owner in America. There is little of a sublime nature here. Instead there is the struggle to survive and overcome the obstacles that poverty and insignificance of birth create for Moll from the start. Moll's world is firmly rooted in the social and historical realities of her time.

Defoe   drew on the picaresque tradition that existed in England through the translations of Spanish works such as *Lazarillo de Tormes* (c. 1554) and the native imitation of them in *The English Rogue* (1665, 1668, 1671) of Richard Head (c. 1637–c. 1686) and Francis Kirkman (1632–c. 1680). These works often have a central narrator, but his or her story is generally mixed in with those of other criminals or, in some cases, with wholly different tales, sometimes in a romance style very different from the realism of the picaresque. Like most picaresque works, *Moll Flanders* is written in the first person, but whereas the thrust of earlier works in the form is outward, Moll is very much engaged in a kind of dialogue with herself as well as with her audience. The complexity of the work arises from that inner dialogue. Looking back on her life from a secure old age, she finds much that happened to her amusing and much that is very sad. She is often ironic about the men she encounters, and she has little respect for the society that forces her out on the streets to steal and play the prostitute. But this does not prevent her from showing real emotions on occasions. Since she is telling her own story, she will often colour her role in it to suit her self-image. Her effort to tell it as a spiritual autobiography is undercut by her obvious pleasure in some of her criminal activities and by the preface in which the 'editor' complains that he had to revise her real language because it would have been too offensive, and states that she is no longer as penitent as she was when faced by the likelihood of being taken out of Newgate and hanged. The reader likes her because she refuses to yield to despair and has enough resilience to act when life seems most terrible. Any reader who finds Moll to blame when, hungry and without any means to survive, she steals for the first time, is misreading the novel. Ultimately it is the failure to try to save oneself that is viewed as the real sin. Moll's Bank Manager husband, who yields to despair, is far more guilty than Moll.

Defoe communicates these ideas to the reader in a number of ways. Sometimes, as has been suggested, the story itself clarifies the situation. If she upbraids herself for stealing when hungry, or for marrying her lover's brother when confronted with the possibility of being thrown out of the house of her

Colchester family, we can judge the degree of her guilt better than she can. Occasionally Defoe will use word-play to underscore the ambiguity of a situation. Moll is adept at puns, and the reader has to question Moll's surface account on these occasions. Sometimes the story itself has its ironies. When she is seduced by the elder son of the Colchester family, she presents her lover as a typical rake, but her own motives are certainly mixed. She is vain, ambitious, attracted by the money he offers her, and sexually aroused. She sees herself as an innocent victim, but we have to question the nature of her 'love'. Perhaps Defoe was trying to say that all love is composed of mixed emotions, but there is nothing terribly innocent about Moll from the start. The Colchester family is attracted by her naïveté in wanting to be a 'Gentlewoman', when she is merely an orphan without protection or money. But when her idea of a gentlewoman turns out to be a laundress who has given birth to a number of illegitimate children, the irony turns in many directions – on the very idea of gentility, on the price that is sometimes paid for financial independence and on what seems, at this moment in the book, to be a likely prediction of the course her life will take.

As a hero, the narrator of *Colonel Jack* (1722) is much less ambiguous than Moll Flanders. He is born into a social group in London that regards thievery as a trade and, but for his belief that somehow his real parents were of gentle birth (Freud's family romance), he might have followed the usual career of the young thief of the time who seldom lived to the age of twenty without being sentenced to the gallows or to transportation. But as Jack grows out of the ignorance and poverty of his early years among the street-boys who sleep in the sand of the glass-manufactory to keep warm, he learns the use of money and comes to realise that he is not suited to a life of crime. Transported to America by some ruffians specialising in supplying labour to the colonies, he works in the fields as a white slave. But his diligence eventually makes him a supervisor of the slaves, and his economically efficient system of getting the slaves to work out of gratitude wins him his freedom. He obtains his own plantation, grows rich, educates himself with the help of another transported felon, and journeys to Europe to seek the status of gentleman that has been his goal from the start.

Although the first part of the novel is more or less straightforward narrative in which we wonder at Jack's success, the second half is a series of half-comic adventures in a society that is strange to him. Although he succeeds in obtaining a commission and thereby achieves the technical status of a gentleman, he fights for the wrong cause and is eventually haunted by his participation in the Jacobite rebellion of 1715. And his effort at finding a wife who will be faithful to him is thwarted only slightly fewer times than that of a fictional correspondent to one of Defoe's newspapers, Tom Manywife, who blithely ignores the laws of England to continue his quest for an honest woman. Defoe exploits various social themes, as one of Jack's wives is seduced while drunk, and the first turns up at Jack's plantation as a transported felon and a woman who now realises her mistakes. Jack remarries her, and she makes an excellent wife. Another of Jack's wild adventures terminates in disaster as his effort at the illegal trade with Spain's American colonies results in a shipwreck. At the end, Jack returns to his plantation and his wife and his quiet life to settle down in happiness.

Both *Moll Flanders* and *Colonel Jack* were quickly abridged. A ballad of *Moll Flanders,* with the story so changed as to be hardly recognisable was squeezed into one page, and Jack appeared as a real criminal in some of the collections of criminal lives. Much the same type of change occurred with *Robinson Crusoe.* It is often the fate of those who create myths to have no control over their future. But this was not the fate of Defoe's last and most complicated work of fiction, *Roxana* (1724). Roxana is almost the reverse of *Moll Flanders.* Her crimes are committed with a full sense of the weight of the sin. Like Moll, Roxana tells her own story, but Roxana begins as a member of the bourgeoisie with a good education and an inclination to enjoy dancing. When she is plunged into poverty by the folly and desertion of her husband, she embarks on a career as a courtesan. At first she resists the arguments of her maid, Amy, that she must become the mistress of the Landlord, who has generously allowed her to stay in her house and even provided her with food and clothing. Amy preaches the doctrine of 'Necessity' and self-preservation. Faced with starvation, a man or woman will do anything to survive. Roxana gives in, but she refuses to deceive herself about the moral wrong she has committed and compounds the sin by forcing Amy to lie with her landlord as well.

Having risen to the heights of prosperity as mistress of the King, Roxana gradually retires with her wealth to the home of a Quaker woman, and tries to find some of her former lovers to see if they might not make suitable husbands. She finds a Dutch merchant who had offered her marriage, and now accepts him. They take up a title and retire as members of the nobility. Unfortunately for Roxana, she is pursued by her daughter, Susan, whom she had tried to help. But Susan, who is familiar with the career of the lady Roxana, wants more than money. She wants her mother. Roxana, who knows that the revelation of her real life would ruin her, tries to keep her daughter away. Amy, who feels no tenderness toward the girl, threatens to murder her, and after Roxana becomes infuriated at this suggestion, Amy disappears. The reader senses that the murder has been committed, and Roxana ends the novel on a note of despair.

Some critics have defended the ending as sufficient. But the curiosity of the reader is left unsatisfied. In 1740 another writer added a sequel, but this hardly supplies what is wanted. In this novel Defoe showed that he could create brilliant characters, reveal their psychologies in subtle ways, and bring them into dramatic interaction in a way that only the greatest novelists have succeeded in doing. Whether Defoe wanted to go any further with a fiction that was profoundly explorative of human feeling is impossible to answer. He probably thought that it was hardly the kind of fiction that would be popular. Everyone loved Moll Flanders and Robinson Crusoe and could identify with their struggles. Roxana, with her tendency to irony and occasionally bitter feminism, has had to wait until our century to be fully appreciated.

Defoe turned his interests away from fiction after 1724, writing accounts of real islands and real criminals. Between 1724 and 1726, he wrote his *Tour Thro' the Whole Island of Great Britain*, a brilliant view of the state of the nation at this time, and followed it with a series of economic and geographical surveys of Great Britain and the world. And he wrote lives of Jonathan Wild and John Sheppard, the great criminals of his time. He never gave up fiction entirely where he felt it would express his ideas more fully than any other form. In 1724 he wrote a fictional account of a voyage around the world, and in his account of piracy, published between 1724 and 1728, he created what the material demanded – a revolutionary pirate interested in freeing oppressed sailors and slaves and in establishing a utopian colony on Madagascar. These works continued to be read throughout the century, and if Defoe the man needed to be re-discovered toward the end of the century, a large number of his works continued to be reprinted and to exert their influence on the age.

II   Sublime analogies

Defoe's interest in a sublime and often terrifying nature found its echo in the poetry of the period, particularly in what proved to be one of the most popular poems of the century – James Thomson's (1700–48) *The Seasons* (1726–30). Thomson was born at Ednam in Roxburghshire where his father was a minister. Shortly after the family moved to Southdean. Thomson went to school at Jedburgh and later to the University of Edinburgh. Although he wrote some poetry while in Scotland, his career as a poet really began after he moved to London in 1725. In the second edition of 'Winter' the first section of *The Seasons* to appear, Thomson wrote a preface in which he called for a return to sublime poetry which has been the inspiration of mankind 'from Moses down to Milton'. He proceeded to argue for the seriousness of poetry and for a rejection of what might be considered rococo style:

> To insist no further on this head, let poetry once more be restored to her ancient truth and purity; let her be inspired from heaven, and in return her incense ascend thither; let her exchange her low, venal trifling, subjects for such as are fair, useful, and magnificent; and let her execute these so as at once to please, instruct, surprise, and astonish: and then of necessity the most inveterate ignorance, and prejudice, shall be struck dumb; and poets yet become the delight and wonder of mankind.

He called for the choice of 'great and serious subjects' and the rejection of 'little glittering prettinesses, mixed turns of wit and expression, which are as widely different from native poetry as buffoonery is from the perfection of human thinking. A genius fired with the charms of truth and nature is tuned to a sublimer pitch, and scorns to associate with such subjects'. The true poet sings of nature and loves solitude. Seeking for models, Thomson points to the Book of Job and Virgil's *Georgics*.

Although Thomson dropped this preface in subsequent editions, perhaps because he thought it might offend some of his contemporaries, the sentiments were representative of the new thinking of the time. Thomson thanks Aaron Hill (1685–1750) in the preface, and Hill, a literary critic and dramatist, was one of the earliest proponents of a literature of sincere feeling. Also Thomson's statement was far from an isolated response. In 1724, Leonard Welsted (1688–1747) had written his *Dissertation concerning the Perfection of the English Language,* attacking too much imitation in poetry and advising poets to follow nature and the bent of their genius. And in his essay 'On Lyric Poetry' (1728), Edward Young (1683–1765) argued for the necessity of originality and sublimity in writing odes. Now Pope argued for originality and for following nature in his 'Essay on Criticism', but it is hardly surprising that of the writers named in this chapter, Defoe, Hill and Welsted find a place among the dunces of Pope's versions of the *Dunciad.* The new emphasis on more open and emotional forms was very different from what Pope had in mind.

Not only is Thomson absent from the *Dunciad*, Pope's scathing attack on bad art and bad morals, but there was a persistent rumour that Pope had aided Thomson in writing parts of *The Seasons.* The rumour was false, but it suggests that contemporaries saw in Thomson's rewriting of Virgil's *Georgics* many of the same qualities that they had come to think typical of Pope. Thomsons's original version of 'Winter' was shorter than later versions and more of a descriptive poem, dominated by the terrifying image of the power of nature's fiercest season. But if it lacked some of the narrative expansion of later versions, it still contained that analogy between man and nature, human and animal, that contained, within a large metaphysical image, the seeming helplessness of humanity before the terrors of life. Winter's coming seems like the end of life itself:

> 'Tis done! dread winter has subdued the year,
> And reigns, tremendous, o'er the desert plains!
> How dead the vegetable kingdom lies!
> How dumb the tuneful! *Horror* wide extends
> His solitary empire.

Thomson quickly slips into moralising about man's life, its brevity, its sins, its 'secret Guilt', and concludes the poem with a vision of death and divine judgement as the moment of revelation when all will understand why the poor suffered while those who lived in luxury seemed to thrive. Such moralising remained in the poem as it went through numerous revisions, and Thomson sought out new areas where he might comment on the life of the times in both specific and general terms. The poem did not collapse under such pressures, but it became a somewhat different type of work. The nature passages remained as powerful as ever, but society loomed ever more important in *The Seasons*.

Thomson's insistence on his analogy between man and the animal world has often been criticised as unrealistic and indirect, but he succeeds in humanising animals in a half-comic fashion and in making man a victim of nature little different from his animals. As a storm approaches, both animal and man seek protection:

> The wanderers of heaven,
> Each to his home, retire; save those that love
> To take their pastime in the troubled air,
> Or Skimming flutter round the dimply pool.
> The cattle from the untasted fields return,
> And ask, with meaning low, their wonted stalls,
> Or ruminate in the contiguous shade.
> Thither the household feathery people crowd,
> The crested cock, with all his female train,
> Pensive and dripping; while the cottage-hind
> Hangs o'er the enlivening blaze, and taleful there
> Recounts his simple frolic: much he talks,
> And much he laughs, nor recks the storm that blows
> Without, and rattles on his humble roof.

Oddly enough, in this scene, it is the cock who seems to worry about the storm and what it might mean. The cottager laughs without concern and tells his stories. The humanising of the animals plays against the animalisation of man. The cattle 'ruminate' and the birds return not to their nests but to their homes. If the notion of 'household feathery people' seems a long way about for a simple term for birds, we have to measure the gain of significance against the loss of conciseness.

More than the other seasons winter is a killer, and one of the most frequently illustrated scenes from *The Seasons* was that of the swain lost in the snow and eventually sinking down in the drifts. Thomson conjures up a scene of sentiment as he depicts the wife and children waiting for him to return, but the death is realistic enough:

> In vain his little children, peeping out
> Into the mingling storm, demand their sire
> With tears of artless innocence. Alas!
> Nor wife nor children more shall he behold,
> Nor friends, nor sacred home. On every nerve
> The deadly Winter seizes, shuts up sense,
> And, o'er his inmost vitals creeping cold,
> Lays him along the snows a stiffened corse,
> Stretched out, and bleaching in the northern blast.

In spite of all the moralising, the social commentary on prisons, hunting, cruelty, it was mainly the scenes of violent death and the inset narratives that were the favourites of readers. Thomson was at his best in creating vivid images that seem to expand to larger symbolic meaning. His terrifying shark following the slave ships and the plague that devours whole cities are like parts of a universe that seems ready to exterminate man with as little concern as we might carelessly step on an insect. Thomson's picture of the city struck by pestilence is very much like Defoe's London in 1665:

> Empty the streets, with uncouth verdure clad;
> Into the worst of deserts sudden turned
> The cheeful haunt of men – unless, escaped
> From the doomed house, where matchless horror reigns,
> Shut up by barbarous fear, the smitten wretch
> With frenzy wild breaks loose, and, loud to Heaven
> Screaming, the dreadful policy arraigns,
> Inhuman and unwise.

The commentary on quarantining houses might have come directly from Defoe's work.

Thomson's blank verse has sometimes been thought of as an imitation of Milton's. Certainly Milton's reputation was extremely high, and there are numerous borrowings. But for the most part, Thomson's verse is his own in both its virtues and defects. It is a splendid vehicle for the sublime and terrifying, and slightly silly when Thomson turns to celebrate the pineapple or to upbraid the savage for not being civilised. In his poem 'To the Memory of Sir Isaac Newton' (1727), he makes wonderful use of it for a sublime picture of Newton as a surrogate of the divine intelligence ordering the Cosmos. He pictures Newton dispelling the false image of the universe suggested by Descartes:

> The heavens are all his own, from the wide rule
> Of whirling vortices and circling spheres
> To their first great simplicity restored.
> The schools astonished stood; but found it vain
> To combat still with demonstration strong,
> And, unawakened, dream beneath the blaze
> Of truth. At once their pleasing vision fled
> With the gay shadows of the morning mixed,
> When Newton rose, our philosophic sun!

Thomson also demonstrated his ability to use other verse forms in his 'Castle of Indolence' (1748), an imitation of Spenserian allegroy and Spenserian stanzaic form, but by that time the revival of Renaissance subjects and forms was beginning in earnest.

Poems like these have often been labelled 'Whig panegyric verse', because they tended to sing the accomplishments of the century, attack sloth, and urge the reader to further efforts at improving society. Such categorisation often blinds us to the individuality of the poems and the poets. Thomson was not a personal poet in the sense that Wordsworth (1770–1850) dramatised himself in his poetry, but neither is he wholly absent. Thomson is everywere in his poem feeling the experiences of nature and directing the reader's horror at natural catastrophes by his own expression of horror. And even the encouragement to industry in the 'Autumn' section of the *Seasons* and 'The Castle of Indolence' has roots in his personal melancholy and sloth. In the same year as Thomson's 'Winter', the painter and poet John Dyer (1700–1758) published his 'Grongar Hill'. Written in tetrameter couplets with their incantatory resonance, this poem too follows the pattern of Thomson. Although the title should remind the reader of Denham's 'Cooper's Hill', Dyer's poem is not at all political. Instead we have the poet hymning the beauty of nature and trying to evoke his sense of the scene and his emotions for the reader. The message of this and some of

Dyer's other poems is simpler than Thomson's analogy: Nature has a purity and beauty that is only corrupted by contact with human civilisation. Dyer converts this observation into a myth and asserts it as an article of faith. In this form, rather than in its more complex manifestations, it was to have a dramatic effect on future poetry.

III Plays for the reformed town

Like prose fiction and poetry, the theatre was undergoing a change in the direction of more feeling and less complexity. In comedy, George Farquhar (1678–1707) preserved some of the complexity of meaning from Restoration comedy while avoiding the difficult wit and verbal interactions of Congreve and Vanbrugh. *The Recruiting Officer* (1706) and *The Beaux' Strategem* (1707) may be regarded as the last flowering of the old comedy or the unfulfilled possibilities of comedy that might have survived Collier's attacks. But Farquhar's serious discussions of marriage and divorce and the amazing freshness of his lovers were probably doomed even if Farquhar had not died so young. Susanna Centlivre (1667–1723) wrote a series of comedies using a lively intrigue plot with rakes who were not very rakish and ladies all of impeccable virtue, the best of which were *The Busie Body* (1709) and *A Bold Stroke for a Wife* (1718) with its good-natured fool, Marplot. The possibility of using the stage for exploratory social sex and marriage commentary, however, was over. When Charles Johnson (1679–1748) tried to stage a play in 1732 that featured the madam of a bordello, it was hissed off the stage.

The dominant new mode was the sentimental comedy of Cibber and Steele, but what was probably the best of this form, Steele's *The Conscious Lovers* (perf. 1722; pub. 1723) was also different from earlier plays in focusing on a major social problem (duelling) rather than on some aspect of love and family relations. Steele's play set the form for sentimental comedy during the century. The hero, Bevil Jr. is a man of exemplary morals, who has rescued a young lady, Indiana, from poverty and the advances of an unscrupulous man to establish her in London. Everyone assumes that he is keeping her as his mistress, but he never even raises the question of love to her, a matter which even has Indiana puzzled. Bevil Jr.'s father wishes him to marry the daughter of a merchant, Mr Sealand, who is indignant at Bevil Jr.'s behaviour. On coming to see Indiana, Mr Sealand finds himself overwhelmed by her dignity and beauty, and by some suggestions and the help of his long-lost sister, he discovers that Indiana is his daughter by his first wife. With this knowledge, Mr Sealand bestows Indiana on her admiring and sentimental lover while giving his other daughter, Lucinda, to her true admirer, Mr Myrtle.

The comic part of the play is borne by Mrs Sealand and her choice for Lucinda's hand in marriage, Cimberton, by the witty servants, Tom and Phillis, and by Myrtle, who, in one scene of low comedy, joins Tom in playing two incomprehensible and bumbling attorneys, Serjeant Target and Councillor Bramble. Cimberton is amusing in his absurd views of marriage and the proper breeding of children, based on the analogy between women and animals. But Tom and Phillis now fill the role of the gay couple of Restoration comedy. Like the un-neurotic children of the poor in Freud's picture of social life, they are able to kiss and act in a more or less uninhibited fashion, while Lucinda marvels at their freedom. That Steele gave the parts of the witty lovers of Restoration comedy to the servants is commentary on the change from the style of Dryden and Wycherley. In Steele's play, the truly admirable couple, Bevil Jr. and Indiana, engage in long conversations filled with 'sentiments' of the highest morality. The sentimentality of the play arises from what must be regarded as a stereotyped view of society: education and a life free of labour impart a refinement that makes Bevil and Myrtle superior to the good-natured Tom or to the talented musician, Signor Carbonelli. Between the lovers there is only a meeting of minds and an exchange of sincere and delicate sentiments.

Steele builds into his play two serious moments. In the first, Sealand presents a heated defence of the new merchant class. He mocks the idea of titles of nobility and descent and questions the morals of Bevil Jr.; it is *he* who demands some sign of true nobility – nobility of character – from his prospective son-in-law. In the second, Bevil Jr., stung to anger by Myrtle's accusations, almost agrees to a duel, but he regains control of his passions and by a calm explanation, succeeds in calming Myrtle's anger. Myrtle is ashamed of his own behaviour and concludes due!ling is foolish, an action undertaken out of fear of appearing cowardly before the world. He praises the true manliness of Bevil Jr. in refusing to yield to such pressures. This scene is only one in which various characters show their awe at the goodness and sincerity of Bevil Jr. The creation of such an exemplary character for a hero became a deadly formula for the literature of the time, and while Steele's play has enough comedy to sustain itself, the same was not true of many of the imitations that followed. The critic John Dennis (1657–1734), attacked Steele's play as a bewildering and confused mixture of romance and nonsense and saw in it the demise of true comedy, a prediction that had some basis in the waning of true comic talent during the decades that followed.

Tragedy followed a different course. The sentimental tragedies of John Banks (*fl.* 1696) with their tearful heroines and vague historical settings were predictive of the type of 'She Tragedy' that dominated the eighteenth-century stage. Nicholas Rowe (1674–1718), a much better writer than Banks, followed him in writing tragedies that appealed to the pity of the audience. His English themes were varied, moving from the time of the Anglo-Saxons (*The Royal Convert,* (perf. 1707; pub. 1708) to the sixteenth century (*Lady Jane Gray*, 1715). In *The Ambitious Step-Mother* (perf. 1700; pub. 1701) and *Ulysses* (1705), he treated classical subjects, and in *Tamerlane* (perf. 1701; pub. 1702), he used the story of the barbaric monarch to make a political commentary. One of his most effective plays, *The Fair Penitent* (1703) was taken from a play written in the early seventeenth century by Massinger and Field, and draws on the type of domestic tragedy that was to interest George Lillo·(1693–1739) several decades later. In some ways even the historical tragedies, like *Jane Shore* (1714), call on the pathos that belongs to the tragedies of ordinary life.

Rowe's tragedies take place in a world heavily governed by Providence. Life is painful, but as in Thomson's 'Winter', there is assurance of guiding spirit that will bring overall good to mankind whether in this life or the next. In *Lady Jane Gray,* the prologue states that the intention is to 'touch the tender heart', and in scenes in which Lady Jane Gray is discovered at her prayers just before her execution at the hands of Queen Mary, Rowe comes very close to effective and moving tragedy. But although he was a favourite of Samuel Richardson (1689–1761), and although his plays remained popular on the stage throughout the century, Dr Johnson was probably right in arguing that he tended to be too 'general and undefined' in depicting the emotions and too shallow in his approach to his subjects. Johnson admired him, but he had reservations. A major problem with the plays is a tendency to abstraction, a fault shared with much of the tragedy influenced by what the English perceived to be French and classical ideals. Thomas Otway (1651–84) was the only English dramatist to convert the passionate tragedies of Racine into great original works. But there was a sense of real issues and characters in Otway that Rowe never achieved. Rowe, of course, claimed to be following Shakespeare in some of his plays, particularly *Jane Shore,* but Johnson's judgement on this is apt. 'In what he thought himself an imitator of Shakespeare', wrote Johnson, 'it is not easy to conceive. The numbers, the diction, the sentiments, and the conduct, every thing in which imitation can consist, are remote in the utmost degree from the manner of Shakespeare; whose drama it resembles only as it is an English story, and as some of the persons have their names in history'.

One of the most popular tragedies of this period was Addison's *Cato.* Although the argument for liberty is generalised enough, the play drew cheers from Whigs and Tories alike. By 1713, the cry for 'liberty' had been annexed by both parties, though, in spite of Addison's affiliation with the Whigs, it played a particular role in the opposition to Walpole's government during the period 1720–40 until once more captured by the radical side. That *Cato* (1713) continued to be thought of as the best-made tragedy of the age by Englishmen and foreigners alike is strange in view of its incorporation of characterisation and structure from Restoration models. Sempronius, with his sado-masochistic attitude toward sex, and Syphax, with his Hobbist view of human bestiality, would not be out of place in some of Dryden's extravagant heroic plays. And Cato is so unmoved in his stoicism as to be almost wholly predictable as a character.

The very rigidity of Cato's virtue calls much of what he does into question. Addison had suggested in *The Spectator* that Cato's character was not very amiable, however impressive he might have been. And the Cato of Addison's tragedy is motivated by a belief that the world itself is evil. He sees in Caesar a considerable number of virtues but demonstrates that they are not the virtues compatible with Rome. As for himself, he adheres to the stoic ideal of the man who is above all human passion – an ideal that many contemporary satirists attacked as essentially inhuman. But Cato is capable of emotion over the stoic ideal itself, an ideal that includes the concept of an after-life. Thus he is almost happy at the end and confuses Lucia, who believes that he is looking forward to life rather than to the suicide that will free him from life. That he dies without knowing of Pompey's revolt is one of many ironies at the end. Even his dignified suicide is tainted by his doubts about the wisdom of such an act. With their involvement in Greek and Roman history, the audiences of the eighteenth century found many political parallels with their own time in Addison's tragedy, but it seems fair to say that for the modern reader only the final act is entirely successful.

These plays were all products of the early years of the century, and while the drama was less changed by the new developments in prose and poetry than might have been expected, one playwright was very much part of the new developments – George Lillo (1693–1739). Just as Defoe tended to build new myths from old, Lillo took the old ballad of the apprentice led astray by a wicked woman, and in 1731 produced *The London Merchant, or the History of George Barnwell.* Like Steele, Lillo celebrated the greatness that the English merchants had brought to the nation, but he did it not so much through a realistic view of society as by a kind of ritualistic drama in which everything seems to be acted out beforehand. George is inevitably seduced by the vicious Millwood, a woman who uses her sex to destroy men. Driven by her demands, he murders his uncle, as a sympathetic nature reflects *without* the storm what such a murder means *within* the state of society. George goes to his death completely repentant, as both his friend and the virtuous woman who loved him tell him of what might have been had he remained honest. Millwood, trapped with a pistol in her hand, spews out her hatred of men and the society that gives them superiority over women.

London apprentices were let out once a year to see the play as a salutary lesson for them to follow, and it would be easy to interpret the simple structure of the play as the mark of an incompetent playwright. But the mythic force of character and action is extraordinarily powerful. And the death of the uncle is a remarkable scene. Unlike the plays of Rowe and those who followed him, *The London Merchant* arouses terror rather than pity. Millwood is so forceful as the male-hating, self-hating, woman that there is nothing quite like her on the stage until *Hedda Gabler*.

Less successful but still interesting is Lillo's tragedy, *Fatal Curiosity* (1736). Whereas *The London Merchant* achieved a mythic effect and thereby succeeded in bypassing the deadly injunction of contemporary criticism, that all good tragedy must involve a generalised representation of the passions, *Fatal Curiosity* begins with a sociological and historical fact. The time is 1618, and Sir Walter Raleigh has been executed unjustly. From the very beginning we are in a world in which virtue seems to be not merely unrewarded but actually punished. The perception of such a world causes Old Wilmot, a poor man, to resolve on acting on the basis of self-interest, self-preservation and necessity. When their long-departed son arrives from the West Indies with considerable wealth in jewels and decides to conceal his identity just to see how his parents will behave, he sets off a series of events which result in his murder at the hands of his father and the subsequent deaths through murder and suicide of his parents. The ironies are painful and relentless in the manner of Thomas Hardy (1840–1928) more than a century later. Lillo shows a number of nice dramatic touches in having the father start the wrong way as he goes to murder the guest who turns out to be his son. But what is most significant is the search for new systems of meaning and new myths for the literature of this period. It remains from this point forward a crucial element in the literature of the time.

5

Scriblerian satire

The group of writers who made up the Scriblerus Club included some of the greatest of their age: Swift, Pope, Gay, Arbuthnot, as well as the talented Thomas Parnell (1679–1718). But Dr Johnson was right in warning literary historians against trying to see their times through their eyes:

> In the letters both of Swift and Pope there appears such narrowness of mind, as makes them insensible of any excellence that has not some affinity with their own, and confines their esteem and approbation to so small a number, that whoever should form his opinion of the age from their representation, would suppose them to have lived amidst ignorance and barbarity, unable to find among their contemporaries either virtue or intelligence, and persecuted by those that could not understand them.

Such a warning is all the more cogent because in the two hundred years since Johnson's 'Life of Pope' it has been thoroughly ignored.

Although the Scriblerus Club came into being as a literary group in 1713, two of its founding members, Swift and Arbuthnot, were the most effective propagandists for the Tories, who controlled the government and public opinion from 1710 until the death of Queen Anne in 1714. The Whigs already had their literary group in the Kit-Cat Club, a combination of critics and literary men – Garth, Congreve, Addison and Steele – the publisher, Jacob Tonson, and a number of the leading Whig politicians. There were many other clubs, like the half-mythical Jacobite October Club and the republican Calves' Head Club. Swift had tried to form a club of writers and friends earlier, and it was inevitable that, at a time of violent factions, a group with conservative political attitudes and similar literary tastes should come together in defence of what they considered to be the true standards of writing.

The Scriblerians remained close friends for most of their lives, despite an occasional quarrel and considerable differences in age and background. Swift and Arbuthnot were both born in 1667 and were twenty-one years older than Pope. Gay and Pope tried to avoid politics until their later years, while Arbuthnot's family had leanings toward Jacobitism. Pope was a Catholic; Swift was ordained as a minister of the Church of Ireland. Both were friendly with Henry St. John, first Viscount Bolingbroke, who was close enough to them in his politics but a deist in religion. Deists believed in a universe created by a god who had long ago ceased to interfere in the particular events that occasionally interrupted the smooth operation of his natural laws. They shared with more traditional Christians of the eighteenth century an admiration for the order of the universe, but they thought of the earth as a mere speck in the universe and of man as one of many species to be discovered on other planets. Such differences created occasional problems. The Scriblerians may not have understood one another perfectly but they certainly liked each other. As a literary group, they shared a pleasure in satire and literary spoofs. Swift had already set the pattern for their type of satire in his *Tale of A Tub* and *The Battle of the Books,* those very unorthodox literary defences of established literary modes in which he had mixed prose narrative with essays that constantly digressed, mock-epic descriptions of battle and even animal fable. In one of his poems, *An Epistle to a Lady who Desired the Author to make Verses on Her in the Heroick Stile* (1734), Swift expressed his somewhat mocking dismay at the request. The heroic was not really his style. Comedy and satire were the best ways to make serious statements. Tragedy and epic often became ridiculous by striving too hard for raised effects. The results were usually bathos rather than sublimity, and Pope's Scriblerian *Peri Bathos or the Art of Sinking in Poetry* (1735) offered a number of sure formulas for bad writing in the heroic style.

Together the friends embarked on *The Memoirs of Martinus Scriblerus,* a prose satire not published until 1741. An amusing attack on pedantry, the *Memoirs* served in many ways as a treasure-house of ideas for future projects. The model was Swift's favourite writer, Rabelais, and Cornelius's effort to raise his son, Martin, in accord with his abstract theories of education, draws strongly from that author. François Rabelais

(c. 1494–1553) wrote his *Pantagruel* (1533) and *Gargantua* (1535) in a style that was explorative of language itself and as a satire on the knowledge of his time. Swift learned much from Rabelais, from the exploitation of the grotesque to the use of the imaginary voyage as an absurd quest after impossible answers to the problems of the human condition. But the satire on self-love and pride, the making Martin into an Anatomist interested in dissecting bodies, and the general attack on science bear the strong stamp of Swift's interests. The broad comedy toward the end involving Martin's passion for Siamese twins, with the legal entanglement over whether they ought to have one husband or two, is more in the manner of Pope and Arbuthnot. But Martin's increasing misanthropy, as a device for satirising the absurdity of human pride, shows a pessimistic view of mankind that Swift, Arbuthnot, and, to a lesser extent, Pope, held in common. *The Memoirs* is a clever prose satire, but, for the most part, it lacks the peculiar turn of wit and layered prose that were to make Swift's *Gulliver's Travels* a true masterpiece.

Another joint project was a comedy, *Three Hours after Marriage* (1717), written by Gay, Pope and Arbuthnot. Broadly farcical, with undertones of obscene and scatological comedy, *Three Hours after Marriage* was a typical product of the Scriblerians in its satire on pedantry. Although Pope blamed Colley Cibber, the manager of the theatre, for its failure, it was not the type of comedy that was likely to please the audience of 1717. Satire often used obscene material as part of its basic material and neither Swift nor Pope was going to abandon it. That both Swift and Pope were considered by many readers to be offenders against decency, irreligious and improper, suggests the degree to which they were not entirely representative of contemporary taste. On the other hand, those readers with some degree of literary sophistication recognised their genius and understood that satire will use offensive language and imagery to increase awareness and sharpen the sting. *Three Hours after Marriage* was less satire however, than the broad humour that would have passed without adverse comment in the Restoration, but which was now out of fashion.

The real successes of the Scriblerians were individual efforts. John Arbuthnot (1637–1735), physician in ordinary to Queen

Anne, had already published his *History of John Bull* and *The Art of Political Lying* in 1712, before the creation of the Scriblerian Club. These were effective political satires in support of the Tory government. Arbuthnot was particularly skilled in creating political satires that communicated through thinly-disguised but witty fables. John Gay (1685–1732) showed his particular talent early with a burlesque, 'Wine' (1708), a poem in blank verse, with Miltonic echoes in the manner of Philips's 'The Splendid Shilling'. He parodied pastoral poetry in 'The Shepherd's Week' (1714) and relied upon Virgil's *Georgics* for 'Rural Sports' (1713) and 'Trivia: or, the Art of Walking the Streets of London' (1716). Although Gay's interest in mixing genres and undercutting dignified forms by using them for low and comic subject matter came naturally to him, Swift had some influence as well. Swift's poems on the city, 'A Description of the Morning' and 'A Description of a City Shower' published in the *Tatler* during 1709 and 1710 mingled exact observation of city scenes with a dignified style. The results are oddly ambiguous. Swift's vision of London is mixed: a den of vice as the maid returns to her own room after sleeping with her master; grotesque as the shower carries garbage, dead cats, 'Dung, Guts and Blood' in its streams; and oddly beautiful in the gestures of the maid taking her clothes off the line before they are drenched. Gay's London is more charming. References to a quarrel in the rain as avoidable by remembering the fate of Oedipus, and Gay's creation of the goddess Cloacina, guardian of the filthy tides of the city, mock the pretensions of modern city life; yet even Cloacina's appearance, turnip tops on her head, an eel around her middle and rags behind, does not detract from the delight of her imagined gift of the art of shoe shining to a poor London orphan.

Gay was to use this ability to keep a balance between dignity and the comic to excellent effect in his *Fables* (1727–38), but he scored his real triumphs in the theatre. Here again, he was interested in mixing genres. *The What D'Ye Call It: A Tragi-Comi-Pastoral Farce* (1715) has a preface in which Gay claims to have invented a new form of art – one which lay 'in interweaving the several kinds of the Drama with each other, so that they cannot be distinguish'd or separated'. The work opens with a play within a play as the Steward of Sir Roger

puts on a drama that will suit his master's tastes and include all
forms. The play is about a cruel squire who sends away
Filbert, his son, to serve in the army, leaving Kitty, his
sweetheart, pregnant. In the end, Filbert returns to wed Kitty
and all ends happily and confusedly as the audience and the
Squire learn that the stage marriage was a real wedding and
that his son, Thomas, has married the Steward's daughter.
There are ghosts, including one who sings a song and another
who is the ghost of an embryo. There is a reprieve before an
execution and a mad scene in the manner of Ophelia's in
Hamlet.

Gay had experimented with a 'Tragi-Comical Farce' some
years earlier in *The Mohocks* (pub. 1712) , but while the earlier
work has a prostitute named Jenny and some absurd Justices,
it bears little resemblance to that advanced technique of
blending stage action with real action in *The What D'Ye Call It*
that was to be used even more effectively in *The Beggars' Opera*
(1728). But by the time Gay came to write his *Beggar's Opera* he
had not only experimented with the techniques of farce and
burlesque that were essential to the fabric of that work; he had
also tried his hand at standard theatrical genres: comedy with
The Wife of Bath (1713) and tragedy with *The Captives* (1724).
And if he did not write an opera libretto until 1732, when *Acis
and Galatea* was set by the great composer Handel, he had
already written some excellent ballads for music including
'Twas When the Seas were Roaring'. Although the musical
score for *The Beggar's Opera* may have been something of an
afterthought, a glance at Gay's early work makes his sudden
triumph with his ballad opera of criminal life less surprising.

I   'The Beggar's Opera' and 'Polly'

The suggestion for a 'Newgate pastoral' first came from Swift,
but the writer of burlesque pastorals and the poetic
topographer of London hardly needed much encouragement.
The Beggar's Opera was a theatrical success of a kind London
had never seen before. It ran for thirty-two consecutive nights
and became the rage of the town with an entire industry of
artefacts – playing cards, fans, plates, paintings springing up
to depict scenes of Polly Peachum and Captain Macheath. It

created a new genre, the ballad opera, which had considerable influence on composers like Wolfgang Amadeus Mozart (1756–91) and may be seen as the origin of the modern musical. It has never been off the stage for long, and it inspired Bertolt Brecht's (1898–1956) brilliant modernised version, *The Three Penny Opera*. Brecht's collaboration with the composer Kurt Weill (1900–50), who combined serious modern music with jazz and other popular musical forms, almost parallels Gay's partnership with Pepusch. Gay's work came at a crucial point in modern history. In 1721–22 came the first great financial crisis with the collapse of the South Sea Company and its inflated stocks. Those years saw the rise in the crime rate, and criminals could find hiding places in what was now the large metropolis of London. Defoe had drawn some of these events together in his pamphlets on Jonathan Wild, the criminal fence, and Jack Sheppard, the clever thief. The remark of one of Brecht's characters, 'What is the robbing of a bank to the founding of a bank', would have found numerous echoes in the thinking of Gay's time, when many had not fully accepted the hazards of the new capitalism or even the idea of the Bank of England, which was established during the reign of William III.

The Beggar's Opera is best viewed as a satire on three aspects of contemporary life: music, politics and the drama. Although not everyone raged against opera to the degree that the critic John Dennis did, there were few men of letters in the time who did not find considerable absurdity in the spectacle of an audience that might not pay to view legitimate theatre spending a great deal to hear songs in a language they did not understand. Gay complained to Swift in 1723:

> As for the reigning amusement of the town, it is entirely music; real fiddles, base-viols, the hautboys, not poetical harps, lyres, and reeds. There is nobody allowed to say, 'I sing', but an eunuch, or an Italian woman. Everybody is grown now as great a judge of music, as they were in your time of poetry, and folks that could not distinguish one tune from another, now daily dispute about the different styles of Handel, Bononcini, and Attilio.

George Friedrich Handel (1685–1759) had tried to establish opera in England as early as 1711. Giovanni Battista Bononcini (c. 1672–c. 1752) came from Italy to Britain

around 1720 as a rival to Handel. Atilio Ariosti (1666–
c. 1740), another Italian composer of operas, was in England
during 1716 and again in 1722. The three shared the
directorship of the Royal Academy of Music dedicated to
opera. Much of the conversation about singers focused on the
castrato, Senesino and a few years later, after Handel had
started his opera, he shared it with the divas Faustina and
Cuzzoni. The quarrel between the two sopranos grew violent
in the years before Gay's satire, with fights occurring on the
stage. When Captain Macheath finds himself torn between
Polly and Lucy, he is showing an obvious, if ironic,
relationship with Senesino under somewhat similar
circumstances.

For music Gay offered, not operatic arias, but versions of
contemporary ballads arranged by John Pepusch (1667–1752).
Ballads had been experiencing a literary rise since Addison's
advocacy of them, and Ambrose Philips (c. 1675–1749) had
edited the first modern collection in 1723. Instead of the
repetitions, both musical and verbal, of Handel's operatic
style, Pepusch gave the audience simple and frequently
beautiful songs that assumed a new dimension in a theatrical
setting. Often the songs are so lovely that the listener forgets
both the context and the meaning of the words. A typical
example is the song 'Over the Hills and Far Away', a duet
begun by the 'heroic' thief Macheath:

	Were I laid on Greenland's coast,
	And in my arms embraced my lass,
	Warm amidst eternal frost,
	Too soon the half year's night would pass.
POLLY	Were I sold on Indian soil
	Soon as the burning day was closed,
	I could mock the sultry toil,
	When on my charmer's breast reposed.
MACHEATH	And I would love you all the day,
POLLY	Every night would kiss and play,
MACHEATH	If with me you'd fondly stray
POLLY	Over the hills and far away.

Because the music is so charming we forget that it is a song
about one of the grimmest of contemporary events: the
transportation of criminals to work as slaves in the colonies for
a period of time. Pepusch did not hesitate to use a chorus from

an opera of Handel, *Rinaldo* (1711) as the setting for one of Gay's lyrics, and if it may be seen to some extent as an attack on opera, *The Beggar's Opera* may be better regarded as offering an alternative type of musical drama.

If Gay's satire against contemporary political and social life seems tame next to that of Brecht, it was nevertheless strong enough for its time. Swift wondered if the prime minister, Walpole, did not see himself in the figure of Peachum, the arch fence, or even Lockit, the keeper of Newgate. Peachum, like Jonathan Wild, operates as an impeacher of criminals while actually controlling their depredations against society. Having employed his criminals until they have outlived their usefulness, he turns them in for the reward. Both Peachum and Lockit live by a code of self-interest. Lockit remarks, 'Of all animals of Prey, Man is the only sociable one. Everyone of us preys upon his Neighbour, and yet we herd together'. They see society in Hobbist terms as pure convention. Hence, when Mr and Mrs Peachum discover that Polly has married Captain Macheath, they are outraged that she should follow such a silly and dangerous convention, one that they never bothered with. At the same time that they dismiss such legalities, they ape the middle class. Though their business or 'Trade' is only such by an ironic analogy, they consider their work more honest than that of supposedly honest business and professional men. At a time when the middle classes were insisting on what Foucault has called 'the illegality of Right' – the freedom to commit certain illegalities in the name of business – why should the criminal class perceive any difference between their activities and those of the respectable bourgeoisie. When we see Peachum acting the gentleman and complimenting Mrs Trapes on her brand of gin, that he detects through a friendly kiss, Gay questions the values of the middle classes at the same time that he laughs at the absurdities of his upwardly mobile criminals.

Although Captain Macheath is sometimes known by a name that suggests Walpole, he belongs more to the side of *The Beggar's Opera* that involves literary satire, for unlike the older generation, the Peachums, Lockit, and Mrs Trapes, he attempts to imitate the heroes of romance and pastoral rather than any middle-class ideas. If his relationship with Polly and Lucy has sometimes been viewed as somewhat like Sir Robert

Walpole's with his wife and mistress, Molly Skerrit, he remains, for the most part, a believer in honour among thieves and a scorner of the upper classes. In one of his last songs, he implies that the 'ways of the court' have so corrupted social life that all the personal values of friendship have been destroyed. He tends to idealise all his relationships. He is Polly's pastoral swain and lends her books on romance. When he feels that he must have other women and calls in the prostitutes, he refuses to think of them as anything but charming ladies until they betray him. And in his surprise that one of his gang turns him in, he shows his initial naïveté.

As for Polly, she is completely innocent and charming within the possibilities allowed to a young woman passionately in love with the daring Captain Macheath. If her pastoral attitudes and expectations appear ironic amidst the betrayals of the criminals and prostitutes, she and Macheath are able to transcend that reality, partly through the transforming power of the music and partly through the power of pastoral. The lovely song quoted above is a confession of their belief that not even the worst climate of the colonies can change their love. Admittedly, Polly has a moment in which the thought of seeing Captain Macheath riding in a cart to the gallows at Tyburn with heroic bravery is almost enough to make her wish him condemned but the thought of his death awakens her from this momentary lapse into the pleasure of imagining herself the widow of a folk hero. And if her quarrel with Lucy arouses her more combative instincts, she soon returns to a profession of her entire love. The modern critic, William Empson, (b. 1906) has argued that the images contained in that love are not without reference to the gallows, and certainly Gay was not without irony in dealing with Polly's love as a literally choking experience. But all this is part of the layered irony throughout the ballad opera. It is a world in which everything wears one kind of disguise or another, in which Mrs Trapes's song about her youth may be read either as a charming statement of her amorous nature or as a whore's willingness to turn a trick. On the whole, the sense of reality and the seaminess of life among Gay's criminals comes as a delayed reaction and never destroys the illusion of gaiety.

In addition to the play with pastoral and romance characterisation and language, Gay constructed his ballad opera as a burlesque in the manner of Buckingham's *The Rehearsal*, a play produced originally in 1671 (pub. 1672) but rewritten throughout the Restoration and eighteenth century to suit later audiences. George Villiers, second Duke of Buckingham (1628–87) built his play around the rehearsal of a new play by Bays. Smith, a visitor to London, and the audience watches in disbelief as Bays instructs the actors in the best ways of performing his awful play. Gay's work opens with a conversation between the Beggar-playwright and a Player. The Beggar has brought his ballad opera into the legitimate theatre after having acted it among the poor. In its original form, Macheath is supposed to be hanged, but in compliance with the expectation of the audience, the Beggar agrees to have an absurd happy ending. A reprieve is called for and the Beggar bows to popular taste. He comments on the 'similitude of manners in high and low life', remarking that the poor are generally punished for their crimes. By implication it would seem that the rich escape. But the end belongs to Macheath, who confesses that he was really married to Polly alone among all the wives who appear at the end to claim him. Whereas *The Rehearsal* closes with the abandonment of the play, *The Beggar's Opera* leaves the stage to the performers. Or are they performers? Gay closes his work on a note which leaves both the world of illusion and reality in doubt. Macheath appears to belong to both worlds.

Gay tried to follow his success with a sequel, *Polly,* but this time the government moved to suppress it. Gay published it in 1729 and perhaps gained greater attention by the Lord Chamberlain's rejection, since the publicity created an interested audience. As the poet, once more in conversation with the player, remarks, works like *The Beggar's Opera* are unlikely to have successful sequels. Gay attempts to expand the irony of his masterpiece by transporting Polly to the West Indies where her virtue is under attack by the plantation owner, Ducat. Macheath, now transformed into a complete villain, has become a pirate, 'married' the prostitute Jenny Diver, and renamed himself Morano. Gay brings in a tribe of virtuous Indians to comment on Europeans and their lack of morality. Cawwawkee, a brave noble Indian, falls in love with Polly, and after Macheath has been hanged and the claims of Ducat rejected, Polly gives a half-consent to marry him.

Taking his hints from Defoe's *History of the Pirates*, Gay has Polly disguise herself as a man, and it is she who captures Macheath for the Indians. *Polly* has possibilities, but Gay's moralising is heavy-handed. When one of the pirates speaks of honour, Jenny remarks, 'For shame, lieutenant; you talk downright *Indian*'. And indeed Gay's Indians do comment wisely on the degenerate nature of Western man. 'With how much ease and unconcern these *Europeans* talk of vices, as if they were necessary qualifications' says the chief, Pohetohee. Macheath reveals a complete unconcern for anything but power and wealth. Characterisation is stiff and obvious, and for a writer whose main gift was his light satiric touch, *Polly* was a bad idea. He used his talents to better effect in the second series of *Fables,* published in 1738 after his death.

II   'Gulliver's Travels' and other satires

Creating Indians similar to those in Gay's *Polly,* bringing them to Europe and having them comment on contemporary life had been one scheme Swift had toyed with in considering the possible subjects on which he might focus his satire. Instead he turned to the tradition of the imaginary voyage and published his *Gulliver's Travels* in 1726. Swift had been anything but inactive in the years following the appearance of *Tale of a Tub.* A powerful propagandist for the Church of England and Ireland, particularly against the Dissenters, he was soon to turn his talents to political propaganda for the Tories. In 1710 he started writing for the government in *The Examiner,* and in 1711, he wrote *The Conduct of the Allies,* questioning the necessity for continuing the war against France. In 1711 he published one of his finest works of irony, *An Argument against Abolishing Christianity,* using one of his favourite devices – a narrator with little grasp of the implications of the arguments he is advancing. In this instance the writer's defence of Christianity comes down to the idea that its abolition would cause too many inconveniences and that since no one actually believes in Christianity, it is completely harmless. Swift was to use a similar ironic device in 1729, when the humble social engineer of *A Modest Proposal* suggests that the best way of solving Ireland's difficulties with beggars and famine would be to raise the young children for food. Swift was aiming his barbs at the voracious appetites of the ruling classes who, having devoured everything else, would be just about ready to turn to cannibalism. And if in 1726 Swift needed any encouragement to launch into a satire upon mankind, he had just won a battle with his *Drapier's Letters* (1724–25), a series of letters supposedly written by a Dublin drapier, attacking Walpole's plan to dump a new and unpopular coinage upon an Ireland that was tired of being mistreated by the London government.

Although there are a number of English candidates as models for Swift's mixture of dystopia and utopia in the fantastic lands visited by Gulliver, from Sir Thomas More's *Utopia* (1516) and Bishop Joseph Hall's *Discovery of a New World* (1609) to Henry Neville's *Isle of Pines* (1668) and *Robinson Crusoe* (1719), and although it is possible to go back to classical sources such as Lucian, (*fl.* second century A.D.) and his *True Story*, a satire on lying tales of adventure, the imaginary voyage was predominantly a form developed by the French. Rabelais's *Gargantua and Pantagruel* concludes with a voyage to strange lands on an impossible quest, and in his mid-seventeenth-century voyages to the sun and moon Cyrano de Bergerac (1619–55) set up the pattern of journeying to worlds where merely being a human being was evidence enough for the inhabitants of those regions to put a voyager on trial for cruelty and viciousness. De Bergerac's tendency toward deism is carried forward in two other imaginary voyages that were translated into English and widely read: Gabriel de Foigny's (c. 1650–92) travels to the land of the winged hermaphrodites, and Denis Vairasse's (*fl.* 1665–81) discovery of a wise and deistical race known as the Severambes. Foigny's work was translated in 1693 and Vairasses's, though first translated in 1675–79, was popular enough to receive a second translation in the eighteenth century (1716). Both of these works preserved a sense of realism at the start in imitation of the many accounts of genuine voyages to newly-discovered lands that seemed only slightly less amazing than these deliberate fantasies. The Accounts of William Dampier (1652–1715) begun in 1697 but not finished until 1709 and of Woodes Rogers (?–1732) published in 1712 were read with delight by a large audience. Rogers's account of the rescue of Alexander Selkirk, who had been living in isolation on the island of Juan Fernandez, attracted the attention of Sir Richard Steele and, even more significantly, Daniel Defoe, who was to use a number of details from Selkirk's experiences for *Robinson Crusoe.*

Gulliver has his brief moments of isolation in Books III and IV, but Swift was more interested in Gulliver's contacts with other societies than with the idea of stripping bare the absurdities of human aspiration. Gulliver is an English surgeon who takes to sea for adventure and to earn a living. He is frequently everyman, often a fool and occasionally a mad man. Sometimes he is naïve and gullible; at the end he is a disillusioned idealist. He can be cruel or cold or act with the detachment of a scientist examining a corpse, and he can be generous and affectionate. But at all times he is capable of living in an illusion, of trying to adapt to whatever society he encounters and of losing himself in the day-to-day effort at sustaining his ego. Some critics have said that such things do not matter because *Gulliver's Travels* is not a novel, and we are not concerned with the characters. Such a judgement is false because in spite of its satire, *Gulliver's Travels* is an extraordinary fantasy in which the hero's fate is of concern to the reader. If we have to pay attention to what Swift is saying in his satire, we would lose much if such attention precluded our pleasure in Swift's imaginative creation of his many worlds.

The first two voyages, to Lilliput and Brobdingnag, which see Gulliver changing his size in relation to the inhabitants, from the 'Man Mountain' to a creature no larger than a 'splacknuck' or cockroach, exhibit Gulliver and mankind in terms of his power and will-to-power as well as his helplessness. Swift may have been drawing on the optical theories of the philosopher George Berkeley (1685–1753), whose *Theory of Vision* (1709) argued that man judges everything seen according to relative size and distance, but the use to which Swift put these ideas was very different. Gulliver's size should give him an enormous advantage in the land of Lilliput, and it is true that he is able to carry away the fleet of Blefescu. But from the very start, when he is tied up and threatened with death by poisoned arrows, his size is only equivalent to a doubtful fantasy of power, particularly masculine power. If this power is translated into a standing army, it is a threat to everyone within the state, and Gulliver's eventual betrayal at the hands of Flimnap is hardly surprising. Although Gulliver hardly understands his position in Lilliput, the reader should be more discriminating. At one point his enormous appetite seems a matter of curiosity. Toward the end, Gulliver seems to be devouring the substance of the country. If the Lilliputians appear ungrateful in their decision to rid the land of him, such steps are occasionally as necessary as Swift's own effort at ridding the country of its greatest military figure, the Duke of Marlborough.

Now it is true enough that the Lilliputians are petty in their attitudes toward politics and manners, that as a true standard of politics, Flimnap's ability to dance on a tight-rope is worse than Walpole's manner of keeping power in England, and that the disputes among the parties and religious groups about whether to wear high heels or low heels or break an egg on its rounded end or the pointed one are more absurd than the analogous English examples that they satirise. Still, the Lilliputians have been capable of constructing a utopia in which children are raised away from the awful influence of parents and superstitious nurses and in which the lines of caste are rigidly maintained. Even if, as Gulliver comments, this system, modelled on some of Plato's ideals, has fallen into disuse, there is something to be said for a society capable of creating such a scheme – at least Swift would have thought so. And we should remember how eagerly Gulliver embraces his status as a Nardac in the court of Lilliput. For all their littleness, the Lilliputians come closest to ordinary humanity of all the people in the *Travels,* and if Gulliver displays a moment of virtue in which he refuses to reduce the sovereign land of Blefescu to a dependent state, he never really questions his right to use his power to destroy the navy of a nation that has done no harm to him.

In Brobdingnag Gulliver is as small as a Lilliputian was to him, but there is a secret wish fulfilled in being small. It is like returning to being a baby, and at one point he is indeed treated as such by the monkey that carries him off. But Gulliver's main reaction is to reject his size and to think up to the size of his hosts. He laughs at the dwarfs, fights battles with wasps and other insects and animals that offer to attack him, and over-estimates his size by showing how he can jump over what is to him a mammoth cow-pat only to fall short and land in nastiness. His effort at proposing to the King the use of gunpowder produces a similar result. The King's reaction to this invention that expands man's capacity to destroy his fellow man and the environment is to pronounce the human species despicable creatures and to confirm his judgement that mankind was 'the most pernicious race of little odious vermin that nature ever suffered to crawl upon the surface of the earth'. But then the king needed little persuading after hearing Gulliver's account of the political institutions of Great Britain. On these occasions Gulliver apologises for the Monarch's narrow views.

The Gulliver who makes these judgements is still, at least nominally, the believer in the greatness of his country and Western man. He identifies furiously with the giants of Brobdingnag and merely wants to bring them what his country can offer. This amounts to weapons of destruction and institutions undercut by bribery and corruption. When rescued after being carried out to sea by a bird, he regards his fellow humans as pigmies and shouts down at them. He admits that while in Brobdingnag he could not bear to look at himself in a mirror. The third voyage furthers the destruction of that pride that reached a height in Lilliput and was severely tested in Brobdingnag. Set adrift by Japanese pirates, Gulliver lands on an island, and this experience of physical isolation may be seen as a harbinger of the mental isolation he will experience after his final voyage. The third book covers a multitude of human fantasies and destroys each one of them in turn.

First Gulliver encounters the flying island of Laputa and is rescued from his island. Although this section contains some political satire in which the island is depicted as a colonial power that reduces its dependent states to its control by hovering over and shutting off the sun, Swift is more concerned with his larger satiric themes. The Laputans are philosophers who have dedicated themselves to the study of abstract science and mathematics as well as music. Gulliver is intrigued at first, since he considers himself something of a scientist, but he is soon angered by their indifference to what they consider his inferior knowledge and becomes eager to leave. In this impulse, he shares something with the wives of these men of lofty thoughts. Gulliver reports a typical case of a wife who runs away to the earthbound land of Lagado where she is found living with a footman who beats her constantly. She is brought back to Laputa but quickly slips down to her lover. The implication is that the Laputans have lost contact with reality, and indeed their imaginations have been allowed to wander out of control. They live in constant fear that the sun will swallow up the earth or that the earth will be hit by a comet. This is Swift's most serious comment on the limitations of the abstracted intellectual life and what it does to man's very limited capacities.

From Laputa, Gulliver descends to Lagado and Balnibari where he encounters a world of practical reason misapplied to social and economic engineering. It is a world of projects in which the 'common forms' of life are turned upside down. Like the Five-Year Plans of some socialist countries, the new order had taken ordinary modes of agriculture and by their 'improvements' induced a famine throughout the land. In the great Academy, dozens of scientists work on such projects as recreating food from excrement, producing naked sheep and soft marble, and building houses from the top down. Books are written by a machine that arranges words arbitrarily, and the problems of meaning are solved by having people carry objects about to point to. What to Rousseau was a positive good, the concern with things rather than words, is here mocked by Swift who, in a deliberately conservative stance, suggests that the proper study of mankind should begin by looking at man and his artefacts as representative of what he can and cannot, should and should not, do.

In Glubbdubdrib he satisfies the fantasy of going back into the past. And while he sees that, compared to the Roman Senate, the English Parliament resembles a 'knot of pedlars, pickpockets, highwaymen and bullies', he also learns that even in the Augustan age, heroism was not rewarded. And in Luggnagg, after discovering that there is a race of immortals, called Struldbruggs, he rhapsodises on the possibilities contained in such a prospect – wisdom, riches, learning. Instead, he learns that they are monsters, 'peevish, covetous, morose, vain, talkative, but uncapable of friendship, and dead to all natural affection'. They lose their teeth, sense of taste, and hair at ninety, and they are unable to communicate with those who came after them because of changes in the language.

Gulliver rapidly changes his mind about them and argues that to bring one to England would arm people against the fear of death.

Although the third book has often been criticised for lacking the unity of the other sections, the description of the Struldbruggs is among the most powerful passages in the work, and the scenes among the projectors of the Academy among the funniest. In departing from these strange countries, Gulliver travels through Japan where he is told that he is the first traveller to refuse to trample on the crucifix. On the whole, the reader is prepared for a Gulliver who is disillusioned but not quite for the sudden conversion that occurs in the land of the Houyhnhnms. He arrives after his own crew set him adrift and finds himself in the land of philosophical horses and disgusting Yahoos. The process by which Gulliver quickly identifies with the horses and rejects any relationship with the bestial Yahoos is the same as his behaviour previously, except that now, in order to align himself with the superior people, he must completely reject any allegiance to mankind. Thus his account of human history reveals his new insight into the reality of human actions. He explains his conversion by stating that 'truth appeared so amiable to me, that I determined upon sacrificing every thing to it'. And it is at this point that the Master points out the 'gross defects' in human reason.

Unfortunately Gulliver is not a horse, and his effort at imitating them is at once bitterly comic and almost tragic. Many critics have tried to find defects in the Houyhnhnms. Their love is governed by rational choice, and their loyalty and affection are beyond dispute. They have passions, but they are capable of governing them. They do not spoil their children. That they have no iron suggests that they belong to a golden age. But it is a golden age in which man can never live. There is nothing cruel about their decision to send Gulliver away; what is cruel is Swift's message to the reader: mankind is capable of conceiving of a utopia but completely incapable of living in it. Horses perhaps, humans never. When Gulliver is forced to depart from the country of the Houyhnhnms, he is bitter to the point of tears and boasts of having received the honour of kissing the hoof of his master before entering his boat of Yahoo skins. The image of Gulliver about to prostrate himself before this wise horse is at once ludicrous and painful. If we do not feel with Gulliver the agony of being cast out of this rational paradise and at the same time realise the indignity of his position, we miss the power of Swift's satire.

Swift's career as a writer did not end with *Gulliver's Travels*. He continued writing prose tracts on political subjects, and his power as a satirist did not diminish. In 1738 he published his *Complete Collection of Genteel and Ingenious Conversation,* a series of dialogues in which the characters speak no piece of 'wit' that has not been around long enough to become completely inane. Swift's hatred for the unexamined life and the unexamined word is never more clear than in this collection of clichés and dull proverbs. The dialogues go nowhere and conclude nothing, but the reader is left with a sense of the absurdity of most social conversation. Swift mentioned his works on conversation long before publication in a letter to John Gay in 1731 and also mentioned his *Directions to Servants*, not published until 1745, the year of his death and a time when he was no longer in control of his affairs. *Directions to Servants* is a mock handbook for servant behaviour. Using that format, Swift indulges in some of his most outrageous irony as he vents his feeling of abuse against a class of people whose behaviour throughout his life has apparently raised his indignation. The ironic device used is that of wrong advice presented with the solemn air of a writer who assumes that everyone knows that the aim of all servants is to please themselves and drive their masters to distraction. As a result, the advice runs along lines of the best methods to swindle the master, the most unsanitary ways of serving food and the most ruinous techniques of cleaning the house.

In recent years Swift's reputation as a poet has been on the rise. The realism of his city-scape poems has already been mentioned, but he also developed a distinct and clever use of tetrameter couplets for purposes of narrative as in his very early 'Baucis and Philemon' (1706), with its witty use of the theme of metamorphosis, for satire, as in his 'Beasts Confession' (1732), with its play with the theme of the rational animal already used in the fourth book of *Gulliver's Travels,* for ironic autobiography, as in 'Verses on the Death of Dr. Swift', written in 1731 but not published until 1739, and for his birthday poems to Stella, Esther Johnson, his close friend until her death in 1728. The charming poem to Stella written in 1718 is a perfect example of Swift's ability to contain emotion with wit as he turns the fact that she has 'doubled' both her years and size since she was sixteen into an elaborate compliment to her mind and virtue. Swift's poetic themes are not different from those of his prose, but they play against an oddly consonant type of rhyme and metre that sets up an ironic contrast between form and content. This is particularly true of a series of poems devoted to the contrast between the appearances of society and the reality of human life. In 'A Beautiful Young Nymph', 'Strephon and Chloe' and 'Cassinus and Peter', all published in 1734, Swift either reveals to the reader the occasional horrors of the body or shows a young man disillusioned by the discovery that the beautiful woman he loves defaecates like any other mortal. The theme is not very different from what appears in *Tale of a Tub*, but the particular image of the realities of bodily functions in relation to the illusions of society are, perhaps, more powerfully stated than in his earlier work.

III   Dunciads

Such poems, along with the final book of *Gulliver,* gave Swift the reputation of a vicious misanthrope, a reputation particularly strong toward the end of the century. But from 1726 until 1728, the Scriblerians seemed to be overwhelming society with their brilliant satire. Swift wrote to Gay in 1728, 'The Beggar's Opera has knocked down Gulliver; I hope to see Pope's Dulness knock down the Beggar's Opera, but not till it has fully done its job . . . . To expose vice, and to make people laugh with innocence, does more public service than all the Ministers of State from Adam to Walpole'. Pope's 'Dulness' was *The Dunciad.* The first version of this poem appeared in 1728, with a version containing editorial apparatus in the manner of Swift's 1710 *Tale of a Tub* and entitled *The Dunciad Variorum* appearing in 1729. Pope changed the anti-hero of the poem from Lewis Theobald (1688–1744), a friend of Addison and rival editor of Shakespeare, to Colley Cibber with the publication of a new fourth book in 1742, and in 1743 he published *The Dunciad in Four Books.*

If Swift's reputation suffered from accusations of misanthropy, Pope's, which had been the subject of a number of attacks before, was now firmly established in the image of the 'Wasp of Twickenham'. He was mocked for his physical deformity, appearing in a famous print as a monkey. The anonymous author of *The Blatant Beast* (1742) attacked Pope as a 'Distorted Elf' whose attacks failed to discriminate between the objects of his satire:

> Like plagues, like death thy ranc'rous arrows fly,
> At good and bad, at friend and enemy.

Since Pope did indeed include some of his acquaintances among the Dunces, the charge was not without foundation, but the degree to which writers ought to indulge in personal satire, as opposed to a more general kind of satire, had always been a subject of controversy. And by mid-century, though still practised by a number of poets, it was regarded as indicating a lack of true feeling and sensibility. The attack on the kind of poetry that Pope chose to write was under way long before the more theoretical objections to his writing that came after the middle of the century.

On one level Pope was certainly venting his anger against a number of his enemies. To achieve this he selected the mock epic form of Dryden's *Mac Flecknoe* (1678), with its satiric plot involving the coronation of the new monarch of bad poetry and the departure of the old master of terrible verse. Although Dryden's poem was mainly an attack on his rival, Thomas Shadwell (c. 1642–92), it contained a larger picture of the world of Grub Street with its hack writers and mean existence. Dryden used the pattern of epic to contrast with the petty and pitiful world of bad art and added allusions to biblical passages, involving the passing on of the mantle of power, to lend depth to his attack on the world with which he attempted to associate Shadwell. Pope took Dryden's hints and made his poem into a systematic attack upon the corruption of modern society. Although that corruption is seen mainly in terms of bad literature, Pope reaches out to the rot in education, politics, manners and morals. The coronation of the new monarch echoes the Lord Mayor's pageant, and the new values of eighteenth-century London – its luxury, its vulgarity, its emphasis on wealth – are attached to the triumphal ascension of first Theobald and later Cibber to the throne of bad poetry.

At the end of the eighteenth century, James Lackington (1746–1815) owned a huge bookshop named 'The Temple of the Muses', which boasted selling more books at a lower price than any competitor. Lackington's *Memoirs* (1791) and *Confessions* (1804) give an account of his career that demonstrates considerable intelligence and a great deal of shrewdness, but his method of selling books, especially remaindered works, put them on the same level as any other commodity. In Pope's time, this attitude towards books was just becoming established. Publishers such as Edmund Curll (1675–1747) made money in any way they could. Curll sometimes plagiarised material, employed an author who signed his work 'John Gay' to make readers believe it was by the real John Gay, and published pornographic titles such as *Onanism Displayed* and *The Nun in Her Smock*. The term 'Curlicism' was coined for this time of literary indecency. In imitation of other industrialists in this age of incipient capitalism, publishers often tried to squeeze whatever they could from their authors, paying them barely enough to keep them alive. Many of these writers worked entirely on what they were assigned to write, turning out their product as quickly as possible. Although these were the *true* Grub Street Hacks, Pope deliberately spread his net much wider, exploiting the satiric technique of guilt by association. But to see Pope as a vicious writer mocking the misery of those less fortunate, less talented than he would be a mistake; Pope was intent on criticising an entire system that was guilty of producing a mockery of genuine literary artistry.

Other writers expressed different views. In his journal *The Manufacturer* (1718), Defoe humorously compared the writer of newspapers to the master craftsman labouring in a factory. And James Ralph (c. 1705–62), in 'The Case of Authors by Profession or Trade' (1758), was to complain that attitudes such as Pope's which seemed to put the author above any concern with money, were destructive to the well-being of writers and harmful to the general distribution of knowledge. Defoe was a man of genius and Ralph a thoroughly professional journalist, yet Pope gave both a place among his dunces. Many of the best writers of our period were forced to labour on a real or metaphorical Grub Street, and by the end of the century, journalism, which seemed to Pope a symptom of the evil he was attacking, had gained considerable respectability. But a single glance at the list of our best-selling books published within the past few months will clarify Pope's position. Perhaps one or two works of genuine merit will succeed in finding a place, particularly if the author is well known, but most of these works are not for the ages. If Gresham's Law may be applied to literary production, with bad books driving out good ones, Pope's feeling that he was witnessing the decline of an entire culture into banality and ultimate self-destruction will be more understandable.

As Aubrey Williams (b. 1922) has shown in his *Pope's Dunciad* (1955), the triumph of Dullness is the fulfilment of Satan's promise to Sin and Death in *Paradise Lost* to restore darkness to the world. Colley Cibber (1671–1757) was a much better vehicle for this, because his remarkable *Apology* (1740), in addition to containing an intimate view of the stage between the Restoration and his own time, was an autobiography of a man whose worldly success seemed to be unaccompanied by any very subtle understanding of art or culture. He took popular success as an indication of his ability, and in his preface to his *Ximena* (1719) actually argued for the superiority of his play to Corneille's (1606–84) *Le Cid* upon which it was modelled. He notes that he wrote plays more or less as his wife produced children and the overtones of that statement go beyond the idea of earning extra money to feed a new mouth. Cibber is a mixture of genuine modesty and unbelievable self-praise. Pope would probably have found the revelation of Cibber's feelings vulgar in itself. True art was not self-expression but a mixture of hard work and genius, learning and craftsmanship.

But by 1742 Pope saw the world of the future belonging to Cibber and his kind, and the fourth book of the Dunciad is an apocalypse in which all the forces of society rush to the feet of Dullness to express their allegiance. Opera with its nonsense is there along with the gentlemen of England and their tutors who have wasted their pupils' time on the grand tour. Dullness gives a monstrous yawn and with that the entire creation begins to return to the darkness from which God in his creative genius had rescued it:

> *Philosophy,* that lean'd on Heav'n before,
> Shrinks to her second cause, and is no more.
> *Physic* of *Metaphysic* begs defence,
> And *Metaphysic* calls for aid on *Sense!*
> See *Mystery* to *Mathematics* fly!
> In vain! they gaze, turn giddy, rave, and die.
> *Religion* blushing veils her sacred fires,
> And unawares *Morality* expires.
> Nor *public* flame, nor *private,* dares to shine;
> Nor *human* spark is left, nor glimpse *divine!*
> Lo! thy dread Empire, CHAOS! is restor'd;
> Light dies before thy uncreating word:
> Thy hand, great Anarch! lets the curtain fall;
> And Universal Darkness buries All.

The world did not end with Pope's vision, but as a prophecy of mankind destroying its world through folly it still stands. And Pope's world – a world in which the connection between God the creator and the artist as creator was real and literal and in which the great work of art formed a kind of system of allusion as immediate and available as nature itself – may indeed have come to an end by 1742.

6

The era of sincerity: mid-century poetry

THE efforts at social and religious reform that marked the beginning of the eighteenth century attacked the very basis of the art of Restoration England and its idealisation of wit. The Scriblerians, with their love of wit, kept the ideals of satire and irony alive to the end of the century, but the dominant movement was away from wit and toward an ideal of sincerity and moral earnestness. In his *Satyr against Wit* (1700), Sir Richard Blackmore (c. 1654–1729) attacked writers who considered themselves wits as immoral and hinted that they were dangerous to the state. In an age that was turning toward improvements in science and agriculture as ways of enriching the nation and feeding the poor, the witty gentleman of Restoration comedy seemed to be a kind of villain engaged in useless activity:

> A Wit's an idle, wretched Fool of Parts,
> That hates all Liberal and Mechanick Arts.

Dissenters such as Defoe and members of the Low Church often justified themselves and their writings on grounds of sincerity, and when Benjamin Hoadly, Bishop of Bangor (1676–1761), a forceful writer on the Whig side, argued in a sermon of 1716 that sincerity was something each man must feel and that no man had the right to question the sincerity of another man's principles, he gave political and theological sanction to the emphasis on openness and sincerity in literature. In France, the rococo did not disappear from the work of Fragonard, but the paintings of Boucher, with their sensual nudes, gave way to those of Jean-Baptiste Greuze (1726–1805), with their realistic picturing of scenes of bourgeois life. Handel was England's most famous composer, but on the continent, Johann Sebastian Bach (1685–1750) was producing music of a more sombre bent.

I   Pope the moralist

Wit did not die, but poets like Pope began to 'moralise' their
song. During the 1730s Pope assumed the role of a spokesman
against corruptions in politics and manners. He did not
abandon the wit that was so necessary for great satire, but
began to use it in the service of moral philosophy. The same
development is clear in the graphic arts where William
Hogarth (1697–1764) began his great series of engravings, *A
Harlot's Progress* (1731), *The Rake's Progress* (1735), *Marriage a-
la-Mode* (1745), and *Industry and Idleness* (1747). Hogarth put his
visual wit to work on scenes depicting the downward path to
ruin for those who do not put their minds and hearts on serious
matters. The idle apprentice ends his life on the gallows, and
other forms of early death relentlessly pursue Hogarth's
wastrels. The entire social fabric was changing as members of
the middle ranks were pursuing the leisured life of the gentry.
More and more servants filled the cities, doing work that
formerly had been performed by the mistress of the house. The
servants too drank their tea with sugar and found time to go on
excursions dressed in a manner not always detectably different
from their mistresses. In his 'Epistle to Augustus' (1737), Pope
lamented the drift toward a society in which the individual
pursuit of secular happiness appeared to be the highest good:

> Time was, a sober Englishman wou'd knock
> His servants up, and rise by five o'clock,
> Instruct his family in ev'ry rule,
> And send his wife to church, his son to school.
> To worship like his fathers was his care;
> To teach their frugal virtues to his heir;
> To prove, that luxury could never hold;
> And place, on good security, his gold.

Such a time has been replaced by the achievements of modern
civilisation, and Pope wryly praises the accomplishments of his
time compared to that of ancient Greece:

> Tho' justly Greece her eldest sons admires,
> Why should not we be wiser than our sires?
> In ev'ry public virtue we excell,
> We build, we paint, we sing, we dance as well,
> And learned Athens to our art must stoop,
> Could she behold us tumbling thro' a hoop.

Pope began composing his 'Moral Essays' and 'An Essay on Man' in 1730 and continued writing them until 1734. The order of publication did not always correspond with the final arrangement or composition. 'Epistle I' of the 'Moral Essays' appeared in 1734, 'Epistle II' in 1735, 'Epistle III' in 1733 and 'Epistle IV' in 1731. The 'Essay on Man' was published anonymously in 1733–1734, in part to avoid some of the attacks that greeted the 'Moral Essays'. The trick succeeded to the extent that some critics did not recognise Pope's hand and praised it while disparaging Pope's other work. If the five poems may be considered as a series of comments on human life and manners, 'The Essay on Man' may be regarded as a general comment on the human condition with the four 'Moral Essays' focused specifically on certain problems of modern life. 'Epistle I, To Viscount Cobham' is the most general, directed toward the concept of character and the way to understand human motivation. Pope develops the idea of a 'Ruling Passion' as the key to each man, and as in many of these poems, gives a list of 'characters' (in the sense of a set description of a character type) who exemplify one or another passion. 'Epistle II, To a Lady', uses the device of the poet advising a painter to draw certain portraits and then gives a catalogue of modern women, each worse than the last and each, significantly enough, possessed of greater power in the state. 'Epistle III, To Bathust' and 'Epistle IV, To Burlington', are devoted to the discussion of the use of wealth in contemporary society. In 'Epistle III', Pope shows the misuse of wealth in hoarding and extravagance and compares it, in 'Epistle IV', to the proper use of riches in charity and in works of magnificence carried forward with a proper sense of good artistic taste.

Pope was not a systematic philosopher, and the reader would do well to remember that he is reading great poetry rather than great original thought. Pope may have considered himself a modern Lucretius and may have thought that his exposition of ideas and Christian doctrine was hardly more controversial in its sphere and for his time than Lucretius's version of the Epicurean philosophy had been for his era of history. That he thought his 'Moral Essays' would be equally uncontroversial is questionable. In any event, Pope's venture into moral philosophy roused considerable controversy on matters of personalities, ideas and religious doctrine. The 'Essay on Man' was attacked by the continental Catholic mathematician and philosopher, Jean Pierre de Crousaz (1663–1750) as deistic and heretical. Pope was defended in 1738 by William Warburton (1698–1779), Bishop of Gloucester, who had recently embroiled himself in religious controversy with his *Divine Legation of Moses* (1737–41), one of the more interesting of the many contemporary treatments of ancient myth and language as a clue to the providential coming of Christianity. Pope was so grateful to Warburton that he made him his literary executor.

The 'Essay on Man' is actually a meditation on the theme, *et ego in Arcadia,* which abounds in the painting of the seventeenth and eighteenth centuries, the idea that death is everywhere, that Death can say, 'I too have lived in Arcadia', that man's life is brief and that he had best attend to finding what happiness he is capable of attaining on earth and to living a moral life that will bring happiness in this world and allow for the possibility of happiness in a life to come. Although Pope's phrase, 'Whatever is, is right', has been taken as an example of his optimism, it may be seen as just the opposite. Pope draws this conclusion from man's dismal state – his ignorance, his sufferings, his seeming insignificance, his short life. Under such conditions, all that man has is hope – hope that there is a meaning to the pains suffered and hope that a limited happiness may be achieved despite his limitations. The first section exhorts man as a species to acknowledge his weaknesses and submit, in his blindness, to a larger power.

Having asserted the existence of a harmony and order in the universe, Pope proceeds in the following books to demonstrate the balance of good in the world. Man's passions may seem an evil but they are vital for his very being. Man is motivated by selfishness, but selfishness leads him to recognise his advantage in living in society and in following the common interest. It is in man's general make-up that the ordering hand of God may be seen. He is made capable of happiness, if he can regulate and balance his passions and restrain his pride. And if he can live virtuously, happiness is always attainable. Those few who can see through the appearances of nature and reach to a perception of God and his plan find a bliss unequalled on earth. Death is never far off in the 'Essay on Man'; each of the four sections starts with some kind of reminder of man's mortality. But the man who can raise his mind above his misfortunes and those of his family will achieve a heaven in his heart and soul.

Crousaz found much to criticise in Pope's system, and despite the work of modern scholars to discover the traditional Christian roots of Pope's thought, the emphasis of Pope's poem is not on Christian revelation but on man's position in a universe that God regulates according to a plan that remains unknown to us. Though most writers in the eighteenth century agreed that God operated through what they called second causes or natural laws, they disagreed on the degree to which God might interfere at any time for an individual case. In Pope's scheme, the machinery is too good to require such tampering, and despite his disclaimers, the general line of thought in the 'Essay on Man' seems to be more Spinoza, Shaftesbury and Bolingbroke than Augustine, Aquinas, Erasmus – that is to say, more secular and contemporary than Christian and traditional. Saint Augustine (354–430) advanced orthodox Christianity against the heresies of his time; Saint Thomas Aquinas (c. 1225–74) codified Christian thought; and Desiderius Erasmus (c. 1466–1536) offered a human image of Christianity, advocating reform within the Roman Catholic church rather than a complete Reformation. Benedict Spinoza (1632–77) argued that moral judgements were relative and that God was best worshipped as a force diffused through the universe. Although it is long since anyone thought that Pope's poem was merely an exposition of Bolingbroke's thought, Pope was in close contact with Henry St. John, first Viscount Bolingbroke (1678–1751) during the writing of his poem, and he may have absorbed some of his friend's deism. While it is true that the Boyle Lectures, established by the scientist Robert Boyle (1627–91), and attracting some of the best theologians of the late seventeenth and early eighteenth century, usually emphasised logical evidence for the proof of God's existence in the universe rather than revelation, few of the speakers neglected any mention of God's intervention on earth and fewer put as much stress on the insignificance of man in the universe as Pope. Pope suggests the possibility of other worlds and other beings, and Crousaz was quick to argue a hint of heresy in such a position.

THE DUNCIAD with NOTES VARIORUM.
His HOLINESS and his PRIME MINISTER.
A Letter to the Publis

1. A satiric cartoon on Alexander Pope.

2. William Kent's frontispiece to Thomson's *The Seasons* (1730).

3. Dr Samuel Johnson by Sir Joshua Reynolds (1756).

4. Mrs Pritchard and David Garrick in *Macbeth*, from a mezzotint by Green after Zoffany in the collection of Mr Harry R. Beard.

5. *Gin Lane* by William Hogarth.

6. Two scenes from *Industry and Idleness* in William Hogarth's Moral series, started in 1730.

Laudatur et Alget
Juven . Sat . I.

7. Daniel Defoe by M. van der Gucht (1706).

8. Samuel Richardson by Joseph Highmore (1750).

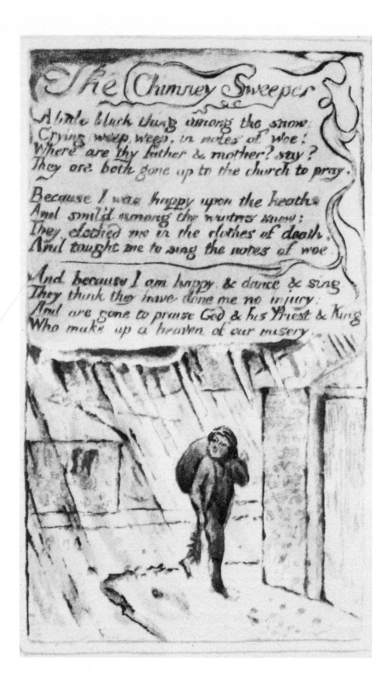

The Chimney Sweeper

A little black thing among the snow:
Crying weep, weep, in notes of woe!
Where are thy father & mother? say?
They are both gone up to the church to pray.

Because I was happy upon the heath,
And smil'd among the winters snow:
They clothed me in the clothes of death,
And taught me to sing the notes of woe.

And because I am happy, & dance & sing,
They think they have done me no injury:
And are gone to praise God & his Priest & King
Who make up a heaven of our misery.

9. *The Chimney Sweeper* by William Blake.

10. The frontispiece of *The Marriage of Heaven and Hell* (1793) by William Blake.

11. *The Man of Feeling* by Thomas Rowlandson.

12. The Tapestry Room at Castle Howard, Yorkshire, which was built by Sir John Vanbrugh between 1702 and 1714.

13. Seaton Delavel, in Northumberland, from a contemporary painting. Built by Sir John Vanbrugh between 1718 and 1728.
14. Chiswick House, outside London, based on Palladio's Rotonda, built by Lord Burlington in 1725.

JANE AUSTEN.

15. Jane Austen.

16. Fanny Burney by Frances d'Arbley.

17. St. Martins in the Fields, London. Built by James Gibbs between 1722 and 1726, who was strongly influenced by Sir Christopher Wren and by Italian architects. This church is widely regarded as Gibbs' masterpiece.

18. The Royal Crescent, Bath, built by John Wood between 1761 and 1765. Wood invented the concave row of houses.

19. Lloyd's Coffee House, 1798.

However, the excellence of the 'Essay on Man' lies not in its doctrinal positions but in its poetry. The ideas allow Pope to express himself in a manner that varies from the satiric to the sublime, and from the first image of Pope and Bolingbroke walking out into a very eighteenth-century field to hunt after the things of the world as well as of the spirit Pope shows his virtuosity. Lines such as:

> And now a bubble burst, and now a world

or the start of the second Epistle:

> Know then thyself, presume not God to scan;
> The proper study of mankind is man.
> Plac'd on this isthmus of a middle state,
> A being darkly wise, and rudely great

or the 'ages of man' speech at the end of the second:

> Behold the child, by nature's kindly law,
> Pleas'd with a rattle, tickled with a straw:
> Some livelier play-thing gives his youth delight,
> A little louder, but as empty quite:
> Scarfs, garters, gold, amuse his riper stage;
> And Beads and pray'r-books are the toys of age:
> Pleas'd with this bauble still, as that before;
> 'Till tir'd he sleeps, and life's poor play is o'er

show Pope's skill in manoeuvring the materials of moral philosophy in poetry. That he was not a truly philosophical poet in Coleridge's sense is also clear enough. Samuel Taylor Coleridge (1772–1834) argued in his *Biographia Literaria* (1817) that William Wordsworth might be the first truly philosophic poet in English, meaning by this a poet expressing an original and creative view of mankind and experience. Pope's notion of a balance of forces in society may be found in a number of writers, but his most immediate debt was probably to Bernard Mandeville; and Mandeville's system shows a callous disregard to individual pain and suffering. Johnson did not like the 'Essay on Man' and in his review of a work by Soame Jenyns (1704–87), he dismissed with contempt the notion that there could be some benefit in human pain or that we can ever find comfort in a system by which our pain may benefit other beings. Without questioning Pope's brilliance as a poet or the cleverness of his mind, we may at times wonder if he thought all his ideas through as much as he ought to have.

The tone of the 'Essay on Man' is hortatory. The 'Moral Essays' are less dramatic, less formal. The 'Epistle to Cobham' focuses on character in a way that allows Pope considerable scope for digression, especially since the unifying 'Ruling Passion' is accompanied by a variety of external characteristics, many of which appear to be contradictory. In 'To a Lady' Pope indulges in some traditional anti-feminist satire as he moves from one vicious woman to another. The arbitrariness of the organisation allows Pope some of his most brilliant portraits, and while Pope holds up the character of Martha Blount at the end as an ideal woman, Pope's method is basically satirical rather than speculative, a portrait of the negative rather than a moral argument. The 'Epistle to Bathurst' returns to the speculative mode and takes up a subject raised in the 'Essay on Man', the inequality of wealth in society. Why should the farmer live close to the subsistence level while others live in luxury? Pope does not answer his question but rather demonstrates the corruption that often comes with wealth and the frequency with which society recycles accumulated fortunes as the heir spends rapidly what may have taken decades to gather. In short, implicit in his account of the real unhappiness in the life of a Sir Balaam is the myth of the real happiness of the poor. The 'Epistle to Burlington' continues this argument with an analysis of bad taste in the use of wealth. Just as the man of Ross in the third Epistle is held up as an example of charity, so Burlington is put forward as an example of the proper use of wealth in building. ''Tis use alone that sanctifies expence', Pope argues, and he ends with an image of public building that improves the lot of everyone in the kingdom.

The writings of the early 1730s contain a good deal of political commentary. The satire on figures like Timon, and references to the Queen and Walpole, suggest the new role that Pope was to take for the remainder of the decade. In his last satires, Pope was to dramatise himself much more than in his earlier work, and he was to present himself as the poet, living among other Englishmen, a victim of corrupt government and a corrupt court. If some of the sombre quality of 'An Essay on

Man' and the 'Moral Essays' disappears, it is replaced by a willingness to risk a certain comic presentation of himself, beleaguered by the requests of bad poets and beset by fools. He struck this pose first in his 'Epistle to Dr. Arbuthnot' (1735). Here Pope presents his life as that of a man intending no offence who has been forced to do battle to save himself and his reputation. The device lends itself to the character-portraits that he had mastered, and in the sketches of Atticus (Addison) and Sporus (the witty writer and political figure John, Lord Hervey (1696–1743)), Pope wrote what were his most finished portraits. But Pope achieves his power from his picture of himself as the good man, in the mode of Horace's satiric rhetoric, and he concludes with a portrait of his father which stresses the ideal of the innocent, harmless citizen:

> The good man walk'd innoxious thro' his age.
> No courts he saw, no suits would ever try,
> Nor dar'd an oath, nor hazarded a Lye:
> Un-learn'd, he knew no schoolman's subtle art,
> No language, but the language of the heart.

Pope gains considerable force by this portrait, and by the end, in which he expresses his friendship for Arbuthnot, he is able to transfer the feeling of sincerity to himself. In a similar fashion, Pope claims to be a lover of virtue in 'The First Satire of the Second Book of Horace Imitated' (1733) and in the work which began this discussion, 'The Epistle to Augustus' (1737). This is one of Pope's most difficult poems. It plays ironically with the work being parodied, as its longer title, The First Epistle of the Second Book of Horace Imitated, suggests. Since George II was not interested in the arts at all, the comparison with Augustus operates as an ironic contrast, while at the same time bearing direct reference to that Emperor who destroyed the freedom of Rome. Thus the description of George II as 'Great Friend of LIBERTY', is intended to echo the demands for liberty in the propaganda of the Opposition in Parliament.

Pope made his final statement of this position in the two dialogues that appeared in 1738 as *Epilogue to the Satires*. 'Fr.' remarks that Pope is 'too *Moral* for a Wit' and suggests that he restrain his satire as Horace did. But Pope is beyond any restraint now. The entire society has become corrupt, and the virtuous man cannot sit by and let vice triumph:

> Ask you what provocation I have had?
> The strong antipathy of good to bad.
> When truth or virtue an affront endures,
> Th' affront is mine, my friend, and should be yours.

Pope boasts then of his power as a satirist, but it is a power used in the cause of moral good:

> O sacred weapon! left for truth's defence,
> Sole dread of folly, vice, and insolence!

And he concludes his part of the dialogue with a heroic stance as the defender of freedom and truth. If Pope was to turn back to the *Dunciad* and Scriblerian ridicule in his final years it may have been out of a sense that he had gone as far as he could in attacking the corruption of the times from a personal position. He had outlasted Walpole, whose hold on Parliament declined after 1739, but the levity of the world had not disappeared with the end of Walpole's corrupt political power. Yet Pope's return to the past should not disguise his common ground with those writers seeking to write poetry and prose that reflected or claimed to reflect a sincerity of feeling and belief.

II   The poetry of night

Contemporary with Pope and claiming an increasing interest among writers and readers was a melancholy literature concerned with night, graveyards and tombs. In the verse of Anne Finch, Countess of Winchilsea (1661–1720) such concerns appear at first glance remarkably similar to the preoccupations of the poetry of the early seventeenth century, but a brief examination reveals that this resemblance is mainly connected with her involvement with traditional Christian themes. Her emphasis on the presence of Providence in nature occasionally brings to mind those writers interested in the sublime, and her poem on the great storm of November 1703 is reminiscent of Defoe's prose treatment of that event in 'The Storm' (1704). She translates a number of Psalms and imitates Milton. But the debt to Milton, though general, is especially evident in her continued use of 'Il Penseroso', a poem which dominated the thinking of many of the poets who followed her.

At her best, the Countess of Winchilsea is an effective meditative poet, brooding over nature and analysing its effect upon her. In her hands the retreat poem of Horace and his follower Pomfret becomes 'A Petition for an Absolute Retreat' (1713) with an emphasis on human mortality and a certain gloom in the 'shade' that surrounds her secret abode. She writes a poem to 'The Spleen' (1713), which dwells on melancholy, and in *A Nocturnal Reverie* (1713), using Milton's long poetic period, she evokes her reaction to the sights and sounds of the night. The use of pure description without some compensatory moralising was regarded as an inferior form. Lady Winchilsea breaks her description at the end with a brief moral, but her obvious pleasure in language that produces sensations of hot and cold, appeals to the sense of smell and to tactile sensation, and evocation of a variety of colours, was very much like that of Keats a century later.

Attracted to similar subject matter was Thomas Parnell (1679–1718), a clergyman and a member of the Scriblerus Club. Parnell was also drawn to classical subject-matter and could write 'Augustan' verse in the manner of his friend Pope, but Pope would have been unlikely to write poems such as 'Meditating on the Wounds of Christ' (1722) or 'On Divine Love' (1722). In his 'Hymn to Contentment' (1714), Parnell used 'Il Penseroso' as a model while making the chief end of his retreat 'heavenly vision' that will give him the power to write religious poetry:

> While silver waters glide along,
> To please my ear, and court my song:
> I'll lift my voice, and tune my string,
> And thee, great *source* of *nature* sing.

In *A Night-Piece on Death* (1722), Parnell sets the pattern for many works to follow. He meditates at night on the idea of death and mortality and on the graves of the unknown men and women who lie underneath the earth. Suddenly he thinks he sees the ghosts of the dead burst from their graves and the voice of death seems to speak. The message he delivers is one familiar to any reader of the metaphysical poets. Man should not fear death. The body is but a cage for the soul which, released, rises to 'Blaze of Day'. What is distinctly eighteenth century about the poem is the initial description, which takes up more than half the work and presents the mood of the speaker as well as evoking the terrifying landscape of night and the tomb. Parnell seeks in the appearance of nature the key to God's presence in the world and therefore justifies the use of description as a form of worship. But the very real drift toward description as a statement of the poet's feeling is also evident.

The fascination with meditative writing of this kind extended to prose as well as poetry. Elizabeth Singer Rowe (1674–1737), in her fictional letters, *Friendship in Death* (1728), and James Hervey (1714–58), in his *Meditations among the Tombs* (1746), appealed to just such an interest. And in *The Complaint* (1742), commonly known by its subtitle, *Night Thoughts,* Edward Young (1683–1765) wrote the most popular extended poem on this subject. Young had already achieved considerable reputation with his *Universal Passion* (1725), collected in 1728 as *Love of Fame,* a series of formal satires on social themes that attempted many of the same moral goals that Pope was to pursue in his 'Moral Essays' and satires. Young was a great defender of originality, but there is more artistry in the couplets of his satires than in the more original blank verse of *Night Thoughts.* The popularity of *Night Thoughts* is a good indication of the vogue for meditative, melancholy poetry, but it says little for Young's poetic talents. Cliché follows cliché as Young fails to rise to anything more than flat or dead metaphor. In the tragic figure of Lorenzo, Young creates a character of some interest, but *Night Thoughts* is effective only on an emotive level. If a reader is in a mood to be sad, Young's brooding melancholy may touch him. Young may call on Milton to inspire him, but the inspiration never came. His blank verse functions as a kind of prose poetry not very different from the lugubrious *Meditations* of Hervey.

If the nine books of Young's *Night Thoughts* may be said to have any organisation at all, it is not an obvious one. Criticism had been voiced about Thomson's *The Seasons* on the grounds that it lacked any 'method', and the same is true about another poem on melancholy, *The Spleen* (1737) by Matthew Green (1696–1737). Acknowledging this fault, Green quickly excused it on the grounds that the imagination required freedom:

> The want of method pray excuse,
> Allowing for a vapour'd muse;

> Nor, to a narrow path confin'd,
> Hedge in by rules a roving mind.

Green then wanders over various methods for curing melancholy or spleen, finding the solution mainly in a retreat from the world that will provide calm and contentment and in his faith in a creator. Green's tetrameter couplet is livelier than Young's blank verse, and his method of running away from the dreams of melancholy, the residue of childhood fancies, along with his attack on imagination, do not disguise his fascination with excessive indulgence in melancholy. A modern reader of *The Grave* (1743) by Robert Blair (1699–1746) might well wonder why this poem went into so many editions, or what the eighteenth-century reader experienced in his picture of the ghosts rising from the cemetery at night:

> Rous'd from their slumbers,
> In grim array the grisly spectres rise,
> Grin horrible, and, obstinately sullen,
> Pass and repass, hush'd as the foot of Night.
> Again the screech-owl shrieks – ungracious sound!
> I'll hear no more – it makes one's blood chill.

We should not forget the presence of death in this period. The childhood mortality rate was astoundingly high, and few families escaped without the deaths of some children. Smallpox vaccination was tried by a few. Lady Mary Wortley Montagu (1689–1762) witnessed a method of inoculation in Turkey, had it administered to her son, and encouraged the practice in Britain, but for most families it was a continual plague. Johnson's friend, Hester Thrale (1741–1821), had thirteen children, only a few of whom survived into adolescence. Without an understanding of the ways by which micro-organisms attacked the body, physicians were incapable of curing most diseases. Many of these poems of melancholy had a theraputic value. They eased the grief of the readers.

The moment of grief and mourning was the ideal time for a display of the deepest feeling by the poet. An emphasis on the poet's personal sincerity merges with the presentation of himself in the poem as capable of deep emotion and sensibility. The sincere man of feeling cannot display too much organisation in his poetry. Such design would demonstrate excessive control and suggest a lack of true emotion. The tendency for form to disintegrate in poetry is more obvious in the second half of the century, but the admiration for Milton's wandering organisation in 'Il Pensoroso' and 'L'Allegro' suggests a general trend. Melancholy was more than a subject for verse; it was an experience for Englishmen particularly associated with the national character. In 1733, Dr George Cheyne (1671–1743) published *The English Malady*, a treatise on nervous disorders, and more and more writers seemed to suffer from degrees of melancholy or 'hypochondria' as the century progressed.

III   Poetic enthusiasm

At the Restoration, the religious excesses of various cults were blamed for the rebellion and consequent death of Charles I. Imagination unrestrained by the reason was considered the worst of evils for the state, established religion, and the individual. Swift argued this point in his *Tale of a Tub* (1704), but by mid-century key words that in the Restoration had evil connotations, now became ideals. Novelty, originality, imagination and enthusism were soon to become words to conjure by in poetry. Addison's advocacy of imaginative literature – ballads, fairy tales, ghost stories – was to carry the day. The ornate and imaginative poetry of Spenser found an advocate in Thomas Warton the elder (1688–1745), and his sons were to join those who championed a new kind of poetry. A new religious enthusiasm also was sweeping the nation. John Wesley (1703–91) and his brother, Charles Wesley (1707–88), were to advocate a certain degree of enthusiasm in religion. With Charles Wesley, hymn writing, which had a fine if relatively restrained master in the Dissenter Isaac Watts (1674–1748), took on new and fervent life. Fielding might shake his head at the Methodists and continue to advocate the ideals of control and ridicule as the best procedure for art, but other forces were gaining strength. An enthusiasm for gardening and landscape that had been strong in the 1720s emerged as a kind of passion by the middle of the century. Pope had been one of the more original designers of gardens, and his garden grotto at Twickenham seemed to symbolise a cave of poetic imagination. And if Pope, whom many of the younger poets considered a poet lacking in true feeling, could assume such a stance, what might not a true enthusiast do?

Along with this enthusiasm for nature and emphasis on introspective melancholy came a revival in lyrical forms, particularly the ode, elegy and ballad. Dryden had sneered at writers of 'Songs', and Pope had echoed his opinion, but despite such influential judgements, there was, from the 1690s onward, a fascination for brief poems displaying deep feeling and emotion. In his preface to the love elegies of James Hammond (1710–42), published in 1743 but written a decade earlier, Lord Chesterfield (1694–1773) praised the 'fancy and imagination' of the young poet and noted that 'sincere in his love as in his friendship, he wrote to his mistresses, as he spoke to his friends, nothing but the true genuine sentiments of his heart'. This quest after sincerity of feeling had implications for biography as well as poetry, but its influence on poetry was particularly vital in turning poets to shorter forms in which emotion could be expressed most intensely. Hammond abandoned the couplet in a number of his elegies and went to an iambic pentameter quatrain with alternate lines rhyming. For the most part the poems display the sadness of the lover at the cruelty of his mistress, and while there was ample classical precedence for such poetry in the poems of Tibullus (c. 54– c. 18 B.C.), it was clearly a very different model from that of Horace and Juvenal so admired by Dryden and Pope. The harsh satires of Decimus Juvenalis (c. 60–140 A.D.) may well have been of greater significance to the age than those of Horace whose urbanity seemed, somehow, less sincere, but satire itself was becoming suspect.

William Shenstone (1714–63) may be regarded as a typical poet of this period. After publishing a volume with an imitation of Spenser, 'The School-Mistress', in 1737, he retired to perfect his garden at Leasowes, a garden that became an influential model for the period. He continued publishing through the collections of the miscellaneous writer and publisher, Robert Dodsley (1703–64), which appeared originally in 1748, 1755, and 1758 and were reprinted six times before the end of the century. His works were collected after his death in 1764. Although Shenstone wrote a number of long poems, most of his work is in the form of ode and elegy. In an essay on elegy, Shenstone praised that form as the best mode for expression of deep grief. An admirer of Milton's 'Lycidas', Shenstone claimed to be expressing his deepest feelings in his elegies, and Dodsley claimed that he was the true master of that form in English. In addition to the elegies, Shenstone wrote songs, ballads and odes, and the ode now began to take the form that we know best through the romantic poets and particularly John Keats. Shenstone's odes were usually meditations on subjects like memory and indolence. But he also devoted some to the subject of love, and at least in the pose of the poet, there is little difference between the elegies and the odes. Elegy XI begins:

> Ah me, my friend! it will not, will not last!
> This fairy-scene, that cheats our youthful eyes!
> The charm dissolves; th'aerial music's past;
> The banquet ceases, and the vision flies.

In such poems, Shenstone is very much the poet of sensibility as well as sincerity, but unlike the poets of the later eighteenth century, he keeps his syntax and moral relatively clear.

Writing at the same time as Shenstone was Mark Akenside (1721–70). His great work was a versified version of Addison's *Spectator* essays on imagination, *The Pleasures of Imagination* (1744). Akenside was as much a disciple of Shaftesbury as of Addison, and his poem is filled with the kind of enthusiasm for nature and the presence of God in nature to be found in Shaftesbury's *Characteristics*. Following the practice of Thomson and perhaps the more expansive traditions of the North, Akenside, who was born in Newcastle-on-Tyne and educated at the University of Edinburgh, composed his poem in blank verse, but it was without the kind of allusive quality and wit that made Thomson's poetry so much a part of the age dominated by Pope. When he re-wrote his poem toward the end of his life, it was even more dominated by grand periods that gave it the feeling of breathless sublimity that Wordsworth was to master. In addition to following Shaftesbury in his sense of awe before the design of nature, Akenside began to develop a theory of sympathy – a tie between man and nature that was based entirely on passion and emotion. It was an idea that was developed by a number of writers, but nowhere so thoroughly

as in the first book of *A Treatise on Human Nature* published in
1739 by the philosopher David Hume (1711–76). Akenside's
Odes on Several Subjects published in 1745 extended the concept
of the ode to a variety of types, from imitations of the formal
Greek ode to generalised lyrics on subjects such as sleep or
poetry or even poems to friends. Although his syntax is
traditional enough and his statements clear, Akenside, like
some of his contemporaries, began experimenting with a
sense of suspension at the end of his poems that made the poem
turn in on itself.

The master of this technique, however, was William Collins
(1721–59), the most experimental of the poets of the forties. If
Akenside's poetry turns to the very aesthetic problems of
poetry itself, Collins appears to strive toward making the poem
a subject of objective contemplation in which didactic
problems exist merely as part of an artistic text. In his *Persian
Eclogues* (1742), he took advantage of an oriental theme to
introduce a rich vein of imagery and picture into pastoral. And
at a time when many critics regarded Shakespeare's mixed
metaphors and emotional rants as errors in taste, Collins, in
his 'Epistle Addressed to Sir Thomas Hanmer' (1743),
conjures up pictures of Shakespeare's characters from the
pages of the text and finds genius in every line. Collins also
imitated some of Shakespeare's techniques in his lovely 'Song
from Shakespeare's *Cymbeline*' (1744). Yet it was in his *Odes on
Several Descriptive and Allegoric Subjects* (1747) that Collins
achieved his real success. Cultivating a sense of wonder and
sublimity, Collins threw an almost magical effect over these
poems. He lengthened the opening sentence of the 'Ode to
Evening' to the point of leaving the reader with the sense of
floating through beautiful imagery and language unconnected
with any real meaning. In fact, there is a statement made, and
the final lines might belong to any number of contemporary
odes, but the very ordinariness of the close makes it irrelevant.
The reader is swept away by the personified figures of the
seasons and only dimly-stated ideas about nature and its power
and magic. Pure description and language loaded with
maximum effect dominate the odes. In the 'Ode to Fear' and
'Ode to Pity' Collins confronts the two elements of sublimity
in tragedy and uses repetition to achieve a sense of the failure
of language to express overwhelming emotion:

> Ah Fear! Ah frantic Fear!
> I see, I see thee near.

Other odes were typical of contemporary choice of subject matter. The 'Ode on the Poetical Character' is a poem on the progress of poetry to England, and the 'Ode to Liberty' had become a set piece for poets. Two later poems are of special interest however. In his 'Ode Occasioned by the Death of Mr. Thomson' (1748), Collins not only exploited the image of Thomson as a druid, a magical priest of poetry, but he varied the last line, 'In yonder grave your Druid lies', from 'the Druid' of the first, to move from the impersonal to the personal. And in a fragment, not published until 1788, 'An Ode on the Popular Superstitions of the Highlands', Collins sketched out the subject-matter in the folklore of the Highlands that might lend itself to the imagination of the poet. Both of these poems suggest the direction that Collins might have followed had he lived.

Less effective as poets but influential as critics were the brothers, Joseph Warton (1722–1800) and Thomas Warton (1728–90). In *The Enthusiast: or, The Lover of Nature* (1744), Joseph Warton idealised nature in a verse that drew its inspiration partly from Spenser and partly from Milton's shorter poetry and the richer, descriptive passages of *Paradise Lost*. He asked:

> What are the Lays of artful *Addison*,
> Coldly correct, to *Shakespear's* Warblings wild?

And in his picture of the superiority of the country to the city, he depicted the din of the city as a kind of nightmare. The best of his Odes (1746) is 'To Fancy', in which he once more praises Shakespeare and imagines himself wandering through 'a fairy grove' with Spenser. In 1756, Joseph Warton brought out the first volume of his study of Pope's poetry, declaring that 'wit and satire are transitory and perishable but nature and passion are eternal'. By these standards, only Pope's early poetry deserved real attention. Warton admired the gothic imagery in 'Eloisa to Abelard' but criticised Pope for a lack of invention and passion. The second volume of Warton's study did not emerge until 1782, but by then Warton's opinion was even more set against Pope.

Thomas Warton's 'The Pleasures of Melancholy' (1747) is written in blank verse, but the major influence behind the poem is Spenser:

> Thro' Pope's soft song tho' all the Graces breathe,
> And happiest art adorn his Attic page;
> Yet does my mind with sweeter transport glow,
> As at the root of mossy trunk reclin'd
> In magic Spenser's wildly-warbled song.

In 1754, he published his *Observation on the Faerie Queen of Spenser* and attempted to distinguish between the critic and the reader. Spenser, he argued, makes us suspend our judgement. He appeals directly to the heart and to the imagination. Warton acknowledged that Spenser's allegory did not appeal to contemporary audiences, but he stressed the importance of the appeal to the imagination. Warton's greatest contribution to English letters lay far in the future when he was to bring out his *History of English Poetry* between 1774–81. In this work he was to rediscover the poetry of the past, but by this time the poetry of the Anglo-Saxons, the ballads and the literature of the Elizabethans had taken on a magical aura.

IV Gray's early verse

Before turning to Thomas Gray (1716–71), the best poet to emerge after Pope's death in 1744, we should recall that from Thomson to Akenside, many of the poets have been grouped together as writers of 'Whig Panegyric' verse. Certainly many of these poets wrote poems to liberty and celebrated British institutions of government, but such a term is best limited to the Georgic tradition which tended to celebrate some branch of English commerce. At their most insensitive, poems such as *The Sugar-Cane* (1764) of James Grainger informed the reader about the best slaves to choose for a plantation and the way to select them for their ability to work well. But poets like Akenside wrote against slavery in impassioned tones. What may be said is that the celebration of man in the natural environment of England tended to attract poets sympathetic to the concepts of freedom that emerged out of the fight against Walpole by an opposition composed more of disaffected Whigs than Tories. Certainly Dr Johnson, in making his judgements on these poets, detected a political attitude different from his own and passed his judgements on to posterity. If experiments with various forms and their presentation of themselves as men of moral sincerity have been emphasised, it is because that aspect is more *distinctive* in their poetry.

Gray's most famous poem 'Elegy Written in a Country Churchyard' (1750), draws together many of the strands discussed in this chapter. At the end, after contemplating the lives of the dead in the cemetery at Stoke Poges, he imagines his rustic poet's (and his own) epitaph after he too has joined the dead without achieving any notable fame:

> *Fair Science frowned not on his humble birth,*
> *And Melancholy marked him for her own.*
> *Large was his bounty and his soul sincere,*
> *Heaven did a recompence as largely send:*
> *He gave to Misery all he had, a tear,*
> *He gained from Heaven ('twas all he wished) a friend.*

Gray presents himself as the man of deep feeling and honesty and therefore well qualified to comment on the sadness of life, but the 'Elegy' is much more than another graveyard poem. The opening stanza, with magnificent economy, achieves a sense of isolation and withdrawal into the self that make the perceptions of night and darkness that follow somehow more resonant than in the poems of Parnell and Blair. And Gray's meditation on obscurity and death, while calling on the commonplaces of a Young, produce a different effect as the poet broods over the fate of poverty, the genius and energy that remains forever unused. In contemplating the achievement of greatness, Gray pictures it in terms of brutality as well as triumph. But 'Their lot forbade' them any aspect of public fame:

> Far from the madding crowd's ignoble strife
> Their sober wishes never learned to stray;
> Along the cool sequestered vale of life
> They kept the noiseless tenor of their way.

The poem ends with a contemplation of the death of the poet and his epitaph as he joins the stream of history.

The poem is resonant with ideas of death, history, time,

fame and of living passion transformed into the pathos of a barely literate inscription. The 'sigh' that is the poet's only real response to the entire spectacle replaces statement with a form of gesture. And the withdrawal from the poem through the imagined swain, who notices his absence from the fields and reports his death, followed by the epitaph, distances the poet from his own experience while allowing him to present himself as the ideal poet of wild emotion and sensibility. Though the poem is generalised as a study of human mortality, it is actually about the striving of the poet after fame. Like Keats in his sonnet, 'When I Have Fears that I May Cease to Be', the poet eventually despairs of solving the overwhelming questions raised by his meditation. Death closes the poem as it closes life, but in the work of art the end is an illusion that defies the reality of history and the cemetery. In part, the greatness of Gray's poem lies in the unresolved tension between art and life, achievement and failure, generalised history and the life of the individual man, and the effort of mankind to seek for answers and the reality of death which answers everything but in an unsatisfactory way.

The 'Elegy' is typical of Gray's early poetry. In 1742 he wrote his 'Ode on the Spring' and 'Ode on a Distant Prospect of Eton College'. Dodsley published the latter in a pamphlet in 1747, and both appeared in Dodsley's *Collection* of 1748, that repository of the best poetry of the period. The 'Ode on the Spring' treats the subject of time as a relative experience. Beginning with a very traditional description of the spring, Gray moves to a description of the brief life of the insects that flutter in the air and, with the help of 'Contemplation's sober eye', to an analogy with the life of man which for all its self-importance is merely different in degree rather than kind. Although Gray turns his 'Ode on the Spring' back to the life of the poet at the end, it is a far less personal and profound poem than the Eton 'Ode' with its heavier use of personification. Gray begins his poem with an address to the spires of Eton as seen from Windsor, but quickly turns the poem to himself and the way experience gradually destroys the happiness of childhood. If Gray depicts childhood in a manner that seems to ignore the problems of youth – as a type of Eden from which humans are driven by time and age – he never lapses into condescension. He writes as a poet who has felt 'pain' deeply, and his view of the 'Little victims' at play incorporates within the time of childhood the inevitability of suffering. Although Gray and Collins have been criticised for their use of personified figures like 'Shame', 'Fear' and 'Despair' they regarded such images as aspects of the sublime, powerful, concrete and concise poetic figures, and it would be hard to see how Gray could be more effective in his picture of adult life as a kind of living hell. Gray ends his poem with a paradox. Warning the children of what they are likely to suffer is futile because the unhappiness of adult life cannot be avoided. Knowledge would only remove them from their paradise a little sooner. Pain and anguish are simply part of the human condition.

7

Mid-century fiction and drama

Between Defoe's last novel of consequence and Samuel Richardson's *Pamela* (1740) a period of sixteen years elapsed in which no English writer stepped forward to build upon Defoe's achievements. During that time French writers dominated prose fiction, and their fiction showed a steady growth toward more complex forms than the novels of the late seventeenth century with their emphasis on passion and their lack of interest in character. Robert Chasles (c. 1659–1720) stressed bourgeois situations and greater realism in his collection of tales *The Illustrious French Lovers,* first published in 1722 and translated into English by a minor writer of fiction, Penelope Aubin (*fl.* 1721–29) in 1727. Alain René Lesage (1688–1747) introduced a distinct bourgeois hero into the picaresque with his *Gil Blas,* first published in 1715 but not completed until 1735. Pierre Carlet de Marivaux (1688–1763) depicted the rise of a poor but very handsome peasant in *The Fortunate Peasant* (1735) and of a charming shop girl in *The Life of Marianne* (1731–42). Marivaux was the master of a third-person style that influenced Fielding in its detached amusement toward protagonists and in its rococo stylisation of character and event. There was Antoine Prevost (1697–1763), a dedicated writer of fiction whose *Manon Lescaut* (1729), part of a larger work, *Memoirs of a Man of Quality,* explored the hopeless love of the Chevalier des Grieux for a beautiful girl who loves him in her own way but cannot remain faithful. In addition to such influential works, the French were particularly attracted to imaginative forms such as the fairy tale and philosophic tale. Voltaire (1694–1798), one of the giants of the eighteenth century, did not produce his masterpiece of prose fiction, *Candide,* until 1759, but tales such as *Zadig* (1748) and *Micromegas* (1752), with their ironic view of the human condition, appeared early enough in the century to establish his particular fictional manner. This is a brilliant array of writers, but the great masters of fiction in the eighteenth century were English.

I   Richardson

Samuel Richardson (1689–1761), a successful printer in London, agreed to embark on a volume of letters that would serve as models for anyone wishing to write a letter similar to the kind provided and would entertain the reader by offering miniature fictions. These fictional letters included a writer whose character was to emerge in the style of address, a person addressed, who sometimes also emerged as a character, and a subject. The 'Familiar Letter' was a popular form in the age, and Defoe used it not merely in his journalism but as a means of lending an informal tone to works like *A Tour thro' the Whole Island of Great Britain*. And from the time of the anonymous *Letters of a Portuguese Nun* (1669, tr. 1678), it had been adapted to works of fiction dealing with passionate love relations. Richardson completed his *Familiar Letters* in 1741, but before that date, he had turned aside, intrigued by some of his own creations – letters from a serving girl concerning the attempts of her master to seduce her. *Pamela or Virtue Rewarded* was published in 1740 and its success launched Richardson on a career as a novelist.

Perhaps the most striking aspect of *Pamela* was its moral tone, for it was the first respectable novel published in England. Its respectability was partly a genuine attempt to inculcate a moral point of view and partly a matter of changing times. There was nothing immoral about *Robinson Crusoe* but at the date it appeared (1719), the middle classes, or those with strong roots in the Dissenting movements of the seventeenth century, disapproved of all novels and plays. Richardson wrote an attack on the immorality of the theatre earlier in his career, and the idea of novels immediately conjured up French tales of passion or the English versions of Mrs Haywood. Dr Johnson remarked on how the theatre gradually became more acceptable to Londoners, even those of the middle ranks. This was accomplished by a strict moral code in public theatres. Such a code could not be enforced with novels, but Richardson set this tone for future fiction.

Pamela was an unusual novel. The heroine, through her virtue, holds out against the seductions of Squire B----- and, too much in love to carry his assaults against the virtuous servant girl beyond threats of violence, he finally proposes marriage. The marriage occurs in the middle of the novel, and the remainder of the work reveals Pamela's efforts to hold her position in the face of objections from the Squire's relatives. The novel is composed entirely of letters from Pamela and therefore gives a limited point of view. We never know how the Squire actually feels, and we learn about everything from Pamela's account of her abduction to the country and the efforts of upper servants like Mrs Jewkes to persuade her to yield. Scenes such as that in which the Squire disguises himself as a serving girl to get into Pamela's bedroom while Mrs Jewkes holds down her arms are told with such naïveté that many critics have been uncertain whether the comedy was deliberate. And moments when Pamela is afraid to escape because there seems to her a ferocious bull in the pasture turn to comedy as the bull turns out to be a harmless cow.

Although Richardson, who always maintained a pose of high morality, is not much help in clearing this matter up, it may be argued that *Pamela* is essentially a comic novel. However virtuous she may be, Pamela is a servant whose struggles with her libidinous master teach the reader about her humanity and the need for personal integrity in every rank of society. But servants were usually the subject of comedy, and however much the reader may learn from her struggles, however much he may admire her Christian principles, the reader will feel superior to her and also amused. More problematical is Richardson's exploitation of scenes involving somewhat explicit sexual titillation, what the modern critic, Ian Watt, suggested was a kind of Puritan striptease in which the moral sitaution might allow considerable room for the treatment of sex. But here again we should recognise what Richardson's attitudes would have been toward a young girl on the way to matrimony. City festivals allowed some libertine scenes, and modern readers should not overestimate contemporary objections to sex within the arena of marriage.

Richardson brought out a second part of *Pamela* at the end of 1741, partly as a response to a number of unauthorised imitations. Even his biographers point to this work as

Richardson at his worst, dull and pompous. The excellence of the original had been in Richardson's ability to draw the character of the serving girl, in an exciting plot at the beginning, and in a realistic depiction of setting, situation and character. Pamela is given the ability to describe everything in great detail, and Richardson's creation of grotesque minor characters like Colbatch and Mrs Jewkes adds to the sense of what is essentially comic realism. The second part was more static. Pamela finds that she has a rival for Mr B-----'s affection, and that lends some drama to the work, but for the most part, Pamela writes about what she thinks and knows. She had already shown a certain insufferable moral superiority at the end of the first part, and she picks up where she left off in the sequel.

But Richardson was already working on his masterpiece *Clarissa*, and he brought out the six separate volumes between 1747 and 1748. Now treating a heroine whose station in life placed her just below the aristocracy, Richardson cast Clarissa as a person capable, in her sensibility and intelligence, of bearing the weight of a story whose tragic power remains unmatched in the English novel. The story is simple: Clarissa rejects the suitor selected by her family, and after threats and intimidation, she searches for help from outside the inner circle of the Harlowe family. Lovelace, a former suitor of Clarissa's sister and now an enemy of the family, offers his help, but Clarissa is afraid to trust him because he has a reputation as a rake. Caught in the machinations of Lovelace, Clarissa is forced into a coach and carried away. She resists all his advances, though abandoned by her family and housed in a house of prostitution. Despairing of winning her affection, Lovelace drugs and rapes her. Instead of succumbing, Clarissa gathers herself together for a death that will guarantee her moral superiority over her seducer and family. She escapes and with the help of some friends, lives long enough to put her faith in Christ and an afterlife. Compared to the hectic ravings of Lovelace, Clarissa is serene in her death. Eventually, Lovelace is killed in a duel, but his life has been ruined by the awareness that an action that seemed trivial enough to him had destroyed the chance he might have had of gaining Clarissa. Nothing in the story alone can reproduce Richardson's brilliant delineation of the real duel of the novel – that between

Clarissa and Lovelace. The letters plunge deeper and deeper
into the characters' minds and hearts, into what they know
about themselves or think they know and what they reveal of
half-concealed motivations. Lovelace is a libertine of mythic
proportions. He has the libertine's philosophy of pleasure and
predatory attitude toward women. Marriage is merely a
convention for those enslaved by the laws of society. But his
'philosophy' is merely a covering for an uncontrolled will and
raging passions. He is driven to destroy Clarissa for reasons he
never understands. Clarissa, on the other hand, may feel some
attraction for Lovelace but, between her reason and her
Christian faith, she is capable of controlling her passions.
Richardson surrounds the antagonists with some brilliantly
realised characters. The Harlowe family and their candidate
for Clarissa's hand, Soames, emerge with vivid realism as do
the friends of Lovelace, rakes, whores and the madam, Mrs
Sinclair.

Richardson abandons the use of a single correspondent and
manoeuvres the letters in a dramatic fashion. We are hundreds
of pages into the volume before we have a letter from Lovelace,
and reading Clarissa's correspondence with her friend, Anna
Howe, describing her situation, we might hope that Lovelace
is not really so bad as some have said. When Lovelace's
correspondence with his friend Belford reveals that he is a
complete villain, the reader is dismayed and fascinated. Some
letters are used to create character through odd spelling and
mannerisms, but for the most part, they are used dramatically
and for psychological depth. Belford takes a large part in the
correspondence toward the end, and he is very much a realistic
narrator giving exact details of surroundings and objects. His
description of the prison in which he finds Clarissa after her
second escape is a set piece in which a room is allowed to tell its
own history by the effects of human life through time, and his
description of the death of Mrs Sinclair, howling with pain and
surrounded by a terrifying and terrified crowd of prostitutes
directly out of Swift, is allowed to stand in contrast with the
calm death of Clarissa.

Richardson was a friend of Aaron Hill and shared with him
the concern about sincerity as well as the faith in an afterlife
that informs some of the poetry and prose of the period.
Clarissa's choice of heaven as her goal and turning away from

life comes at a time when the pleasures of life were becoming everywhere more appealing, although as we have seen, because of the primitive state of the medical profession the deaths of infants and of mothers in childbirth were everyday occurrences. Surrounded by the continual reminder of death, a number of writers on Christian themes argued that real faith would rejoice in an early departure for heaven. Once Clarissa turns away from the chance of happiness in this world, she seizes upon a Christian death as her real opportunity for vindication. If we are tempted to see in her decision the desire to put all those who mistreated her in the wrong and to make them feel guilty for having made her suffer, we would not be far from wrong. Lovelace makes an effort to see her and displays emotions that border on madness, and the most vicious members of her family come around to hoping that she does not die. But there is also a positive side to Clarissa's decision. Within her own terms, she achieves a sense of self-worth that she could not have attained in any other way. She becomes a kind of Protestant saint in rising above a Lovelace who is witty, charming, imaginative and intelligent. As readers, we literally switch from a fascination with his wild longings, dreams and daydreams to the still normative but intense morality of Clarissa.

Richardson's final novel, *Sir Charles Grandison* (1753–54) was a retreat from the intensity of *Clarissa* but in some ways an impressive achievement. No one could follow Richardson's success with *Clarissa,* though numerous shorter versions of her seduction and destruction continued to be written for the next two hundred years, but *Grandison* created a tradition of novels that were essentially comic in outcome while treating serious subjects and dramatic events. Jane Austen not only acknowledged her debt to *Grandison* but attempted to dramatise it as well. Admittedly, *Grandison* does not have a great deal of action. The heroine, Harriet Byron, is brought into contact with Sir Charles and, like everyone else, comes to admire his goodness. He rescues her after she is abducted from a masquerade, and she is more than grateful. Unfortunately for Harriet, Sir Charles, when in Italy, had fallen in love with a lovely but unstable woman, Clementina. Her noble family is catholic and not entirely happy with Sir Charles's offer of marriage. They regard him as a heretic and somewhat alien to their ways. By the time Harriet Byron meets Sir Charles, the relationship with Clementina seems to have ended, and he feels almost free enough to fall in love with Harriet. But Clementina's nervous condition weighs heavily on his mind, and he must feel entirely free before he can propose and be accepted by Harriet. Richardson keeps this somewhat quiet plot alive by a variety of secondary characters who are used to illustrate some of the problems with marriage and love in contemporary England and by conversation on various aspects of life and letters. The letter technique is far more obvious than that used in Clarissa. At one point Harriet obtains and reads the correspondence of Sir Charles. The simpler device of flashback would have been easier. And without some excitement in the plot, the general awkwardness of the epistolary novel becomes obvious. Richardson argued that Fielding's use of a third-person narrator commenting on the events at his 'own dull Pace' created 'dry' narratives without psychological interest, but *Grandison* demonstrates the advantages of Fielding's method.

II   Fielding

Henry Fielding (1707–54) may have been inspired to write prose fiction in response to Richardson's *Pamela,* but he had been the major writer for the theatre during the 1730s. Although some critics have theorised that Fielding's plays were becoming too complex for stage presentation and that a turn to fiction was necessary, the chances are that Fielding found the techniques of the stage fully adequate and that the passage of the Licencing Act in 1737, with its success in stamping out stage satire, was an ample explanation for Fielding's turn to prose fiction. After the success of *The Beggar's Opera,* a number of new theatres opened to take advantage of an interest in fresh productions. The two patent companies preferred to perform plays already in the repertory, since there was a saving on the fees to be paid to the author and new costumes and sets were not required, but some of the smaller theatres were willing to experiment with fresh material. Fielding began his dramatic career with *Love in Several Masques* in 1728. It was a regular comedy and was performed at Drury Lane with little success.

After a trip to Leyden to study law, he returned to London and began writing a series of farces for the New Haymarket theatre. That theatre was dedicated to performing farce and burlesque since its opening in 1720, and in 1729, Samuel Johnson of Cheshire (1691–1773) had scored a huge success with a strange mixture of tragedy and absurdity called *Hurlothrumbo*. In something of the same vein, Fielding undertook to satirise the techniques of tragedy in his *Tom Thumb*, first performed in 1730 and enlarged in 1731 as *The Tragedy of Tragedies*. Fielding was particularly hard on the heroic tragedies of the Restoration, but many of his parodies on heroic speeches would do well as burlesques on some of the speeches in Shakespeare. Like Swift, Fielding distrusted the grand, heroic or tragic in literature. The hero, Tom Thumb, enters with some gigantic prisoners to the admiration of all. The princess Huncamunca loves him passionately and thereby raises the jealousy and wrath of the villain Grizzle whose death after a lengthy soliloquy shows Fielding at his best in the burlesque vein:

> But Ha! I feel death rumbling in my brains,
> Some kinder sprite knocks softly at my soul
> And gently whispers it to haste away.
> I come, I come, most willingly I come.
> So when some city wife, for country air,
> To Hampstead or to Highgate does repair;
> Her, to make haste, her husband does implore,
> And cries, 'My dear, the coach is at the door'.
> With equal wish, desirous to be gone,
> She gets into the coach, and then she cries – 'Drive on!'

In the same year as the first production of *Tom Thumb*, 1730, Fielding began his series of farces on political themes. These attacks on Sir Robert Walpole and his government reached their high point of abuse in 1736 with *Pasquin* and *Historical Register for 1736*. Although there was a rumour that the government suppressed an even more savage satire, 'The Golden Rump', Fielding's attacks were sufficiently direct to bring the Government to act, and the first violator of the Licencing Act of 1737 was unceremoniously thrown into jail. Fielding's career as a playwright was over. In addition to his farces and political satires, Fielding wrote a number of regular comedies. The best of these was *The Modern Husband* (1732) with its attack on contemporary manners. His *Don Quixote in England* (1734) is interesting for its attack, through the eyes of the seemingly mad Quixote, on self-interest and what passes for ordinary morality. Fielding was to return to a more effective assault on the manners of his day in his fiction.

Shamela (1741) was Fielding's first response to Richardson's novel. The letter-writer is now a scheming, most unvirtuous servant named Shamela. She makes the same kind of little proverbial observations on what happens to her, but her observations are often filled with sexual innuendo. Her master marries her eventually, but having discovered her together with her lover in bed, he is in process of taking legal action against both at the end. Fielding found Richardson's morality and his sense of reward for 'virtue' particularly vulgar. Next year he produced his *Joseph Andrews* about the brother of *Pamela*. Fielding introduces Pamela at the end of the novel along with her husband whose name is now known – Squire Booby, but whatever parody Fielding may have intended at the outset is swallowed up in a work with its own integrity. Joseph Andrews is virtuous in the same way as Pamela but for different reasons. One of his main reasons is his love for Fanny, a country girl of great beauty and good sense, who returns his love. Lady Booby, who tries to seduce Joseph, is motivated not by love but by lust, and Fielding advances his own idea of human motivation. Good characters are good because they are motivated by love, which, in a larger sense, may be translated as charity. Christian teachings counsel us to control our passions. As his example of the good Christian, Fielding gives the reader the wonderful character of Parson Adams, the teacher and counsellor of both Joseph and Fanny. With the exception of these three figures along with a few others, Fielding's world is inhabited by vicious squires, justices, inn-keepers and clergymen. After rejecting the advances of Lady Booby (much to that Lady's surprise), Joseph, on his way back to the country, is attacked by thieves and stripped bare. A coach filled with travellers refuses to help, and only the action of the coachman saves Joseph. That the coachman is soon to be sentenced to transportation for robbery is a sad commentary on the general charity of the world.

The plot of *Joseph Andrews* involves a meeting on the road between Joseph, Fanny and Parson Adams and their trip back to their village. On the way they encounter the family of Mr Wilson, who has withdrawn from society after living the life of a man of the world. His pastoral life, away from the problems of London, is established as a rather eccentric norm for the book. After a tense moment of revealed identities Wilson turns out to be Joseph's real father. Fanny emerges as the sister of Pamela, and after a moment in which they fear that they are brother and sister and therefore without hope of marrying, Wilson recognises the mark of his lost son on Joseph. Fielding uses some obvious plot contrivances, including a pedlar who reveals many of the mysteries at the end, but the mixture of brilliant comic sense and a profoundly pessimistic view of human nature establishes *Joseph Andrews* as an important work of fiction.

Between 1742 and 1749, when he published his best novel *Tom Jones,* Fielding worked at a number of tasks. In 1743, he published his *Miscellanies* with two works of fiction among the dialogues and essays: *A Journey from this World to the Next* and *Jonathan Wild.* The first is a voyage to the underworld in the manner of Lucian. Fielding tells of his death on 1 December 1741 and his coach ride to the underworld. On the way those in the carriage visit the Palace of Death where the most honoured guests are military heroes like Alexander and Charles XII of Sweden. Soon they arrive at the place where Minos judges those who seek entry into Elysium. Fielding describes how rich men are rejected while a thief who stole from need is admitted. The stories of various figures are repeated, including the transmigrations of the soul of Julian the Apostate, the last pagan emperor of Rome, and the life of Anne Boleyn, second wife of Henry VIII. The best that can be said of this work is that it shows Fielding experimenting with various fictional devices. *Jonathan Wild* is better, but again it is more important for the stance Fielding assumes as an ironic narrator of the life of Jonathan Wild. Wild is pictured as a man who may rightly be distinguished for being 'great', for greatness, in Fielding's definition, is almost the opposite of goodness. To achieve great things, a man has to take advantage of his fellow human beings and be willing to do anything to rise to the top. Wild, in his complete disregard for anything but self-interest, tries to take advantage of everyone he encounters, and Fielding adds the story of Mr and Mrs

Heartfree to show how the innocent are victimised and betrayed by villains like Wild.

Jonathan Wild is a considerable achievement. As a view of society it is almost Swiftian in its unwillingness to compromise with the pervasive sense of evil in the world. Its problem is the failure to break through the irony at any point into a more humane way of seeing the relationship between the good and the great. Fielding had not yet achieved the 'humanity' that he named as one of the chief qualities of a writer of fiction. The feeling of pity, or refusal to pass judgement, that pervades *Tom Jones* is lacking in *Jonathan Wild,* with the result that the irony gradually becomes cloying. In his 'An Essay on the Knowledge of the Characters of Men', published in the same year as *Jonathan Wild,* Fielding expressed his sense that in a world in which the crafty continually wear disguises, almost everyone is forced to take up some kind of mask or risk ridicule. When he wrote *Tom Jones,* Fielding seems to have allowed himself to become more sanguine about those who try to live without disguises.

By the time *Tom Jones* appeared, Fielding had become a Justice of the Peace for Westminster. His journalism for the government in *The True Patriot (1745)* and *Jacobite's Journal* (1747–48) brought some support from the party in power, and he had long been the recipient of patronage from Ralph Allen, the model of Squire Allworthy, and from the Duke of Bedford, who added to his position by helping him to become a Justice of the Peace for Middlesex. Now he could write with some sense of security and perhaps with less bitterness than informs his early fiction. *Tom Jones* has its villains in Captain Blifil and his son Blifil, in Thwackum, and in Dowling, the lawyer, but it is a work in which goodness prevails, not by the half-ironic device of the pedlar of *Joseph Andrews* but by the workings of the plot which fits together beautifully in much the same way that Fielding's world fits together in the novel. At one point, Fielding informs us that we would be mistaken to think that goodness usually triumphed in the world. Fielding was too much a disciple of Mandeville to believe that. But within the novel good does triumph over evil and that is the only thing that matters.

Tom Jones may be read as a simple parable. The novel begins at Paradise Hall governed by a Mr Allworthy. Two youths grow up in this ideal place, Tom, an illegitimate child of unknown parentage but genuine goodness, and Blifil, the son of Allworthy's sister, a person incapable of any love except self-love. Tom's capacity for love, both sexual and spiritual, creates problems for him, and through a misunderstanding he is cast out of Paradise Hall and must leave Sophia (Wisdom), the girl he was hoping to win in some way for his wife. Though he makes many friends, Tom, pursued by the hatred of Blifil, and the love of a number of women, ends in jail. But eventually he is rescued; his identity is established as an illegitimate son of Bridget Allworthy; he is reconciled with his foster father, Allworthy, and marries his Sophia. Read in this way, *Tom Jones* is a kind of allegory in which goodness of heart wins out over evil self-interest, since it is the 'perfect happiness' that Jenny Waters feels in her relationship with Jones that leads her to tell Allworthy of Tom's true identity. Sophia's last name is Western and the return from London to the Western countryside is very much a retreat to a new Eden.

Fielding tells his story in a manner that establishes the narrator as a character within the work. Indeed the novelist and critic Henry James (1843–1916) thought Fielding was the only personality in *Tom Jones* who achieved anything beyond the standard stereotypes of fiction. Certainly Tom Jones surprises the reader on the few occasions that he actually speaks in his own voice, seeming, at those moments, almost out of character. Fielding, as already mentioned, believed that the true novelist had to have 'humanity', but he also included in the composition of his ideal writer of fiction learning, genius and experience. Fielding introduces each of his eighteen books with an address to the reader, often on the subject of fiction itself and occasionally on matters of manners and morals. But in addition to such formal occasions for criticism and ethical discourse, Fielding fills every page with commentary of this kind. Thus *Tom Jones* is both a novel about novel writing and a discourse on life in eighteenth-century England and on existence in general. Fielding uses his knowledge of epic to indulge in some scenes of comedy in which the similies common to heroic poetry are contrasted with low subject matter, and his knowledge of the drama gives him a particularly good sense of the way plot should be used. A large part of the delight in the novel rises from the way Fielding brings his characters together for surprising encounters within the context of a plot that makes these extraordinary meetings at once natural and amusing. But ultimately it is that combination of ingredients that lends to *Tom Jones* the feeling that the panorama of scene and character is important to us as readers. *Tom Jones* is a great novel because it entertains us while telling us some vital truths in the way that only literature can.

Both *Joseph Andrews* and *Tom Jones* were turned into memorable films by a single director, Tony Richardson, and they were films that tell us much about the nature of Fielding's narratives. *Joseph Andrews* opens with a glorious view of the countryside on May Day and soon changes to a vision of London during the time of its amazing expansion. The eighteenth century saw the construction of some of the magnificent London squares, and before the writing of *Joseph Andrews*, Hanover, Grosvenor, Cavendish and Berkeley squares were either completed or in various stages of construction. Richardson shows building stones and ropes everywhere and the difficulties of manoeuvring through the streets of a city that was in process of becoming what Defoe called a 'monster' city. *Tom Jones* is far less self-indulgent in its camera work, but it too has some wonderful contrasts between the beauty of the country and grim scenes of city life. Oddly enough, however, what these films suggest is the degree to which Fielding holds the reader trapped in his commentary. There are certainly sketches, descriptions and scenes in these two novels; indeed Fielding refers to Hogarth in his preface to *Joseph Andrews* and by way of compliment, Hogarth referred the viewers of his prints back to Fielding. But this was mainly on the nature of character as opposed to caricature. There is little free play of the visual in Fielding's novels and nothing resembling description for description's sake. We are told that Lady Booby walks with Joseph in Hyde Park, but that is all. Fielding's narrator is too intent on telling us how the reader ought to think about the significance of what is experienced through his narrative to indulge in a description of contemporary London. Richardson transposes many of Fielding's humorous narrative techniques to the camera with great success, but the remarkably vivid scenes of eighteenth-century life are all the work of the modern director. Fielding was concerned with other matters. We may be able to visualise a scene from *Tom Jones,* such as the one involving the country girlfriend of Tom, Molly, in the fields with her clothes covered with specks of manure and her looks revealing how sexually available she is, but Fielding is more concerned that we *think* about what such a scene might mean than that we should be capable of visualising it in our minds.

Fielding's next novel, *Amelia* (1751) is, in a sense, Fielding's *Grandison.* Like Richardson, Fielding tried to write a novel that strove for a middle way between comedy and the serious or tragic. He stumbled at the beginning by giving Amelia a slightly broken nose. It was an effort to bring realism to his portraiture and to remove his heroine from the realm of romance, but it was an awkward device. Also *Amelia* was essentially the story of a marriage rather than the usual romance that ends with the wedding and a brief account of children to come. The protagonist, Booth, is deeply in love with his wife, but he tends toward a belief in human self-interest and egotism. As a result, he conducts himself with a degree of scepticism. Not that Booth is wrong about most of the characters he meets. He is betrayed by his best friend and meets evil wherever he looks. But at the end he and his wife are rescued by the benevolence of the kindly Dr Harrison, and Booth learns to appreciate his wife's love and the joys of human kindness when it is to be found. Fielding based his book on epic material drawn from the *Aeneid*, but such a structure is more of a prop for Fielding as a writer than a necessary allusion for the reader. *Amelia* is a book that improves on re-reading but suffers from a certain distrust of fiction itself. In his final work, a travel book titled *A Voyage to Lisbon* (1755) recounting his quest for better health abroad, Fielding expressed some regret that he did not write history instead of fiction. Some of that feeling creeps into *Amelia* in Fielding's adherence to what he felt to be real motivation for character and in his refusal to fall into what he could do best – write scenes of hilarious comedy. But in his avoidance of extremes, Fielding realised one important route that the classical novel was to travel. Neither Booth nor Amelia take on significance beyond the limits of their own lives, and in that sense, they resemble the great mass of novelistic characters that were to people the bourgeois novel.

III Smollett

Compared to Defoe, Richardson and Fielding, Tobias Smollett (1721–71) was not a great innovator. His first novel, *Roderick Random* (1748) is not a great advance over Lesage's *Gil Blas* which Smollett translated in the same year. But Smollett had a unique way of seeing the world, and the picaresque form allowed for something close to autobiography. Like Smollett himself, Roderick is a Scotsman and a doctor, and like his creator, he burns with indignation at the way the world treats him. Roderick never forgets that his father was a gentleman, and while he undergoes many of the adventures of picaresque rogues, he is never without a sense of the injustices done to him in relationship to what ought to have been his station in life. If it would be a serious error to read *Roderick Random* as autobiography, so it would be a mistake to miss the degree to which Smollett felt compassion for his hero. We laugh at him in some of his awkward moments, but we feel with him in his pain and anguish too. His discovery of his long-lost father and the recovery of his position in life provide a satisfying conclusion to his wanderings and sufferings.

In his preface, Smollett claimed that he was writing satire, and for all Fielding's picture of an indifferent and self-interested world, it was Smollett who pictured that world as genuinely cruel and even sadistic. Roderick's personal experiences in the navy and his sufferings merge into the larger picture of the mishandling of the Battle of Carthagena in 1740 during which thousands of men were slaughtered needlessly. Thus we move from the magnificently comic-satiric scene of Captain Oakum's insistence that the sick are merely pretending to illness, only to have many of them die on the deck (culminating in the release of a madman who attempts to strangle the captain), to the bitter picture of bodies floating in the sea at Carthagena. The element of cruelty in Smollet's comedy makes him a master of the grotesque and of a type of comedy in which human beings often act like mechanisms or like the figures in an animated cartoon. All of this takes place in an ambience of corruption and ignorance. The talented members of society seem excluded from the important positions in the arts, professions, and politics they deserve, while madmen, sadists and fools appear to have a direct route to success.

Smollett's other mid-century novels show his figures moving through a similar world, though the degree of toughness gradually gives way as feeling and sensibility become the dominant forces in literature. In *Peregrine Pickle* (1751), Smollett created a cast of characters around his hero who belong to the tradition of the comic grotesque that was eventually to influence Charles Dickens, but the action of the work is constructed around Peregrine's practical jokes – jokes that are built into a moral philosophy as practical satire. By playing such jokes on those who deserve punishment, Peregrine, under the influence of his mentor, Crabtree, takes the revenge on the wicked that society itself refuses to administer. Individual scenes, such as a wonderful dinner of food in the ancient manner prepared by a lover of the ancients, which turns everyone's stomach, show Smollett's brilliance as a writer of comedy, but Peregrine is probably a 'hero' admired only by Smollett. In *Ferdinand Count Fathom* (1753), Smollett selected for a protagonist a villain of the Jonathan Wild type, who endears himself to the reader only by his overall lack of success. Ferdinand is always betrayed by his own passions into acts that destroy all his vicious plans. He is brought to complete misery by the end, and is rescued by those whom he sought to hurt, Renaldo Count de Melvil and Serafina. Imagery of black and white, villain and hero, along with scenes involving banditti and an apparent ghost, are strongly suggestive of the Gothic. Smollett also mingles scenes of melodrama, in a raised style reminiscent of contemporary tragedy, with scenes of low comedy and satiric grotesque. In his preface, suggesting the idea of the novel as a 'diffused picture' of life, Smollett argues for a mixture of styles, but while occasionally both styles work together, Smollett is best at satire. A good example of his satiric style appears in his description of the madam of a bordello visited by Fathom and some acquaintances:

> they were received by the venerable priestess, a personage turned of seventy, who seemed to exercise the functions of her calling, in despite of the most cruel ravages of time; for age had bent her into the form of a Turkish bow. Her head was agitated by the palsy, like the leaf of the poplar tree; her hair fell down in scanty parcels, as white as the driven snow; her face was not simply wrinkled, but ploughed into innumerable furrows; her jaws could not boast of one remaining tooth; one eye distilled

a large quantity of rheum, by virtue of the fiery edge that surrounded it; the other was altogether extinguished, and she had lost her nose in the course of her ministration. The Delphi sibyl was but a type of this hoary matron, who, by her figure, might have been mistaken for the consort of Chaos, or mother of Time. Yet there was something meritorious in her appearance, as it denoted her an indefatigable minister to the pleasure of mankind.

In contrast to these set pictures are some remarkably good scenes of adventure and social life that reveal Smollett as a writer with a fine sense of realistic detail.

Smollett's *Sir Launcelot Greaves* (1760) might well belong in the chapter on sensibility, but the impulse behind this work is still satiric. The basis of the work is Cervantes' *Don Quixote*. He had used Cervantes' model in *Roderick Random* to an extent in treating the relationship between his hero and his faithful servant Strap, and he had translated *Don Quixote* in 1775. But *Sir Launcelot Greaves* is based on a contemporary idea – the principle of the stewardship of wealth. Smollett's rich young hero is not mad except as the injustices of the world would make any sane man mad. At times Roderick's fury approaches madness, but his reaction is produced by his helplessness. Sir Launcelot Greaves rides out, not with a lance, but with a great deal of money, and in one of his adventures, he simply outbids one of the villains he encounters. At other times Smollett's knight hires lawyers to defeat his villains. At the end, he marries a woman of equal benevolence, Miss Darnel, whose heart was 'incapable of disguise or dissimulation; frank, generous, and open'. This should indicate how far, by 1760, the age had travelled from its admiration for disguise.

IV   Other mid-century novelists and dramatists

Smollett's effort at a quixotic novel is more interesting as a document in the history of ideas than as a work of fiction. The idea was slight and Smollett had difficulty sustaining it, even though it gave him an opportunity to satirise the evils of the time. A far better novel on a similar structure was Charlotte Lennox's (1720–1804) *Female Quixote* (1752). A friend of Dr Johnson and the future author of a study of the sources of Shakespeare's plays, *Shakespeare Illustrated* (1753), she created a heroine whose mind and sensibility were dominated by the French romances of the seventeenth century in much the same way as Don Quixote was befuddled by the romances of chivalry. Lennox had obviously read the romances carefully. They were still available and still a dominant force on contemporary fiction. Arabella, the heroine, expects men to act as dashing heroes or as despicable villains and insists on being regarded as a romance heroine. Her admirer treats her with considerable patience as a person afflicted with a disease of the imagination, and as readers, we hover between disbelief, laughter and sympathy. Lennox is aware to some extent that Arabella is using her dream world as a kind of latency period, and she does emerge eventually to become a woman capable of loving her admirer. Jane Austen did it better in *Northanger Abbey* (1818), but *The Female Quixote* is a novel with considerable charm and some skilful writing.

One other novel should be mentioned, though until its re-publication in the twentieth century its fame was mainly limited to word of mouth and to copies sold surreptitiously to special customers. *Fanny Hill* (1748) by John Cleland (1709–89) was one of many works of pornography produced during the eighteenth century, but it is unusual in a number of ways. The vitalism, the belief in sexual fulfilment and sexual energy, that underlies the work is not unusual for works drawing on philosophic libertinism for their outlook, but such works were seldom merely pornographic. In fact, *Fanny Hill* has some fine scenes of comedy and satire, and unlike works written entirely for titillation, it develops its characters with some care. Fanny undergoes the usual career of the prostitute of literature, from innocent country girl to sophisticated courtesan, but she tells us much about herself and the men she encounters. If there is the usual masculine daydream material, there is also satire to invade the sexual fantasy. Cleland was a philologist, and his fascination for language emerges at a number of points. In one section Fanny discusses the inability of language to describe the individuality of sexual experience. In language such events must appear monotonous with the same words used over and over again. While *Fanny Hill* can be classified as pornography, it does nevertheless have literary qualities that work against the daydream fantasies of most pornography. Like Moll Flanders, who influenced Cleland's creation, Fanny ends happily. She comes gradually to see that sexual freedom is not the best answer to life and manages to come back together with her first lover in a marriage that appears to leave both parties contented. Although Cleland, reviewing his own novel, argued that it was far more moral than *Tom Jones,* he could not win anyone to agree with him. He was warned against writing such a work again by the government, and his next work, *Memoirs of a Coxcomb* (1751) showed little of the skill displayed in *Fanny Hill.* Cleland's only work of consequence made a considerable splash on its appearance, and we should not underestimate the degree to which censorship deprived it of a wider audience through the centuries.

Charlotte Lennox's work on Shakespeare was indicative of some movements in drama and dramatic criticism. At the start of this chapter, Fielding's trouble with the Licencing Act and his change over to fiction was mentioned as a crucial turning point in the history of the drama. Fielding was not alone in his disappointment. Smollett blamed politics, theatrical and otherwise, for the failure of the theatrical managers to accept his tragedy, *The Revenge,* and politics was unquestionably behind the refusal to perform *Gustavus Vasa* (1739), an effective tragedy which Henry Brooke (c. 1703–83) published with an impressive subscription list. Edward Moore (1712–57) wrote an effective attack on gambling in *The Gamester* (1753) a play that was more directed at reform than at evoking a generalised sentimental response, and some elements of Restoration comedy survived in Garrick's rewriting of Wycherley's *The Country Wife, The Country Girl* (1766), in excised versions of Congreve's comedies, and in comedies that attempted to reconstruct Restoration comedy along moral lines, such as *The Suspicious Husband* (1747) of Benjamin Hoadly (1706–57). But the pattern of performing old plays already in the repertory continued, and looming larger than ever before in the repertory was William Shakespeare.

At the beginning of the century, most critics agreed that the only comedy of Shakespeare that could be acted, apart from spectaculars like *The Tempest* that had been made into an opera, was *The Merry Wives of Windsor.* But from 1744 onward, Shakespeare's romantic comedies grew in popularity. David Garrick (1717–79) was unquestionably a major force in the general popularity of Shakespeare on the stage. More than Thomas Betterton (c. 1635–1710) and Cibber, both actor-managers, Garrick dominated the stage of his time. He wrote some brisk comedies like *Miss in Her Teens* (1747), collaborated with George Coleman on the highly successful *Clandestine Marriage* (1766), and created a school of acting that contemporaries considered 'natural' compared to the more formalised gestures and positions of the past. Garrick was a great booster of Shakespeare, and in 1769 staged the great Shakespeare Jubilee at Stratford-on-Avon, an event that established Shakespeare as the national bard and Stratford as a permanent tourist attraction.

Garrick's fame as Hamlet is immortalised in *Tom Jones,* where Partridge, Tom's companion, is so convinced of the reality of Garrick's feelings and so terrified at the appearance of the ghost that he turns pale and trembles. And when Tom tries to persuade him that Garrick was merely acting, Partridge points to the absolute naturalness of the way Garrick gradually returned to his initial calm as evidence that no one could pretend to such real emotions. But Garrick's admiration for Shakespeare did not extend yet to the bardolatry that regarded every word of the text sacred. In his version of the fifth act of *Hamlet,* he removed what he called the 'rubbish' of the gravediggers, made Laertes into an innocent party in Hamlet's death, and kept the Queen alive for repentance. Hamlet was killed accidentally in running upon Laertes's sword while trying to aid his fainting mother. But *Hamlet* was always cut, and it was in Garrick's version (1772) that one of Hamlet's best soliloquies was first heard on the stage.

Interest in Shakespeare was reflected in criticism and editions as well as in stage attendance. The first modern edition was Rowe's (1709), followed by Pope's (1725), Lewis Theobald's (1734), Sir Thomas Hanmer's (1743), and William Warburton's (1747). Warburton's edition, with its arbitrary emendations, produced a rash of criticism, most notably that of Thomas Edwards (1699–1757), in *The Canons of Criticism* (1748). Literary criticism of Shakespeare's plays in contemporary journals as well as reviews of performances had become commonplace. William Dodd (1729–77) wrote two volumes, *The Beauties of Shakespeare,* in 1752, pointing out the best passages; Zachary Grey (1688–1766) mingled antiquarian lore with miscellaneous notes in his *Notes on Shakespeare* (1754); but it was Garrick, defending his interpretation as an actor or his revisions as an adaptor, or Garrick under attack for his various changes in Shakespeare's lines, who seemed to keep Shakespeare before the public. Smollett was one writer who was not entirely convinced that Shakespeare demonstrated that the rules of the French critics were nonsense and that imagination was all. But in measuring Shakespeare's greatness against other writers, Mark Akenside writing in *The Museum* in 1746, rated Shakespeare at the top of the scale. He received a 0 on a scale of 0–18 in the category of 'Critical Ordonnance' of judgement and only 10 in taste, yet he still emerged with an 18 along with Homer. The lesson was clear: imagination and invention were in and imitation and regularity were out. When Edward Young wrote his *Conjectures on Original Composition* (1759), he dedicated the work to Samuel Richardson as the inventor of a new species of writing in his novels and praised Shakespeare for a genius that needed no learning. For better or for worse, the road to greatness seemed to rest with originality. The type of 'errors' that critics thought they had perceived in Shakespeare now seemed merely minor sins.

8
The age of sensibility

The modern critic, Northrop Frye (b. 1912) is responsible for naming the last part of the eighteenth century by the title assigned to this chapter, and by his arguments he added strength to those critics who found, in the frequently used categorisation of this period, 'Pre-Romanticism', a contradiction to the aesthetic ideals of the time and a reading of literary history that saw the fulfilment of those ideals in the nineteenth century. One of Frye's most striking points was his argument that the art of the time was unique in stressing the artistic process rather than the finished product, but concepts like that of the *non finito* – the argument that the unfinished work of art, such as Michelangelo's (1475–1564) slaves, were in some ways superior to his finished pieces because they remained in a state of potential greatness – had been around since the Renaissance. One of the major questions about Frye's taxonomy would involve the problem of exact beginnings. Collins, with his difficult syntax and obscure connections is certainly a poet of sensibility, and the same is true of Gray, the best of whose poetry was treated in the last chapter. The answer to such questions is that, to a degree, the entire eighteenth century was an age of sensibility but that not until the 1740s and 1750s did it become the dominant movement.

I   New modes of thought and taste

The changes in attitude were accompanied by revisions in the criticism of this period. In 1753 Robert Lowth (1710–87) published a series of lectures that he had been presenting in Latin between 1741 and 1750 on what was, in its English title of 1787, *The Sacred Poetry of the Hebrews*. Lowth stessed the sublimity and power of biblical verse, particularly that of Ezekiel, and, in the process, tended to break down the distinction between a poetry tied to rhyme and metre and that based on a kind of free verse. In 1756, Edmund Burke (1729–97) published his treatise on *The Sublime and the Beautiful,* arguing that the pleasure of the sublime arose from sensations of pain that varied from the terror experienced in viewing a mountain to feelings of discomfort in what was obscure to the senses or in experiences of deprivation such as solitude. A psychology that suggested a degree of pleasure derivable from pain was subject to all kinds of criticism and revisions in one direction or another, but Burke became the starting point for a type of aesthetics that focused on the effect of art on its audience. When Henry Home, Lord Kames (1696–1782) published the first edition of his popular *Elements of Criticism* in 1762 he announced that great literature turns the reader into a someone who re-lives the experience of the work through a kind of 'ideal presence'. Kames was basically a formalist, but like so many critics of his time he wanted to explain the emotions experienced by the reader in the presence of the literary work, a concern that may reflect a more intense involvement between the reader and the printed page during the eighteenth century than that experienced by the modern reader. Finally, critics and writers alike developed a fascination for older literature and older forms. The publication in 1765 of *Reliques of Ancient English Poetry,* a collection of English ballads edited by Thomas Percy (1729–1811), brought with it a new interest in the literature of England's past and a rich source of inspiration for future poets.

What, it might be asked, do such developments have to do with sensibility? Percy's ballads are a good example. Although he edited them so as to make them more readable for his audience, they remained poems that reflected 'natural' feelings and passions very different from the society verse that was common at the time and that even Thomas Gray practised in his light moments. Since stanzas had been lost over the years, they appeared fragmentary in their way of telling a story. Poems involving ghosts and witches appealed to ideals of the sublime, and Percy put in numbers of poems from contemporary imitators of ballads, including himself, that involved sentimental love scenes suitable to the taste of the most tender readers.

Parallel to these changes in taste were the new ideas in philosophy, particularly in epistemology and moral philosophy. Locke's assertion of a real world behind the ideas entering the mind was challenged by George Berkeley (1685–1753) in his *The Principles of Human Knowledge* (1710) and *The Dialogues of Hylas and Philonus* (1713). The mind, argued Berkeley, can only understand mental events and what is not available to the mind cannot be said to exist. Berkeley's argument that all ideas exist in the mind of God represented an idealism only fully appreciated by the followers of Hegel in the next century, but he helped to undermine the faith in a solid and verifiable world. David Hume (1711–76) went further. He demonstrated that such apparent certainties as cause and effect could be reduced to a method of thinking rather than something concrete, and he showed the mind as operating from patterns of association and juxtaposition rather than reason. In *An Enquiry concerning Human Understanding* (1739), he even questioned whether human identity could be anything more than the fitful memory of an illusory continuity of the self. In the 1748 edition of this work, he printed the section 'Of Miracles' in which he suggested that miracles depended on the testimony of individual men and that however much we may believe in such testimony, miracles can never be proved to be true. The *Enquiry concerning the Principles of Morals* (1751) established more fully the system of benevolence and sympathy with which we live in society. However much man may be ruled by self-love he subordinates those drives to the social conditions in which he chooses to live.

Hume was one of those men in Great Britain who most fully embodied the ideals of the Enlightenment as it was developing in France under the guidance of the editor of the *Encyclopédie*, Denis Diderot (1713–84). Hume tried to write useful works like his *History of Great Britain* (1754–61), and he tried to see clearly. His *Dialogues concerning Natural Religion*, published after his death in 1779, reflects his doubts about the evidence for the existence of God. But he was no propagator of a cold theory of reason. Rather he contributed to a concept of mankind that showed him ruled by his passions and feelings. He accepted institutions as the product of human existence and like

Edmund Burke later in the century, maintained that the contract theory of government was merely a political fiction. If the great philosopher of sensibility was Jean-Jacques Rousseau (1712–78), it should be no surprise that, however much they may have fallen out later, Hume befriended him and brought him to Great Britain for a time.

Rousseau, as a moral philosopher, drew on almost fifty years of British speculation on the ethical nature of mankind, particularly on Shaftesbury's argument that man had an innate moral sense associated with his sense of beauty and proportion. Shaftesbury's ideas had been expanded by Francis Hutcheson (1694–1746) in his *Inquiry into the Original of our Ideas of Beauty and Virtue* (1725) and *Essay on the Nature and Conduct of the Passions and Affections* (1726) into a system of mathematical formulae which demonstrated that we act in such a way as to promote the general happiness of mankind. As Professor of Moral Philosophy at Glasgow, Hutcheson passed his ideas on to an entire school of Scottish philosophers, among whom was Adam Smith (1723–90), whose *Theory of Moral Sentiments* (1759) argued for a sympathy between men that operated with an almost obligatory power forcing them to act benevolently and morally. Rousseau, however, moved even further toward a faith in human benevolence. He argued that mankind had been corrupted by civilisation. His passions and affections could be improved by an education in contact with things rather than words. Rousseau did not long to return to the jungle, as some of his detractors suggested, but he regarded the road to civilisation as one of many roads that might have been taken. Many of these attitudes appeared in his two *Discourses* (1750, 1754), but he expanded on them in *Émile* (1762). His novel, *The New Eloisa* (1761), dealt with a passionate romance that gradually cooled into a philosophic relationship between the former lover and Julie. Passion is still there, but it is under control. Among other influential aspects of Rousseau's novel is a magnificent scene in the Alps where the lover, Saint-Preux, finds consolation for his hopeless passion. It would be impossible to overestimate the influence of these works; his *Social contract* (1762), and his autobiography, *The Confessions,* published after his death, had a major influence on the eighteenth century and on future periods. Rousseau gave priority to natural feeling and emotion above any official code of morality and to the private self above anything. When Jane Austen satirised sensibility as a code of behaviour that superseded all traditional moral codes, she was not likely to have been thinking of Rousseau, but the path to such an attitude seemed more possible after him.

One other philosopher ought to be mentioned to make the formula for the art of the second half of the century complete. In 1749 David Hartley (1705–57) published his *Observations on Man*. Hartley did not believe in an innate moral sense but expanded Locke's suggestions about the association of ideas into a system by which every action could be ascribed to some kind of seemingly random association. Although the second half of Hartley's treatise was essentially theological, explaining the way in which association fitted into the scheme of Providence, the first section seemed to suggest that human beings were indeed ruled by that irrational associational impulse advanced by Locke as a kind of madness. In conjunction with Hume's picture of human motivation, it suggested that man was hardly a rational creature and that, more often than not, he was moved by some obscure conjunction of associations.

II   The poetry of sensibility

To divide Gray's poetry into a section that was written before 1750 and another after might seem to suggest that he suddenly came under the influence of the philosophical movements I have been discussing. But attempts at relating a poet to intellectual backgrounds are always difficult even if the poet proclaims that he is influenced by one philosopher or another. Gray was certainly a poet of sensibility before 1750 as were Collins and the Wartons. His indebtedness to Dante and Petrarch and his interest in the sonnet form revealed by his 'Sonnet on the Death of Mr. Richard West', written in 1742 but not published until 1775, shows the same concern for earlier poetic forms that impelled Thomas Edwards (1699–1757) to publish his series of sonnets in 1748. Yet there is a change in the later poetry. 'The Progress of Poesy' and 'The Bard', both pindaric odes and both published in 1757, reveal a willingness to take more risks, to make leaps between stanzas and within stanzas that left contemporary readers bewildered.

Gray had suddenly become the leader of a type of poetry that was sometimes considered obscure – and sublime because it was obscure.

'The Progress of Poesy' is not an unusual poem in its subject, the movement of poetry from Greece through Italy to England, where Freedom allowed it to flourish. Similar poems had been written by Thomson and Collins. And the subject of 'The Bard' is clear enough once the historical setting, Edward I's attempt to kill all the bards as part of his conquest of Wales, is understood. The Bard appears suddenly to the King and his army, foretells the future history of Great Britain including the Welsh ancestry of the Tudors and the return of a poetry inspired by Welsh themes, and then throws himself off the cliff. Gray wrote to his friend Mason, 'Nobody understands me, & I am perfectly satisfied'. But in his edition of 1768, Gray added explanatory notes which helped, though only a little. Johnson treats the two poems with broad sarcasm:

> My process has now brought me to the *wonderful* 'Wonder of Wonders', the two Sister Odes, by which, though either vulgar ignorance or common sense at first universally rejected them, many have been since persuaded to think themselves delighted. I am one of those that are willing to be pleased, and therefore would gladly find the meaning of the first stanza of 'The Progress of Poetry'.

Part of Johnson's antagonism toward Gray and the odes is connected to his dislike of Gray's Whiggish ideas of freedom, and he demonstrates that any idea that poetry is necessarily connected with liberty is absurd. This leads him to an analysis of trite poetic diction in 'The Progress of Poesy' and to an objection to 'The Bard' as swollen 'to a giant's bulk by fabulous appendages of spectres and predictions'. He dismisses the praise of Gray's abrupt beginning by associating it with the beginning of ballads (primitive art) and finds in Gray's refrain, 'Weave the warp and weave the woof', only the nonsense of the three witches in *Macbeth* murmuring 'Double, double, toil and trouble'.

In the 1768 volume, along with the new notes to both 'The Progress of Poesy' and 'The Bard', Gray also included a number of translations from Old Norse and Welsh: 'The Fatal Sisters, an Ode', 'The Descent of Odin, an Ode', and 'The Triumphs of Owen, a Fragment'. Gray's involvement with this material was connected with his plan to write a history of English poetry by tracing its origins. But he discovered considerable power in the fantastic mythology of the first two of these poems, and he rendered them into English with a heavy alliterative stress:

> Horror covers all the heath,
> Clouds of carnage blot the sun.
> Sisters, weave the web of death;
> Sisters, cease. The work is done.

Although 'The Triumphs of Owen' was actually a complete Welsh poem, Gray deliberately made it into a fragment. This exploitation of the *non finito* was eventually to find additional support when, in 1775, William Mason (1724–97) published a collection of Gray's poems along with a number of fragmentary pieces. In addition to advancing the idea that an unfinished poem might have its own value, it seemed to suggest that poetry inhered in short bursts of lyric intensity. In effect, Gray's interests reflect an odd combination that emerged in the second half of the century: firstly an admiration for the perfection of Greek art, led by the German critic, Johann Winckelmann (1717–68) and present in Gray's use of the pindaric ode; and secondly a fascination for the strength in primitive art to be found in the glorification of the bards of Wales and their poetry as well as in the imitation of crude architecture, advocated by Sir William Chambers (1726–96) in his *Primitive Buildings* (1759) and depicted in paintings like those of John Cozens (1752–97).

One influence on Gray may have been the publication in 1760 of *Fragments of Ancient Poetry, collected in the Highlands of Scotland,* translated, or supposedly translated, by James Macpherson (1736–1796). This collection of seventy pages brought Macpherson instant fame and eventually bitter controversy as he brought out more 'translations' in 1762 and 1763 to form the collection of works by the bard, Ossian. Although Macpherson had some genuine pieces of Highland poetry, he chose to form his material in a way that would appeal to the desire for primitive and sublime poetry, sounding, somehow, like a combination of Homer and the speech of primitive peoples into a simple and dignified, if highly metaphoric, poetic language. Macpherson's model was more the biblical *Song of Solomon* than actual Highland verse, but to many of his contemporaries, the simple dignity achieved by repetition of phrases, the gaps in the narratives and the measured prose seemed the height of truly primitive poetry. That Macpherson presented his account of Fingal's defeat of the leader of the Scandinavian invaders, Swaran, as an 'Ancient Epic Poem' in six books did not disturb Gray, who believed in the authenticity of the poems as an act of faith. We may agree with Johnson's appraisal that these poems could have been written by 'many men, many women, and many children', but they opened the possibility of verse based on very different principles than customary English metre. That Macpherson's version of ancient Celtic poetry sounded like parts of the Bible and evoked the power of the Druid bards did not hurt their reputation either.

Collins had written of Thomson as a 'Druid', and it might be argued that as the role of the poet in society became less important, the poets began dreaming of the powers of the bards of old as described by Macpherson and by Bishop Percy in his essays appended to his collection of ballads. Certainly critics began placing more stress on the nature of artistic genius. Edward Young's 'Conjectures on Original Composition' (1759) tried to separate the writer who makes an original contribution, like Richardson, from mere imitators, and Alexander Gerard (1728–95) in his 'An Essay on Genius' (1774), located true genius in those writers with comprehensive imaginations that enabled them to make instantaneous associations and to project their own feelings into their literary characters with such intensity as to create works that made the readers feel those passions. Gerard argued that the true genius must be an 'enthusiast', a person capable of stronger and deeper feelings than other men.

Although his writings did not fit the image perfectly, Thomas Chatterton (1752–70) provided the myth of the poet of sensibility that lasted through the Romantic movement. Chatterton killed himself at the age of seventeen, unable to face the crushing poverty that resulted from his effort to live off his writings in London. Chatterton attempted to pass off some forgeries of early poetry as the work of a monk named Thomas Rowley who was supposed to have lived in Chatterton's city of Bristol in the middle of the fifteenth century. Chatterton offered his work to Horace Walpole (1717–97), a writer and antiquarian, as genuine historical documents, but Walpole, having been a believer in Macpherson's *Ossian,* was wary of another hoax and quickly found the contradictions in Chatterton's work. The Rowley poems were not published until 1777, after his death, and, despite the objections of Walpole and the careful scholars, Edmund Malone (1741–1812) and Thomas Tyrwhitt (1730–86), belief in their authenticity became even more confused than faith in the genuineness of *Ossian*, since as an act of faith, some believed both in Chatterton's genius and in the reality of Thomas Rowley. But just as *Ossian* with its ghosts, tragic lovers and free verse inspired many poets, so Chatterton's imitation of Chaucer's language and mannerisms and the effects that he observed in some ancient ballads liberated his poetry from many of the conventions of contemporary poetry. Although Walpole admired Gothic 'gloomth' and built his house, Strawberry Hill, as a Gothic mansion, Chatterton's was the first generation to grow up with the new interest in the English Renaissance and Middle Ages. And if he betrayed the counterfeit nature of his monk by having bits of Dryden here and there in the verse, his encounter with the poetry of the past was more immediate than that of Walpole's generation.

Another poet who broke through the conventions of rhyme and metre was Christopher Smart (1722–71). Unlike Chatterton, who was extremely poor and who had little more than a basic education, Smart was a scholar at Pembroke Hall, Cambridge, an excellent classicist, a translator of Horace and therefore a poet capable of the kinds of allusions that enrich the poetry of Pope. But Smart was very much a poet of his time and that meant a poet of deep sensibility, particularly religious sensibility. Smart left his fellowship at Pembroke Hall to throw himself into the life of writing in London, after distinguishing himself at Cambridge by his wit, excessive drinking, and a number of wild escapades. Gray's comments on him suggest a kind of megalomania, habitual lying and lack of control, which Gray rightly judged would cause him to end up in gaol or the mad-house. While in London writing fables and occasional verse, Smart also competed successfully for the Seatonian prize at Cambridge four times between 1750 and 1756 for poems devoted to the attributes of God. In 1756 he had his first bout of insanity, and he was in one asylum or another until 1763. If Samuel Johnson is to be believed, Smart's madness took the form of religious enthusiasm. He would fall to his knees and pray wherever he might be and insist that those around him do the same.

Smart's two best works, 'Jubilate Agno' and 'A Song to David' appear to have been the product of his period of insanity. The first was left in manuscript until 1939 and the second was first published in 1763, the year of his release. 'A Song to David' is the more conventional composition. Smart showed his ability to write a powerful, strongly alliterated blank verse line in the Seatonian poems on God's power and goodness, and he wrote a number of odes to be set to music. But 'A Song to David' has a use of repetition that appears elsewhere in Smart's poetry only in 'Jubilate Agno', and in reprinting it at the back of his somewhat leaden translation of the Psalms in 1765, he demonstrated the degree to which it seemed inspired. The language of 'A Song to David' is magical in the sense that words seem to have a privileged position acquired by repetition and emphasis. After the constant repetition of words like 'precious', 'beauteous', and 'glorious', he slams the poem shut with the tremendous:

> And now the matchless deed's atchiev'd,
> Determined, Dared, and Done.

If 'A Song to David' shows what Smart could do at the height of his artistic powers, 'Jubilate Agno' reveals him as a poet with an original sense of the possibilities inherent in the ability of poetry to explore ordinary experience.

Smart's first editor, who was his nephew, omitted 'A Song to David' from his collection of his uncle's poetry because he thought it showed signs of madness. What must he have thought of 'Jubilate Agno'! Although the free verse is obviously inspired by the Bible, sometimes it is less poetry than what Pope called 'prose run mad'. Critical theory at the end of the century began turning to the idea that great poetry had to be particular rather than general, and Smart, whether acting out of this critical theory or the belief that William Blake (1757–1827) was later to express, that 'everything that lives is holy', incorporated the events of daily life into his poem. Thus we find dates and even footnotes in the long catalogues:

> Let Egerton, house of Egerton rejoice with Sphragis
> green but not pellucid.
> Let Reading, house of Reading rejoice with Syndontites
> found in the fish Synodontes. 27th July N.S.
> 1762. Lord Jesus have mercy on my soul.
> Let Bolton, house of Bolton rejoice with Polygrammos
> a kind of Jasper with white streaks.

Efforts have been made to show that the lines may sometimes be arranged in the form of a litany of comment and response. While this is evident in some sections of the poem, others will not lend themselves to such an ordering. The passage above reveals Smart's interest in science and natural history, and much in the poem seems to be an effort to connect everything, animate and inanimate, human and non-human, into a single praise to God. Thus the frequently anthologised section on Smart's cat, Jeoffry, besides being the most interesting passage of poetry, is also a section that exemplifies Smart's method:

> For he is of the Lord's poor and so indeed is he
> called by benevolence perpetually – Poor Jeoffry!
> poor Jeoffry! the rat has bit thy throat.
> For I bless the name of the Lord Jesus that Jeoffry is
> better.
> For the divine spirit comes about his body to sustain
> it in compleat cat.

It is in passages such as these that 'Jubilate Ango' takes on the dimensions of great poetry. Otherwise it varies from an obsessively organised catalogue of words, things, persons and thoughts to an occasionally inspired effort at rendering the chaos of free associations.

In much of his verse Smart was as logical a poet as John Gay, but the cult of sensibility encouraged a degree of free-ranging association in poetry. This is certainly true of the work of the best example of the poet of sensibility, William Cowper (1731–1800). There are similarities in the lives of these two poets. Just as Smart was to suffer an early disappointment in his love for Anne Vane, so Cowper had to abandon his hope of marrying his cousin, Theodora Cowper, the Delia of his poetry. Like Smart, Cowper experienced periods of madness associated with his religious beliefs, but Cowper's madness took the form of acute despair and the sense that he was not among those chosen for salvation. After his first mild attack in 1752, Cowper was able to make some effort to prepare to follow the career of a civil servant, but faced by approaching examinations for the position of Clerk of the Journals of the House of Lords in 1763, he experienced a genuine attack of insanity. His recovery never removed him entirely from the threat of a relapse, and his poetry is filled with sentiments involving withdrawal from the active world to some place where a person of deep feeling and true sensibility might survive.

Cowper was a poet of some genius, capable of clever and witty occasional verse and a blank verse that moved with the seeming ease of conversation at times and at others was capable of conveying the deepest feelings. Though withdrawn from the busy world of London for much of his life, he followed contemporary events and politics through the newspapers, and among his poems are those containing satirical comments on current issues – on those advocating patriotism to the extent of violent action, on the burning of Lord Mansfield's Library during the mindless anti-catholic Gordon Riots of 1780, and on the brutality of the slave trade. Cowper treated this last subject in a series of five ballads written in the spring of 1788 that demonstrate his versatility – from 'The Negro's Complaint' in which a slave is allowed to make an impassioned defence of the humanity of African slaves to the satirical 'Pity for Poor Africans' with its attack on the economic arguments justifying slavery:

> I pity them greatly, but I must be mum,
> For how could we do without sugar and rum?
> Especially sugar, so needful we see;
> What! give up our desserts, our coffee, and tea?

He also had an excellent sense of humour, and his account of 'The Diverting History of John Gilpin' (1782) was a popular poem throughout the nineteenth century. He was also capable of satirising sensibility itself where it involved a narcissistic contemplation of one's own finer feelings. In 'The Poet, the Oyster and Sensitive Plant' (1782), the poet, after overhearing a debate that turns on the question of which being has the finer sensibility, attacks them both for their selfishness:

> The noblest minds their virtue prove
> By pity, sympathy, and love;
> These, these are feelings truly fine,
> And prove their owner half divine.

But in his long, blank verse poem, *The Task* (1785), Cowper managed to present his own feelings and aspects of his life with great effectiveness. At one point he pictures himself as a wounded deer, separated from the rest of the herd and seeking peace and refuge. *The Task* is filled with particular commentary on the events of the time and on the world's affairs, but Cowper writes in isolation, and his account of the poetic process as well as his description of the imagination creating its own world suggests a disjunction between the self and the world of sense perception that is bridged only at particular moments of sympathy. Poetry itself seems like an effort to connect outside and inside in a concrete way:

> There is a pleasure in poetic pains
> Which only poets know. The shifts and turns,
> The expedients and inventions, multiform,
> To which the mind resorts, in chase of terms
> Though apt, yet coy, and difficult to win –
> T'arrest the fleeting images that fill
> The mirror of the mind, and hold them fast,
> And force them sit till he has pencil'd off
> A faithful likeness of the forms he views.

The pleasure of poetry lies in the relief from anxiety – an anxiety caused by that ever-present feeling of isolation. It is hardly surprising that Cowper wrote a poem on Alexander Selkirk, the possible model for *Robinson Crusoe,* and that in his most effective short poem, 'The Castaway', written in 1799 but not published until 1803, he attempted to write from the standpoint of a man washed overboard from a ship and realising that his cries will not be heard and that he will drown. Cowper draws the analogy with his and everyone's life:

> No voice divine the storm allay'd,
> No light propitious shone;
> When, snatch'd from all effectual aid,
> We perish'd, each alone:
> But I beneath a rougher sea,
> And whelm'd in deeper gulphs than he.

Like Smart, Cowper wrote religious poetry. His *Olney Hymns* are among the best of the eighteenth century from the standpoint of poetic imagery. They were published in 1779, but Cowper wrote them mainly in 1771 and 1772. Although most of the hymns turn on traditional Christian imagery, Cowper's struggles with despair and sense of being overwhelmed emerge in a number of them. The moving 'Lines Written during a Period of Insanity', composed in 1763, though not published until 1816, give some sense of Cowper's anguish:

> *Him* the vindictive rod of angry justice
> Sent quick and howling to the centre headlong;
> *I*, fed with judgment, in a fleshly tomb, am
> Buried above ground.

Yet Cowper is at his best when he is writing with a degree of calm and only the edge of the darkness showing, or when the feeling of horror is controlled as in his magnificent poem 'On the Loss of the Royal George', written in 1782 but not published until 1803, which begins:

> Toll for the brave –
> The brave! that are no more.

Readers looking for consolation in poetry were to find Wordsworth's connections between self, nature and God more helpful, but Cowper was no Wordsworth manqué. His poetry reflected the sense of fragmentation and isolation experienced and described by many artists at the end of the eighteenth century. In the paintings of Joseph Wright of Derby (1734–97), events, for instance a scientific experiment, are depicted with vivid reality, but no one viewing the scene is shown responding in the same way. Each person is lost in the world of private emotion and sensation. That was a feeling and a reality which the poets of the age experienced and tried to express.

III   Prose fiction and sensibility

Laurence Sterne (1713–68), in publishing *Tristram Shandy* over a period of eight years between 1759 and 1767 and in writing his *Sentimental Journey through France and Italy* (1768), provided a psychology for prose fiction that lasted well into the nineteenth century. When Samuel Johnson put forward the opinion that *Tristram Shandy* was too eccentric to achieve any lasting popularity, he was wrong on a number of grounds, but he was reflecting the degree to which Sterne's work seemed startlingly original to its age. Sterne took many hints from Swift's *Tale of a Tub* and from Burton's *Anatomy of Melancholy,* but his great originality in creating a new kind of novel lay in the exploitation of contemporary attitudes toward human experience. If the philosophers were right, if the world was really filtered through individual nervous systems to the mind, if neither reality nor the structures imposed on the world could be trusted, what was left to make into a novel? Sterne's answer was one that might have been expected of a novelist expressing the ideas of his time. We could trust our feelings – our love and sympathy. The rest – philosophy, systems, logic – was so much nonsense to be used for the creation of delusions with which we passed our time. Ironically enough such delusions give life meaning and purpose. They help us to piece together the fragments of existence and make them into something that appears meaningful.

As the full title of Sterne's novel suggests, *Tristram Shandy* is to be about Tristram's 'Life and Opinions', but Tristram informs us from the very start that he was born with a neurosis involving time and language. At the very moment of conception, Mrs Shandy asked his father if he had remembered to wind the clock, and that question gave such a shock to the homunculus, the sperm cell, that Tristram never recovered entirely. As a result, Tristram's narration is based as much on illogical association of language as on any other device, and as a narrator, Tristram has difficulty keeping his time scheme straight. But Tristram, after all, shares this with the reader who has his private world too. At one point, the reader is given a blank page to fill in his own description. Introductions come toward the end of the work rather than the beginning, and the use of aposiopesis, the fragmentary sentence ending in a dash, leaves the reader free to supply his own interpretation and association. Locke had described a number of cases of obsessive and involuntary association and suggested that it was a kind of madness. Sterne demonstrates that we are all victims of such involuntary mental processes. Once Tristram has given the word, 'nose', a particular sexual implication, the reader holds on to such an association even though Tristram may insist that no such meaning is intended.

Human communication under such circumstances is often an illusion. At one point in the novel, during a conversation between Walter Shandy, Uncle Toby and Doctor Slop, the male midwife, all contact between those present breaks down as Slop continues speaking about his favourite subject and a certain gesture has reminded Uncle Toby, an old soldier, of the movement of troops in Flanders during the War of the Spanish Succession at the beginning of the century. Walter Shandy actually believes that language causes actions, that man is governed by auxiliary verbs or names, but his effort to control his world is doomed to failure. He hates the name Tristram and wants his son named after Trismegistus, the Neo-Platonic philosopher, but the maid becomes confused and can recall only Tristram. And when Walter Shandy tries to have the name changed, the question of relationship comes into dispute, ending in the issue of whether a son may sleep with his grandmother on the basis of *Lex Talionis*. 'You slept with my mother', says the son, 'Why may not I sleep with yours?'

Although Tristram maintains that straight lines are for planters of cabbages and not for novelists, *Tristram Shandy* has a plot and form. In outline it is a kind of parody on the decline of a noble house. But unlike the house of Atreus or the family of Oedipus, the Shandy family suffers from a comic rather than a tragic curse – a lack of sexual virility. Through a complex relationship between language and action, Tristram, whose nose was squashed at birth in a symbolic and prophetic action, is circumcised (or worse) by a falling window when he is four years old. Uncle Toby was wounded somewhere near the groin and has sublimated almost all his sexual energy into building a model of the sieges of the War of the Spanish Succession. Mr Shandy limits his sexual duties severely, and the book ends on the sexual failure of the Shandy Bull.

Sterne's parodic device functions only fitfully throughout the work, and his treatment of it is filled with laughter. The innocent Uncle Toby falls in love with the Widow Wadman and only belatedly understands that her interest in the location of where he received his wound has nothing to do with maps of Flanders. Tristram has his ideal woman, Jenny, to love and admire, and he can find some sublimation in the inspiration of writing. His love for his uncle Toby and the moments of death in the novel bring tears to his eyes, and toward the end, he is engaged in his own very real race against death. He reports the declining state of his health to the reader even as he continues with the narrative of his childhood and education. At one point, he finds himself treating three different time levels at once, and this is, significantly enough, at the point in the novel involving a search for an ancient clock and an attempt to find the early records of Chinese history in a library. But the clock is broken and the library is closed.

Death is sad, and though time may not be measurable on a clock in any real way, its passing is significant enough for the narrator. But we live as much by gesture and feeling as by language. After the death of Tristram's brother, Bobby, Walter Shandy finds relief only in a mass of words, none of which have any connection with the event. Bobby never appears as a character in the work, and for the world of *Tristram Shandy,* his reality is only to be found in the feelings of others. Uncle Toby's servant, Corporal Trim, delivers the message of Bobby's death, not so much with words as with the dropping of his hat to the ground. Toby usually expresses himself with whistling or striking his pipe. And passion is sometimes a matter of touch, as in the account of Corporal Trim's brother, who meets his true love while they are squeezing sausages together. Sterne does not dismiss the hobby-horses which men ride in the conviction that they are pursuing truth or the verbal constructs of the philosophers. But the important things in life involve love and compassion and whatever reaches to our deepest feelings.

Sterne's *Sentimental Journey* is more obviously a collection of fragmented experiences than *Tristram Shandy,* though the argument that Book IX was absolutely the final section of Tristram's narrative is hardly persuasive. In *Tristram Shandy* Sterne had engaged in some parody of Smollett's somewhat ill-tempered *Travels through France and Italy* (1766), with its complaints about the French and Italians and their lack of honesty and uncomfortable inns, but *A Sentimental Journey* is a deliberate effort at a different kind of travel book, one in which the traveller leaves himself open to the experiences of the heart. While there is a degree of humour in the work, as there always is in Sterne, his use of Yorick, the humorous sentimentalist and partial self portrait in *Tristram Shandy* as his traveller, allows him to employ sentimental set pieces like the account of Maria, the mad girl, who had appeared in *Tristram Shandy*. After leaving her, Yorick indulges in an address to sensibility:

> Dear sensibility! source inexhausted of all that's precious in our joys, or costly in our sorrows! thou chainest thy martyr down upon his bed of straw – and 'tis thou who lifts him up to HEAVEN – eternal fountain of our feelings! – 'tis here I trace thee – and this is thy divinity which stirs within me – not . . . mere pomp of words! but that I feel some generous joys and generous cares beyond myself – all comes from thee, great – great in the remotest desert of thy creation.

Sterne goes on to speak of the way in which God has given a degree of sensibility 'to the roughest peasant', who weeps over the dying lamb from another flock.

Sterne's interpretation of sensibility as a mixture of the physiological and the spiritual, of those feelings in the human nervous system that seem to correspond to God's contact with mankind, elevate it to the force underlying human love and charity. That it also has some connection with sexual feeling and passion does not diminish it in Sterne's eyes, though in *The Sermons of Yorrick* (1760–69), this aspect is not stressed. On the final page of the *Sentimental Journey,* however, there is deliberate titillation as, sharing the room with a lady of great delicacy, after making a treaty of separation, his hand encounters her maid, who, hearing the dispute, has come between the two beds. The encounter with this charming twenty-year old Lyonoise is rendered ambiguously:

> So that when I stretch'd out my hand, I caught hold of the Fille de Chambre's
> END OF VOL. II.

Admittedly, before sharing the only room at the inn, Yorick and the Piedmontese lady have made a 'treaty of peace', and Yorick vouches for the 'religion and good faith' behind the treaty. But any reader had to know that treaties were made to be broken.

Sterne's influence on the future of the novel, for better or for worse, was immense, and it was through him and a number of other writers that the novel of sensibility became almost equivalent to the English novel until the end of the century. In 1771, Henry Mackenzie (1745–1831) published *The Man of Feeling,* with its hero, Harley, moving from one scene of sentiment to another. The aim of novels of this kind was to produce tears in abundance. Harley goes on his travels because he cannot bring himself to propose to the woman he loves. He encounters a prostitute in France whom he rescues. The father of the prostitute enters, threatens to kill her, and then he and everyone else break into tears. He learns that his affection was returned by the woman who loved him at the end, but it is too late. Harley dies of a heart too tender for the experiences of this world. Sterne's sentimentality always borders on laughter even in the *Sentimental Journey,* and in *Tristram Shandy,* sentiment is never allowed to dominate laughter for very long. Sentimentality saves *Tristram Shandy* from what might be a cruel view of human life, and the best literature of the last half of the century followed Sterne in blending comedy and sentiment. But much popular literature followed the path of Mackenzie, and sentimentality became one of the major aspects of contemporary fiction.

Sterne also influenced the structure of the novel. Even before *Tristram Shandy, The Life of John Buncle* (1756) by Thomas Amory (c. 1691–1788) blended fiction, biography and essay in a loose fashion, but after Sterne, many writers took advantage of Sterne's digressive style to call any wandering prose narrative a novel. The resulting collapse of fictional form influenced even those works that purported to be written in the tradition of Richardson and Fielding. The use of the dash and of fragmentary sections became commonplace. Such devices are directly attributable to Sterne's influence, but perhaps an age of sensibility required loose structures. Henry Brooke's *The Fool of Quality* (1760–62) and Richard Graves's (1715–1804) *Spiritual Quixote* (1772) both suffer from a lack of form in spite of interesting sections.

The one masterpiece that was directly inspired by *Tristram Shandy* was not in Great Britain but in France. Denis Diderot (1713–84) understood the implications of Sterne's treatment of time and created in *Jacques le Fataliste* (1766) a narrative with two possible endings and a sceptical view of experience. Diderot was also one of the few writers who saw into the dangers of sensibility. In his *Neveu de Rameau,* published after his death, he created a character of sensibility but neither charity nor compassion, a man of mediocre talents whose emotions might eventually find an outlet in destruction rather than creation. Diderot was a man who saw into the complexities of eighteenth-century thought as well as into its contradictions, but he was not the only writer to find in sensibility something a little suspect. In one of her early parodies, *Love and Friendship,* Jane Austen showed her contempt for the idea that sensibility might replace traditional morality, and in another work that she left unpublished, her only finished epistolary novel, *Lady Susan,* she created a vicious woman, who, although she claimed to be motivated by the highest ideals of sensibility, was cruel to her daughter and dishonest in all her relationships. But defining the limits of sensibility was one of Jane Austen's major concerns in those works that she sketched out during the 1790s.

One novelist who learned much from Sterne, in spite of some heated disputes between them, was Tobias Smollett. In his last novel, *Humphry Clinker* (1771), Smollett depicted a very different world from that which dominated his earlier novels. Most of the characters are ruled by varying degrees of sensibility. Matthew Bramble, who may be considered the main character, is a person of deep feeling and active benevolence, but he hides his feelings behind a facade of scepticism. The novel is constructed around Bramble's travels through Great Britain with his family and his gradual improvement in physical health and openness of spirit. His niece, Lydia, is an example of pure sensibility, while his nephew, Jery Melford, only barely conceals his feelings behind the wit and irony that he pretends to as part of his Oxford education. Humphry, an ungainly servant hired on the road, who turns out to be Matthew Bramble's son, is a Methodist enthusiast, and Winifred Jenkins, the servant whom he marries, mixes her sexual desires and her religious spirit so thoroughly as to make them inseparable. Both the psychology of Winifred and the method by which it is conveyed owes much to Sterne, for her letters to her fellow servant, Mary Jones, are a maze of what we now call Freudian slips. Only Tabitha

Bramble, Matthew's sister, seems to lie outside the circle of sensibility that includes, to some limited extent, the Quixotic figure she marries, the old Scottish soldier and traveller, Lismahago.

Although many epistolary novels had exploited the irony to be achieved by different accounts of the same event, Smollett's novel takes as its starting point the privateness of experience that informed Sterne's vision of the world. Smollett's account of his travels in France and Italy had shown the way one very irascible person might regard such a trip. In *Humphry Clinker,* the reader encounters visions of London, Bath and Edinburgh through the enthusiastic eyes of Lydia, the critical judgements of Matthew, the witty commentary of Jery, and the flow of conscious wonder and unconscious feeling that issues from the pen of Winifred. Unlike Sterne, Smollett, except for brief moments, is not intent on presenting a world which remains fragmented. Rather he shows the ways in which affection and benevolence can triumph. Matthew is reunited with his old friend, Charles Dennison, and the marriage of Lydia to his son, the mysterious Wilson, who had captured her affections at the beginning of the novel, joins the families together. That marriage is accompanied by those of Tabitha and Lismahago and Humphry and Winifred. Smollett leaves Jery out of the circle to comment cynically on marriage, but the novel ends on a strong note of hope as Matthew's health has improved along with his spirits and as he aids a victim of an extravagant wife, Mr Baynard, to repair his finances. Smollett certainly was no convert to optimism at the end of his life, but *Humphry Clinker* holds out the hope that, in spite of the privateness of each man's world, we may, through some balance of sensibility and common sense, find a degree of happiness in the world. In this view – a far cry from the pessimism of the early novels – Smollett was reflecting the spirit of his time.

9
Samuel Johnson: his times and his circle

The Samuel Johnson most familiar to us is the man shaped by
James Boswell (1740–95) in his *Life,* first published in 1791.
Boswell saw Johnson, despite his many weaknesses, as a great
moralist, as a person who held to certain beliefs with an
assurance that seemed lacking in those of his own generation.
And Boswell tended to think of Johnson as a representative of
that more assured past. It was with these ideas in mind that he
shaped his character of Johnson. Although Boswell was one of
the first writers who, through his journals, gives us the vision
of the self as something constantly in flux, something to be
ordered only with the greatest effort of will, he wanted to see in
the great men he sought out – Hume, Rousseau, Voltaire, the
Corsican Patriot, Paoli (1725–1807) – more stability of
character than he possessed. He showed Johnson with many of
his virtues and (what made the work scandalous to
contemporaries) many of his faults, but he tended to show him
consistent – more like a character in a novel than the living,
breathing Johnson.

I The debate over sensibility as an artistic subject

The real Johnson, who was born in 1709 and died in 1784, was
as much a product of the Age of Sensibility as Boswell. He held
his ideas with passion, not because, like some caricature of a
man from the 'Age of Reason', he was proud of his ability to
argue logically, but rather because he felt his ideas deeply. It
was Johnson who hated slavery and the hypocrisy of Americans
who could prate about freedom while denying it to their slaves.
And it was Boswell who stepped out of the character of the
detached biographer to reprove Johnson for his narrow views
on this subject. It was Johnson whose benevolence to those in

need made his house a refuge for some unfortunate persons. And it was Johnson, in his review of Soame Jenyns's *A Free Enquiry into the Nature and Origin of Evil* (1757), who dismissed any notion that human beings could take comfort from all those systems which placed earth at some far corner of the universe and tried to console mankind by informing him that his sufferings were part of some great but unknowable master plan of the Deity. Johnson was not willing to accept human suffering at such a cheap intellectual rate. Whatever else the story of Johnson's kicking a rock to refute the idealism of Bishop Berkeley may indicate, it suggests that feeling supersedes abstract reasoning, and that was one of the primary themes of the Age of Sensibility.

But Johnson also treasured the past and was not ready to abandon everything to sensibility. If he was sometimes cast in the role of defending the aesthetic ideals of Dryden and Pope against the obscurity that he found in Gray, he did so in the cause of continuity and common sense. And in so doing, Johnson was not so far out of the mainstream as anthologies emphasising new developments may make him appear. Satire, which had reached its highest development in Pope, was still very much a part of the age. It forms a large part of *Tristram Shandy* and was present in the lighter poetry of Gray and Cowper. Charles Churchill (1731–64) wrote a series of satires between 1761, when he published his picture of the stage in 'The Rosciad', and 1764, the year of his death, when he published his 'Farewell', a work that showed considerable poetic power. His satires were more open and his versification lighter than the couplets of Pope. They lack Pope's moral force, but they also breathe a more spontaneous air than Pope's work. This opening-out of satire was true of the entire period. Christopher Anstey (1724–1806), in his 'New Bath Guide' (1766), wrote a dramatic satire on the visit of a family to Bath that undercuts the critical stance of the satirist with the kind of light humour that the age appreciated. And sensibility itself was fair game for the satirists, particularly in the connection of sensation, including sexual feeling, and emotion. In 1788, Thomas Rowlandson (1757–1827), who succeeded Hogarth as England's most effective satiric engraver, produced a series of illustrations called *The Man of Feeling,* the title of Mackenzie's novel, with a main figure whose interest in the ladies he encountered was far from sentimental.

At the beginning of this study, it was suggested that the movements of the age might best be seen in terms of a dialectic. By the end of the century, one of the major conflicts involved those urging rational and moral restraint on feelings and those who believed that emotions ought to be freely indulged. The members of Johnson's circle were by no means on one side of these issues, and they often exploited this conflict for artistic purposes. Thomas Warton, one of the leaders among those praising the poetry of Spenser and the author of the first thorough account of English poetry before the eighteenth century in his *History of English Poetry* (1774–1781), could compose his 'Verses on Sir Joshua Reynold's Painted Window at New College Oxford' (1782) at the end of his life as a kind of renunciation of his love for 'Gothic' poetry and architecture in the face of Reynolds's 'classic' style:

> Sudden the sombrous imagery is fled,
> Which late my visionary rapture fed:
> Thy powerful hand has broke the Gothic chain,
> And brought my bosom back to truth again.

In reality Warton was paying a compliment to Reynolds while demonstrating how the contrast between what Warton believed to be the richer imagination of medieval and northern Renaissance art and an art built on the principles of the line, shape and colour that produced the best paintings of the Italian masters could be used to write an effective poem. Warton admits that Reynolds's art commands the symmetry that the Gothic cathedral lacks, but he does not surrender to Reynolds's greatness before establishing the magical attraction of the 'richly rude' art of the past.

In his *Discourses,* published as separate lectures between 1769 and 1790, Sir Joshua Reynolds (1723–92) set forth the argument for beauty that dominated Samuel Johnson's thinking, and while Johnson's aid to Reynolds was mainly stylistic, there can be little doubt that he influenced his thought as well. According to Reynolds, the greatest painting was to be found not in the realism of Rembrandt but in the art (such as Raphael's) that aims at general ideas and permanent images of truth and beauty. But Reynolds painted at least one imitation of Rembrandt, and in 'Discourse XIII', delivered as a lecture in 1786, he appealed to the power of those paintings that affect the imagination 'by means of association of ideas' allowing for the use of Gothic structures as appealing more directly to the imagination 'with which the Artist is more concerned than with absolute truth'. But Reynolds immediately makes a separation between barbaric art and 'Gothic' art, and here again Johnson would have been in agreement. Johnson was a good friend of Bishop Percy, and there is considerable good humour in Johnson's parodies of ballads; but he could see little aesthetic justification for any theory of art that exalted the primitive above the polished work of art.

II   Goldsmith

Another member of Johnson's circle, Oliver Goldsmith (c. 1730–74) may appear, at first, to represent a bias against sensibility within the group. His 'Essay on the Theatre; or, A Comparison between Laughing and Sentimental Comedy' (1773) is certainly an attack on plays like Richard Cumberland's *The West Indian* (1771), but it is necessary to understand what Goldsmith was attacking. Cumberland (1732–1811) constructed his play around scenes that would produce a maximum of tears. Even *False Delicacy* (1768) by Hugh Kelly (1739–77) had a degree of comedy in the manner of Steele, with one couple representing a somewhat cynical view of the sentimental lovers. Goldsmith was objecting to the excesses of a kind of comedy without any laughter at all. Now Goldsmith was not the only person to write laughing comedies at the time, and there were many in the repertory of the theatres. While Shakespeare's comedies were not considered witty by Restoration standards, they certainly were laughing comedies in Goldsmith's sense. And to read Goldsmith's best comedy, *She Stoops to Conquer* (1773), is to recognise the degree to which Shakespeare's good-natured comedy is his model rather than any Restoration model. But while Goldsmith in his earlier play, *The Good-Natured Man* (1768), set out to write a comedy that would display character he succeeded better when, in *She Stoops to Conquer,* he confronted the issue of sensibility directly. Young Charles Marlow, the hero, only fumbles about in the manner of a man of sensibility when he is forced to speak with Kate Hardcastle, whom he thinks of as one of those many ladies whose manners and sensibilities are so rarified that he must converse with them in a sententious, serious and philosophical manner. With girls of the lower ranks, on the other hand, he is forceful and witty. During his formal conversation with Kate, he keeps his eyes averted in embarrassment, never actually observing her features. Then in a later scene mistaking Kate for a barmaid, an error that she encourages, Marlow reveals himself as a very different kind of suitor.

Contrasted with Charles and Kate, who have true sensibility enough, is Tony Lumpkin, the young squire, whose idea of a good time is to drink with his cronies at the Three Pigeons and to romp with a country girl. It is he who prompts the 'mistakes of a night' by directing Charles and his friend, Hastings, to the house of his step-father, Mr Hardcastle, as an inn, with a landlord who considers himself a gentleman. Just as Goldsmith confronts excessive sensibility directly in the lovers, so, in Mr Hardcastle, he presents someone who loves everything old, in contrast to the fashionable lovers. When Kate pretends to be a poor relation of the family rather than a servant, and expresses her affection for Charles Marlow with tears, he is deeply moved and quickly reveals his own love. Having removed from him the inhibitions that the absurdities of sensibility and sentimentality had imposed on a naturally open personality, Kate is able, after some mockery that follows the revelation of her true identity, to step back from her conquest. Her silence towards the end of the play is notable.

In his literary preferences, as stated in his journal *The Bee* (1759) and in the many essays he wrote for journals such as *The Critical Review*, *Lady's Magazine*, the *British Magazine* and the *Public Ledger* during the 1760s, Goldsmith was an admirer of that line of poetry that went from Denham through Dryden to Pope. Yet his great contribution to poetry was the exploitation of the sense of loss and nostalgia. In 'The Traveller' (1764), a poem in couplets, Goldsmith drew upon his own wanderings about Europe and his impressions of the various peoples he encountered. But his wandering is the product of a kind of restlessness. His heart is always with his brother and his native land, and he concludes that for all the blessings to be found in any one nation, there are also faults. He concludes with the very Johnsonian sentiment that man's happiness is not dependent on institutions or individual rulers:

> How small of all that human hearts endure,
> That part which laws or kings can cause or cure.
> Still to ourselves in every place consign'd
> Our own felicity we make or find.

Goldsmith's greatest poem 'The Deserted Village' (1770), dedicated to Reynolds, is probably the best example of the way the Georgic tradition might be adapted to a personal lament over the social and economic conditions of England. Goldsmith, like Smollett before him, laments the way in which 'luxury' has destroyed the English countryside, causing depopulation and the destruction of villages like Auburn. He effectively blends an idealised picture of village life in the past with attacks on present luxury reflected in the state of the village as seen by the poet at the moment of writing:

> Thus fares the land, by luxury betrayed;
> In nature's simplest charms at first arrayed;
> But verging to decline, its splendours rise,
> Its vistas strike, its palaces surprize;
> While scourged by famine from the smiling land,
> The mournful peasant leads his humble band;
> And while he sinks without one arm to save,
> The country blooms – a garden, and a grave.

Goldsmith's poem is best understood in the context of feelings expressed by John Brown (1715–66) sometimes known as 'Estimate' Brown, in his 'An Estimate of the Manners and Principles of the Times' (1757), a work which went through six editions in its first year of publication. Brown expressed his dismay at what he considered to be a nation in decline. He praised the bravery of common British sailors and soldiers while attacking the 'effeminate' cowardly nature of their officers. His complaint about 'Luxury' was merely a way of putting everything into one word: 'For Vanity, Luxury, and Effeminacy, (increased beyond all Belief within these twenty Years) as they are of a *selfish,* so are they of a craving and unsatisfied Nature: The present Rage of Pleasure and unmanly Dissipation hath created a Train of new Necessities, which in their Demands outstrip every possible Supply.' Brown blamed the rot mainly on the commercial nature of the English economy with its 'exorbitant Trade and Wealth'. An excess of wealth had corrupted the upper ranks, turning them into absentee landlords with little concern for their tenants. Brown also suggested that Parliament pass a law against the 'most pernicious Practice of *early Travel*' arguing that the Grand Tour, which had become part of the usual pattern of education for the nobility and gentry, brought the travellers into contact with 'Maxims, political, moral, and religious, essentially opposite to those which are the main Foundations of the Stability of our public State'. Since the nation faced 'immediate Ruin' the most stringent measures were necessary.

Some of Brown's jeremiad may be ascribed to the fear of change, but it is true that the changes, particularly in agriculture, had caused an enormous upheaval. Enclosing the commons and waste areas was part of an agricultural revolution. 'Mixed farming', which created an interaction of crop and meat production, was made possible by the extensive use of clover and of turnips which enabled livestock to feed through the winter and fertilise the soil. At the same time, farming in this way eliminated the use of the common by those owning one or two cows. Parliament often compensated villagers by giving them small plots of land, but more often than not, the compensation was inadequate. The number of Enclosure Acts increased enormously as the century progressed and with them came the creation of a class of country labourers dependent on wages rather than on the living they managed to get from their small plots. The changes in agriculture wrought by men such as Jethro Tull (1674– 1740) and Viscount Townshend, sometimes known as 'Turnip Townshend', enabled British agriculture to flourish as never before and to feed a population that grew by twenty-three per cent between 1700 and 1760 and by thirty-two per cent over the next forty years. But their improvements were perhaps most striking in the increased amount of meat produced through 'mixed farming'. Continental visitors to England seldom failed to comment on the vast quantity of meat devoured during an ordinary dinner, yet it must be understood that such reports always focused on dinners consumed by the upper and middle ranks. The poor, on the other hand, lived mainly on bread, butter and cheese with a little meat twice a week at most. An economist such as Arthur Young (1741–1820), might lament the spread of watery tea and sugar among the poor as a sign of the increasing effect of luxury, but for the most part the poor worked hard and fared hard. They were particularly vulnerable to bad harvests, and in 1766, a rise in the price of bread resulting from such a poor year was responsible for a number of riots. Sections of Britain lost most of their populations as many left their villages to join the pool of workers in the cities or emigrated to one of the colonies. Another economist, Thomas Malthus (1766–1834), was to view deaths through starvation as part of the natural laws controlling population, but in some ways, Goldsmith was the better observer. He may wax too nostalgic over Auburn, his ideal village, but with the eye and heart of a true poet, he knew that the changes occurring in the countryside were better measured by the cost in human misery than by statistics.

The poem concludes with a vision of the spirit of poetry leaving England, since it cannot flourish where virtue has departed. In this and its blend of feeling, meditation over the past, and social concerns, 'The Deserted Village' incorporates many of the themes exploited by Thomas Gray, but Goldsmith is much more involved in the action of the poem and indulges in far more sentimental scenes along with far more social criticism. If the picture of the prostitute shivering in the cold might evoke Thomas Hardy's ironic picture of the prostitute who leaves the village and is all the better for it, Goldsmith balances his scene with his own irony on the seeming 'universal joy' of the wealthy whose parties are held not far from the black gibbet on which the poor criminals are hanged at an alarming rate. He lacks the conciseness of Blake, who was to juxtapose such scenes with greater power, but there is much to be said for Goldsmith's more detailed and expansive techniques.

Goldsmith was always in financial difficulties that forced him to undertake numerous compilations such as his *Roman History* (1764) and *Animated Nature* (1774), but just as he developed a unique poetic style, so in his prose he developed a light personal touch that was free of the more balanced periods of Addison and Steele or of his friend, Samuel Johnson. Like so many of his contemporaries, Goldsmith turned to oriental subject matter for some of his effects. His *Citizen of the World* (1760) uses the technique perfected by Charles de Secondat, Baron de Montesquieu (1689–1755) in his *Persian Letters* (1721) of writing observations of a country through the eyes of a traveller from an exotic land. Lien Chi Altangi's view of life in London is filled with wonder at the strangeness of English ways. Altangi considers the history and ways of China as more civilised than those of Europe in general, and Goldsmith uses such a perspective as a stick to beat contemporary manners and beliefs. His picture of the Man in Black, one of those benevolent misanthropes we have already seen in Smollett, is a lesson in the restraint that has to be practised in a nation that had exalted benevolence to the highest quality in the human character. But the best parts of *The Citizen of the World* for the modern reader may be those in which Goldsmith exercises his gift for imaginative writing, such as the fairy tale of the prince who left his marriage bed to pursue a white mouse with green eyes. Goldsmith devotes one letter to a woman who has formed her idea of China from the absurdities of such 'Chinese Tales' but this merely prepares the reader for his own brilliance in that genre.

In some sense Goldsmith's best piece of fiction, *The Vicar of Wakefield* (1766), is a kind of fairy tale or at least a fairy tale to the same extent that the Book of Job resembles one. Goldsmith tells his story of the sufferings of Mr Primrose and his family as if the ending, with its restoration of the Vicar to good fortune and happiness, were justification enough for all the pains suffered by him and his family. That he takes every reversal philosophically has led some interpreters to perceive a vein of irony beneath the surface sentimentality. And since some of the anguish is inflicted by the person who will eventually be the benefactor of the Primrose family in an effort to try their spirit, the tendency of Mr Primrose to good humour in his sufferings is additionally puzzling. But perhaps it is just as well to take *The Vicar of Wakefield* on its own terms as a charming fairy tale in a realistically-rendered rural setting.

Goldsmith's concerns with social themes in all his writings have to be set against England's growing commercial power. The Industrial Revolution was just beginning to take on the force that would so obviously change England, but the factory system was starting to take hold in the more industrialised parts of England. The real wealth of England was still coming from its foreign trade and colonies, and Goldsmith's insistence that the wealth of a country lay in its people rather than its commodities was to be the cry of artists and humanists for centuries to come. Goldsmith died two years before Adam Smith published *The Wealth of Nations* in 1776, but many of Smith's ideas were drawn from earlier writers of a century of economic speculation. While Smith is thought of as the exponent of *laissez faire* economic principles, he was not entirely against government intervention for the good of the nation. But he did argue for a providential view of trade that was very much like the systems of Pope and others in so far as it discovered the guiding hand of Providence in the very nature of man as an economic animal. In pursuing his own interest, he is usually pursuing the best interest of the nation. Both Johnson and Goldsmith protested against such large schemes that reduced man to an abstraction. The mad projector of Swift's *Modest Proposal* had become the social observer of the century's end. Allow enough economic freedom, and mankind in general will benefit, said the economists; expanding trade and luxury has driven the peasantry from the country, and that is enough to condemn it, said Goldsmith.

III   Johnson

Johnson was able to dominate such an illustrious group of writers not, as Boswell sometimes appears to imply, by the force of his personality, so much as by his intellectual powers. From his earliest years in Lichfield he was an extraordinary student, capable of memorising a page of poetry in little more than a glance. His father was a bookseller of very moderate means, and he experienced poverty deeply and embarrassingly when he ran out of money after a short time at Pembroke College, Oxford. He was an awkward figure, tall, ungainly and with various tics. He suffered from scrofula as a child which added to what his enemies were later to call his 'deformities'. At twenty-six he married a widow in her forties, Mrs Porter, and with her dowry established a school at Edial near Lichfield. When he failed to attract a sufficient number of students to keep the school going, he travelled to London with one of the students, a young man named David Garrick and in 1737 began working as a journalist for Edward Cave (1691–1754) and his *Gentleman's Magazine.*

The Gentleman's Magazine, started by Cave in 1731, was a compilation of original material and works printed in other journals. Before 1737, Johnson's only claim to literary fame was a translation of Father Lobo's *History of Abyssinia* published in 1735. Now labouring in the Grub Street milieu, Johnson began working with the energy of those who have to write to earn a living. It was in these days that Johnson became acquainted with Richard Savage (c. 1697–1743) and saw in him and his desperate life as a writer the kind of career experienced by too many of the poets, dramatists and journalists of the time – a career ending in destitution, drunkeness and an early death. But Johnson was a writer of genius and a man capable of distinguishing himself by his intellectual energy from those around him. He began writing a half-fictional version of the debates in the Commons for *The Gentleman's Journal* with the title, 'Debates of the Senate of Lilliput', and in 1738 produced an imitation of Juvenal, 'London', that attracted the attention of Pope. After a satire against Walpole's government in 1739, 'Marmor Norfolciense', he became involved in the project to print the collection of tracts that appeared as the *Harleian Miscellany* in 1744. Although Johnson merely wrote an introduction for the project and an essay on the importance of the tracts, after abandoning the full task of editing, the knowledge of historical developments in England he gained from this work served him well when, later in his career, he came to write on political subjects. In 1744 he published his life of Richard Savage and a year later his first seminal work on Shakespeare, 'Observations on Macbeth'. His speculative analysis of the textual problems involved in an edition of Shakespeare was to serve him well in the future.

In 1747 he wrote the superb prologue for the opening of London's Drury Lane Theatre, in which he showed his knowledge of stage history, and in the same year, he published his *Plan of a Dictionary,* setting in motion the great *English Dictionary* of 1755. In 1749 he published his best poem, 'The Vanity of Human Wishes', with its sombre view of human actions and aspirations, and was able to view his tragedy, *Irene,* which he had brought with him when he first came to London, performed on the stage with Garrick in the role of the sultan who beheads his beautiful Christian mistress to demonstrate, by his ability to relinquish what he most loved, his strength of character as a ruler. Between 1750 and 1752 Johnson wrote his *Rambler* essays, and this work brought him the fame that had so far escaped him. Johnson had a high regard for the periodical essay as a literary form, and it was in these essays that he showed his ability to wed his style to his ideas in a manner that was unique in his or any other age. The computer may not yet be capable of discriminating between Johnson's style and that of some contemporaries, but the readers of the *Rambler* recognised the force of Johnson's mind as it played over subjects as diverse as the nature of realism in fiction, the benefits of biography, and the behaviour of women in the theatre. But Johnson was probably at his best when he moralised on the uncertainties of life and the impossibility of our predicting the consequences of our decisions and choices.

The *English Dictionary* was published in 1755 after years of labour and three years after the death of his wife, whom he called, affectionately, Tetty. His meditations and prayers on the day of her death are among the most moving of his intimate diaries. A year after the *English Dictionary,* with its wonderful introductory essay on language and usage, Johnson printed his proposal for another major project – a new edition of Shakespeare involving the comparison of all available editions that might have shown Shakespeare's influence. And between that date and 1765, when the edition finally appeared, Johnson busied himself with another periodical, *The Idler* (1758) in which he introduced that remarkable master of all the current clichés about art and nature, Dick Minim. In 1759 he published *Rasselas,* a mixture of the oriental tale and the philosophical journey, dramatising many of the paradoxes of existence that appear in *The Rambler* and 'The Vanity of Human Wishes'. The story is simple enough. Rasselas, like many a prince of Abyssinia, is sent to the Happy Valley to pass his life in a round of pleasures. But Rasselas believes that he must have free choice in determining what kind of life he will lead, and with the help of the poet, Imlac, he finds a way out to the world. Imlac offers to act as a guide, and Rasselas sets out with him, his sister Nekayah, and her maid, Pekuah.

The rest of the novel resembles the kind of imaginary voyage exploited by Swift in the third book of *Gulliver's Travels*; the travellers investigate a variety of schemes of life that appear to offer the certainty of permanent happiness. All are found to be illusory. Johnson takes the opportunity to explore the possibilities that life has to offer in a series of contrasts: marriage opposed to celibacy; family life compared to bachelorhood; contemplation compared to action; city life compared to a life of retirement. Although Johnson may have his characters conclude that one state is superior to another, the choice is always between two evils. Yet life forces us to make choices as part of our humanity. Johnson's set piece on the absurdity of the pyramids is perhaps the least ambigious illustration of capricious choice for they represent a project undertaken for vanity alone. Thousands may have laboured for the whim of one man and yet they exist mainly as a monument to that vanity and folly. At the end the party returns to Abyssinia, but that return is ambiguous. Do they try to re-enter the Happy Valley? Do they abandon all their projects? May they decide to set out again as Imlac did? Is the solution to be found in the hope of an afterlife? Johnson gives us no easy solutions.

When the edition of Shakespeare appeared in 1765 it did not fulfil all Johnson's claims. He complained that he had not been able to obtain all the old texts he had sought. Nevertheless both the notes to lines and the general observations on the readings of former editors were filled with insight. And the preface was one of the great pieces of English criticism. Johnson was not the first to challenge the unities of time and space, so dear to continental critics of the drama, but his explanation of how the imagination is capable of overcoming any concerns about such matters placed these challenges on firm psychological ground. Johnson was not afraid to carry through his argument in the examination of the specific plays. Shakespeare's *Antony and Cleopatra* was acted only once during the eighteenth century because it was thought that the shifts of scene from Italy to Egypt were unacceptable to contemporary taste, but in his notes to that play Johnson argued that such leaps in space were one of the play's brilliant features. If Johnson found new beauties in Shakespeare, he was also the last major critic to discuss what he considered to be Shakespeare's faults as a playwright. The great Shakespeare Jubilee at Stratford was orchestrated by Garrick in 1769 and thereafter it was generally agreed that the best attitudes for the critic of Shakespeare were awe and devotion.

With 'The False Alarm' (1770), Johnson began a series of lengthy works on politics that cover many of the events leading up to the American Revolution. As a contributor to the *Literary Magazine* during 1756, he had already worked out most of his attitudes, and the new works represented a return to the political wars. Although 'Taxation No Tyranny' (1775) and similar pieces were once used to demonstrate Johnson's 'Tory' politics, we now see them less as party pieces than as forceful arguments in favour of examining the true realities of political power. Like Hume, Johnson viewed ideas such as the contract between ruler and ruled as political fictions that had been confusedly raised from the level of allegory to literal acts. Just as he was to tell Boswell to clear his mind of 'cant', so Johnson had little patience for arguments that concealed self-interest and greed behind ideals. If he argued that patriotism was 'the last refuge of a scoundrel', we should remember that the 'patriots' who opposed Walpole surrendered their principles without a whimper when offered titles of nobility. Johnson was certainly wrong in denying any true idealism behind the popular movements in England and America. But he could see the demagoguery behind John Wilkes (1727–97) whose imprisonment caused riots throughout London in 1768, and he might well wonder if a revolution led by Wilkes would result in the greatest happiness for the greatest number.

In 1775, after travelling to Scotland and the Hebrides with Boswell, Johnson published his *Journey to the Western Islands,* a work in which he acted as a social observer of the rapid depopulation of the countryside through poverty, and of the consequent changes in the social structure and manners of the people. After observing the construction of windows in the houses at Bamff, Johnson argued that historical developments often turn on such small matters:

> The true state of every nation is the state of common life. The manners of a people are not to be found in the schools of learning, or the palaces of greatness, where the national character is obscured or obliterated by travel or instruction, by philosophy or vanity; nor is public happiness to be estimated by the assemblies of the gay, or the banquets of the rich. The

great mass of nations is neither rich nor gay: they whose aggregate constitutes the people, are found in the streets, and the villages, in the shops and farms; and from them collectively considered, must the measure of general prosperity be taken.

Many writers have made similar statements. The value of Johnson rests partly on the way such convictions formed the basis for judgements about art and life.

Johnson's last major work began to appear in 1779 as a series of *Prefaces Biographical and Critical to Works of the English Poets*. He completed his work by 1781, and the introductions were issued as *Lives of the Poets*. The entire enterprise represented an exercise in literary history that had little precedent in the scattered writings of this kind during the century. Johnson relied upon his understanding of the historical milieu of the poets to place them in their time, and he was not afraid to draw conclusions based on economic and social observations. His discussion of the stage in the 'Life of Dryden' draws upon the nature of the audience and the taste of the court in determining why Dryden wrote as he did. The collection went no further back in time than Cowley and Milton. He glances back at the 'metaphysical' poets in his 'life of Cowley', to praise Donne for intelligence while dismissing his and his followers' idea of wit as misconceived. But Johnson dealt mainly with what fitted into his notion of a type of poetry open to critical judgement and examination, and earlier poets , like Spenser, were left for those who admired romances and allegories such as Richard Hurd (1720–1808) who in his *Letters on Chivalry and Romance* (1762) had argued that such works have their own kind of unity and aesthetic force. Our judgement concerning Johnson's own complaint, that the booksellers selected the poets to be included, should be weighed against our knowledge that Johnson suggested four or five poets not in the orginal group and our awareness that at its inception the series was to encompass poets from Chaucer to the contemporaries of Johnson.

Johnson's critical principles vary considerably throughout the *Lives,* but remain consistent. He disliked pastoral because it relied on conventions that defied his sense of reality and true feeling, and he therefore had no hesitation in judging Milton's 'Lycidas' as worthless. He argued that, for the most part, religious poetry was doomed to fall short of its subject, and while he acknowledged the greatness of *Paradise Lost*, he also believed that no reader ever 'wished it longer'. He preferred rhyme to blank verse even in the drama. And he believed that a popular poem, like Pomfret's 'The Choice,' had to be credited for the pleasure that it gave to its readers. This particular type of judgement also informed his criticism of Shakespeare. He approved of the happy ending that Tate had given to *Lear* on just those grounds. Shakespeare's ending was too painful for the pleasure that ought to be derived from the drama – even tragedy. In his individual judgements, he defended Pope against his detractors, arguing that if Pope was not a poet 'where poetry is to be found.' On the whole he preferred Dryden to Pope, but these were the two poets he admired most. In his 'Life of Milton', he defined poetry as 'the art of uniting pleasure with truth by calling imagination to the help of reason'. He admitted the greatness of Milton's epic, but Dryden and Pope gave him greater pleasure: 'We read Milton for instruction, retire harassed and overburdened, and look elsewhere for recreation; we desert our master and seek for companions'.

IV   Biography, Boswell and the quest for the self

In writing biographies of the poets, Johnson was indulging in that form which, in *Rambler* No. 60 he praised above all others 'since none can be more delightful or more useful, none can more certainly enchain the heart by irresistible interest, or more widely diffuse instruction to every diversity of condition'. But Johnson also recognised the motives that lead to the hiding of facts and details in recounting private lives, and the weakness of most biographies. Certainly there were few truly excellent biographies in English to select as models. Johnson wrote *An Account of the Life of Richard Savage* in 1744 and some shorter lives of Sir Thomas Browne (1756), Ascham (1761) and Collins (1763). A glance at an earlier *Lives of the Poets* (1753), attributed to Theophilus Cibber (1703–58) shows how little Johnson could learn from earlier biographies of poets.

For a century so concerned with the nature of the self, the eighteenth century provided less than an adequate supply of good biographies. We have fragments of what, in the hands of Boswell, would become a genre rich in possibilities. Fiction had shown what could be done. In what seemed on the surface to be genuine memoirs, Defoe had revealed the inner doubts behind Roxana's success; Richardson had shown how much might be learned of the human heart by reading a purported private correspondence; and Sterne showed that if the reader grasped the emotions behind a life, he was not concerned about the fragmentary nature of external events. Plutarch's (c. 46–c. 120 A.D.) *Lives* had been the model for lives of the great for centuries, and his account of the public actions of the noble Greeks and Romans continued to be of great interest to eighteenth-century readers; but George Lord Lyttelton (1709–73) appealed more to the sensibility of his age when he dramatised the *real feelings* of his historical figures in his *Dialogues of the Dead* (1760–65).

Letters were a rich source of intimate detail for biographers, but, as opposed to the private nature of Swift's *Journal to Stella,* his letters to Pope reveal the degree to which he and Pope wrote for what was called 'epistolary fame'. The letters of Mary Wortley Montagu (1689–1762), published in 1763, reveal her feelings more deeply, but like those of the witty Horace Walpole, they show more of the public than the private person. Autobiography suffered much the same fate. Colley Cibber's *Apology* (1740) tells us much about his experiences and thought about the stage, but much of what we learn about his character comes through his seeming lack of awareness rather than through any insight into himself. Edward Gibbon (1737–94), the author of *The Decline and Fall of the Roman Empire* (1776–86) and a member of the Club, vowed in his *Autobiography* (1796) that he would tell the 'naked truth'. Gibbon is honest enough about his relations with his father, but he seemed incapable of very much self-revelation. Only Rousseau, in the *Confessions* published after his death in 1782–83, and Boswell, in his private journals, were able to probe character to the heart.

Johnson gave his approval to Boswell's notes on their journey to Scotland and approved his keeping a diary, but in the end, he burned many private papers and letters. And as a biographer in the *Lives of the Poets,* he was what may be called a 'philosophic biographer' in the same sense that Voltaire and

Gibbon were philosophic historians. Just as they tried to avoid the kind of polyhistory that tended to compile documents and evidence by judging the import of such materials, so Johnson excelled not as a collector of original documents but as a judge of character and motivation. Remarks such as those on Milton's treatment of his daughters, his 'Turkish contempt of females', and that 'He thought woman only for obedience, and man only for rebellion', are more than pieces of wit. Johnson was trying to make connections between Milton's personal life, his poetic themes, and his politics, and if we might tend to think more highly of Milton's politics than Johnson, he raises the question of whether high ideals can come from someone who treated his daughters so poorly. Johnson is quick to see the passions at work behind seemingly rational excuses. He sees weakness and hurt behind Dryden's pose of contempt for his critics and a certain malice behind Pope's claim that he was merely paying back his enemies in kind by writing his *Dunciad*.

Although Johnson excelled in such judgements about his subjects, he never pretends that they are the result of detached assessment. Johnson remains the moral philosopher as a biographer, and to some extent the *Lives* provide him another area for exerting moral judgement. Johnson was a fervent Christian and a man of large sympathies. He reports the story of Otway's poverty and hunger with a personal anguish, and he expresses the hope that he died in a better state than had been reported. He waxes angry at the court of Charles II for allowing poets to starve. To Congreve's protest that his plays are not as immoral as Jeremy Collier claimed, Johnson refuses to listen. To any pretence that a nobleman such as John Sheffield, third Earl of Mulgrave, may have had to excellence in poetry, Johnson is contemptuous, dismissing the flattery of his contemporaries and judging him to be 'a writer that sometimes glimmers, but rarely shines, feebly laborious, and at best but pretty'. But he finds some mitigation for Sheffield's life in his 'tenderness', and faced by the madness that afflicted Collins, Johnson expresses his personal sadness. This is not biography as it is written today, but Johnson was capable of closing with his subject in a mannner that makes every judgement about character as much a statement about Johnson as about Addison or Gray.

James Boswell emerged as a great literary figure only in the twentieth century. When his biography of Johnson appeared in 1791, it was regarded as a scandalous work, treating Johnson in a manner that was considered too intimate. The question was, how could such a silly person write such a great biography? In his essay of 1831, Macaulay made Boswell into a kind of toady, setting down everything that Johnson had to say and writing a work of genius in spite of himself, as if one had to be a 'fool' of a particular kind to write such a work. But in 1927 a vast hoard of Boswell manuscripts deposited with a branch of the family in Malahide Castle near Dublin were finally made available, and another cache at Fettercairn House, Scotland was uncovered in 1930, though this discovery was kept secret until 1936. The various editions of his writings, particularly the publication of his *London Journal* of 1762–63 in 1950, resulted in a complete reassessment of his abilities. The appearance of journals of Boswell's experiences on the continent and of his contacts with Johnson over the years have increased Boswell's status to the extent that, with some annoyance, writers on Johnson have had to remind us that Johnson was the greater genius.

Before the publication of the biography, Boswell was known for only a few works. After visiting Corsica on his tour of Europe, he wrote an account of the rebellion in that country and of the Corsican patriot Paoli. The *Account of Corsica* appeared in 1768, and in the following year, Boswell appeared at the Shakespeare Jubilee in Stratford wearing a Corsican costume. From 1777 until 1783 he contributed seventy essays to the *London Magazine* under the name of the 'Hypochondriack' and in 1785 he published his account of his travels with Johnson, the *Tour to the Hebrides*. It is in this work that Boswell showed many of the qualities that appear in the journals and the biography of Johnson. As they set off in 1773, Boswell tells the reader that 'everything relative to so great a man is worth observing' and gives a day-by-day account of their adventures. In his account, Johnson was interested in making observations on the areas visited; Boswell is more interested in Johnson and himself as they experience things. His account of himself is a mixture of ingenuousness and vanity, but we see him clearly as he speaks of himself in the third person as a man of thirty-three and happily married:

His inclination was to be a soldier, but his father, a respectable judge, had pressed him into the profession of the Law. He had travelled a good deal and seen many varieties of human life. He had thought more than any body supposed, and had a pretty good stock of general learning and knowledge. He had all Dr. Johnson's principles, with some degree of relaxation. He had rather too little than too much prudence, and his imagination being lively, he often said things of which the effect was very different from the intention.

The personal note is far different from what Johnson gives us, and Boswell is willing to speak of their occasional quarrels and the differences between his tendency to call hills, mountains, and Johnson's to call them protuberances. He shows us Johnson at the spot where Macbeth met the witches and thinks of *Ossian* when they hear a girl singing an Erse song. Johnson passed his sixty-fourth birthday during this journey, but he refused to worry about the considerable dangers attending such a trip at his age and showed himself more capable of enduring hardships than his young companion. Boswell reveals to the reader a Johnson of remarkable physical and mental strength as well as a Johnson capable of great humour and imagination, and he demonstrated his own insight and abilities in the process. It is a delightful book, less formal than the *Life* and more carefully shaped than the journals.

The London Journal gives us some sense of Boswell's real relationship with Johnson. Boswell was young and impressionable when they met, but he was a member of the Scottish nobility and never forgot his own position in the world. He was sensitive to criticism of his native country, shouted at a London theatre audience that showed its displeasure at some of his countrymen and complained that Johnson showed a want of taste in his attacks on Scotland. Life seemed to display itself to Boswell as a work of fiction. His affair with an actress might have come out of an imitation of *Fanny Hill*, and his separation from Johnson, in whom he found a combination of guide, friend and foster father, is the very stuff of which good literature is made. If the journals that recount his stay in Holland and his travels, his search for a proper wife and his meetings with Johnson over the years are somewhat less interesting than this account of his setting out in life, it is only by degrees. His meetings with Voltaire and Rousseau are wonderful set pieces that reveal his own character and the characters of the men he admired. And his struggle with his idea of what he thinks he should be and the mixture of passion and exuberance, depression and desire that he was are told in a unique manner. He notes to himself:

> It is certain that I am not a great man, but I have an enthusiastic love of great men, and I derive a kind of glory from it. I am told that at least I can sometimes conceive an idea of greatness of soul. How many fine things should I not do if I were not hindered by the fear of appearing absurd!

He tells us of how he almost threw himself before the Emperor of Austria in order to speak with him but thought better of it as his 'heated imagination cooled'. Boswell was a great journalist and biographer not because he was a 'fool' but because the very idea of dealing with character and personality aroused his 'imagination' and inspired his genius.

Boswell was not the only person to write a biography of Johnson or to comment on his life. Hester Lynch Thrale, later Mrs Piozzi (1741–1821) published her *Anecdotes of Samuel Johnson* in 1786, and while her picture of Johnson does not match Boswell's, it too presented a 'character' of Johnson in his conversations. She too kept a journal, and her *Thraliana*, first published in 1942, gives a much better picture of her feelings about Johnson than her collection of anecdotes. While a comparison with Boswell's journals would be unfair to her, she was a person of great intelligence and feeling who survived her husband's neglect and Johnson's selfish desire to keep her from marrying the Italian musician, Mr Piozzi. In 1787 Sir John Hawkins (1719–89) published a *Life* along with an edition of Johnson's writings. Hawkins was a more discerning critic of literature and a more detached judge of Johnson the man than Boswell, but he also had a narrower concept of what biography should do. We also have in the *Early Diary* (1884) of Fanny Burney (1752–1840) a picture of Johnson from the viewpoint of a young woman who admired him deeply.

Such works provide a means of judging Boswell's picture of Johnson, and they confirm the greatness of Boswell's *Life*. Perhaps those critics who have complained that it is not the biography of Johnson that those interested in the genius of Johnson would want are right. Johnson was a many-sided personality, and in shaping the character of Johnson in the way a novelist might do it, with clear lines of personality made solid by accurate details, Boswell tended to restrict the scope of his creation. Perhaps the personality Johnson showed to Boswell was somewhat limited or perhaps Boswell only saw what he wanted to see. But the biographer cannot give the reader more than makes sense. The Johnson that Boswell presents to us is a man of high moral principles and great powers of mind who is nevertheless all too human. Boswell shows that humanity in Johnson's foibles – his bad eating manners, his belief that he could behave pleasantly even in the company of a man whose principles he detested, his terror of death. And because Boswell knew that these were Johnson's weaknesses, he brought Johnson into situations that would put him to the test. He would bring up Hume's calm before his death, as an example of a man without religious principles facing the unknown without fear, in order to provoke Johnson to a denial of such a possibility. He introduced Johnson to Wilkes even though he knew that Johnson hated Wilkes's politics as much as he despised his life of immorality and dissipation. And Boswell devotes an entire section to Johnson's opinions on food including a picture of Johnson at dinner, his attention given entirely to his food, gulping down each bite while the sweat stood out on his forehead. In an almost Swiftian vein, Boswell treats us to such a scene and informs us that to a person of any delicacy whatsoever it was a disgusting spectacle.

In recording Johnson in conversation, Boswell used the equivalent of stage directions and it was in his re-creation of conversation, when Johnson's superiority in 'the art of thinking' emerged dramatically, that Boswell excelled. He makes his subject come alive as Johnson argues with Oglethorpe or engages in one of his many conversations about Garrick. And he mixed such exchanges with letters and the kinds of personal details that seem unimportant. Perhaps that is Boswell's real greatness. Johnson had observed that often a very small mannerism or gesture might tell us more about a character than all his writings or pages on the events of a man's or woman's life. Boswell is filled with such details. They allow us to see Johnson whole, and to some extent, more clearly than those studies based on what we think of as modern psychological analysis.

10
The century's end

If Dryden could look back on the accomplishments of his century with some doubts, the same was not true of the artists of the end of the eighteenth century. If their accomplishments were not to satisfy the tastes of the nineteenth-century Romantics, those writing in the second half of the eighteenth century were confident that they had changed their world and its art in significant ways. And how could it have been otherwise? In music, Joseph Haydn (1732–1809) and then Wolfgang Amadeus Mozart (1756–91) had achieved everything that eighteenth-century art aimed for – feeling controlled by great craft and contained by the spirit of comedy. In painting, there was the excitement of experiment. The connection made between the development of modern non-objective art and cubism and the work of this period are clear enough to anyone studying the purely linear depiction of figures in the illustrations of John Flaxman (1755–1826) in England or the compositions of Jacques David (1748–1825) in France. But form was often at the service of ideology as the American and French Revolutions made the prospect of achieving utopia on earth a little more believable than it had been to the doubting Jonathan Swift.

Mozart's three great operas, all of which were popular in England, give some clue to the times. *The Marriage of Figaro* (1786), based on a comedy by Pierre de Beaumarchais that some considered responsible for the French Revolution, plays with the comic and not so comic events resulting from flirtations and attempted seductions. In the process, the entire divisions among the ranks of society disappear as Figaro and the Countess set out to teach the Count a lesson. In *Don Giovanni* (1787), Mozart turned his rich material into an opera about a hero who is an odd mixture of heroic and villainous traits. Should the spectator admire the courage of Don Juan in his defiant meeting with the dreadful statue that will drag him down to hell, or feel that a villain has been removed from the earth? Mozart's opera has something in common with Gothic fiction and drama. And in *The Magic Flute* (1791) Mozart presented an allegory in which the hero strives for the wisdom to be achieved by overcoming doubt, ignorance and fear. Having triumphed, along with the woman he loves, he joins an order of enlightened beings, while his wonderful companion, Papageno, the natural man, is awarded a charming Papagena with whom he will live happily through his passions. But such a small achievement is only for the ignorant savage. The true heir of the Enlightenment seemed about to make his rational utopia.

Although Mozart visited England as a young virtuoso, England was never to produce a composer of his stature. Mozart shared with his times a sense of excitement – a belief that political and social changes were imminent. In 1780 London was put into a state of siege by a mob protesting against a bill liberalising the treatment of Catholics. The insurrection was put down by John Wilkes, once the cause of riots himself. This was as close to Revolution as England was to come. The French Revolution, however, was watched with fascination by many Englishmen. Unlike the American Revolution in which the American Patriots echoed the classical arguments for a republic that were a genuine part of British politics too, the French in 1789 threatened to shake the order of rank within society. In the Terror an effort was made to eliminate the aristocracy entirely, as well as anyone associated with that class. The mob and its leaders ruled Paris, and from Paris they tried to rule all France. Although Reason was proclaimed as a deity superior to any traditional God, it was obvious that Robespierre was not moved entirely by that force. And even before the Revolution a spirit of irrational fervour seemed to grip France. Mesmerism, a mixture of hysteria and self-hypnosis propounded by Franz Mesmer, an Austrian physician, who believed in secret forces acting on all of us, was a subject of great discussion before the Revolution. Britain watched in fascination but followed a different route.

The great ideological enemy of the Revolution was Edmund Burke. Although Burke had sided with the Americans in their rebellion, he saw in the French Revolution a threat to the

structure of society in Great Britain. Always distrustful of laws
that pretended to cover all mankind, he proposed a theory of
political institutions that was essentially organic and
conservative. Government, he maintained in his *Reflections on
the French Revolution* (1790), is based on the slow growth of
laws and the evolution of political bodies like the English
Parliament. Revolutions interrupt this process and destroy the
very basis of nationhood. This was an argument that became
the basis for the modern conservative position in politics, but
its strong appeal, especially moving in Burke's emotional
rhetoric, was not convincing to those who believed that
political processes might be subject to rational control and who
found the status quo less appealing than Burke. Certainly
Burke's magnificent but idealised portrait of the former Queen
of France as a transcendently radiant being created some
sceptics.

Among those doubters were a group labelled the 'English
Jacobins' after their French counterparts. Perhaps the most
forceful of them was Thomas Paine (1737–1809), whose
writings belong as much to the literature and politics of the
United States as to Britain, the nation of his birth. His *Common
Sense* (1776) was one of the great documents of the American
Revolution. When the French Revolution broke out, he went
over to France also, and in spite of his credentials as a radical,
he was imprisoned and barely survived the Terror. It was
Paine, in his book of that name published in 1794–96, who saw
in the eighteenth century the *Age of Reason*. He believed not in
Burke's slow movement of political institutions but in the
progress of the human race. He thought that it was the purpose
of each citizen to make the condition of mankind a little better,
and he saw in Burke's arguments a glorification of what, in
reality, was something less than perfect. Paine mocked the
glorification of British laws in Burke's work. He saw in the
system of English government only the possible framework for
a truly democratic society. Although both Burke and Paine
claimed to have reason on their side, the excitement in what
they wrote emerges from the clash of the convinced and
impassioned conservative against the liberal who feels he
stands for all mankind. How much detached rationality may
be found on either side is questionable, but it was an inspiring
debate, pitting Paine's forceful prose, rich in imagery drawn

from the Bible and common life, against Burke's artful rhetoric.

I   Fiction

The form of literature best able to convey such conflict has traditionally been the novel, and the Jacobin novel was one of the two major developments in fiction during this period. The earliest of the group of novelists advancing 'Jacobin' doctrines was Robert Bage (1728–1801). As might have been expected, he was the least theoretical, but his picture of society differed from the critical judgements of Fielding in suggesting that society could be changed by correcting the vicious penal code and adjusting the inequalities of wealth. In his last novel *Hermsprong or Man as He Is Not* (1796) Bage used the device of the young man who has lived in the more natural world of America returning to England to apply his experience to the English scene. Other novels include *Mount Henneth* (1781), *Barham Downs* (1784) and *Man as He Is* (1792). Bage was not very good at drawing character, and he employs many of the devices of the novel of sensibility. In addition to these weaknesses, he suffers from having no very clearly formulated idea of the way society might be changed. Change is a clear motif, but its presence is sporadic and its formulation imprecise.

The same was not true of William Godwin (1756–1836), who comes closest of all these writers to being a major novelist. Before writing his best and most influential novel, *Caleb Williams* (1794), Godwin composed his lengthy treatise on law and society, *Political Justice* (1793). In Godwin's view, the social system of England had corrupted the spirit of its citizens. With appropriate reforms a new human might emerge out of the system that he envisaged – a human being free from crushing poverty and the degradations of inequality. He saw the vestiges of the system of chivalry everywhere he looked. Chivalry was embedded in the courts, in the system of rank and class, in the false values of revenge and honour that prevailed among the gentry and aristocracy. Rid the world of such old forms and happiness might be possible for all mankind. In one moment of ecstatic utopianism, Godwin predicted that men and women might be able to live forever, but such excessive enthusiasm should not detract from the very able criticism of a system of laws that continued to function because it had not been properly challenged. That challenge, Godwin believed, could come through the proper use of reason, for he believed that all error would vanish if properly confronted with the truth.

In *Caleb Williams* (1794), Godwin applied these ideas not in a mechanical fashion but as a novelist who tended to see matters in ambiguous human terms. The story concerns the aristocrat, Falkland, and his inquisitive librarian, Caleb. In a long narrative at the beginning, Caleb learns that Falkland had gallantly defended those oppressed by the vicious local squire, Tyrrel, who used his power to crush an honest family through the ability of the wealthy to control the courts, and to dominate over his own niece by similiar means. Falkland tries unsuccessfully to thwart his actions. The niece dies and the farmers are ruined; but he succeeds in shaming Tyrrel before his neighbours. This embarrassment leads Tyrrel to inflict a beating on Falkland in public. The squire is found stabbed shortly after, and while some suspicion falls on Falkland, he insists on his innocence and is acquitted.

Falkland's actions are the product of his notions of honour. Not only does he demand revenge for the affront done him, but he insists on maintaining the honour of his name by a lie. Caleb is impelled by an insatiable curiosity to discover whether Falkland is guilty. During a fire, he is discovered by Falkland as he tries to open a cabinet to obtain documents. Falkland confesses his crime to Caleb but insists on pursuing his servant with his hatred. Thus, Falkland, who himself hates the misuse of the law, uses all his power to prevent Caleb from finding any happiness. Caleb escapes from the terrors of gaol to wander through an England made up of beings as diverse as the bandit chief, Raymond, who refuses to obey the laws, and the majority of men and women who simply submit to a system ruled by the rich and powerful.

One of the more curious figures in the book is a brutal member of Raymond's band, Gines, who insists on robbing Caleb of his clothes after Caleb has announced that he has no money. When Caleb resists, Gines strikes his victim with a cutlass. Raymond succeeds in driving Gines from his group for this behaviour, but Gines is later hired by Falkland to pursue Caleb wherever he may go. In so doing, Gines moves from one side of the law to the other, and this has been his pattern for some time. He functions as what we would call a private detective and what was then called a 'thief-taker'. The profession practised with such villainy by Johnathan Wild earlier in the century had become almost respectable in the absence of a regular police force. The famous Bow-Street Runners served this function well into the nineteenth century, when a national police force was established. Gines has a genuine talent for being a 'bloodhound', but he much prefers 'the liberal and manly profession of a robber' to the 'sordid and mechanical' duties of the thief-taker. Though the sketch of Gines is brief, Godwin suggests how thoroughly intertwined are the roles of the criminal and the policeman, of the law breaker and the upholder of the law. Perhaps no other part of Godwin's argument is as well based on practical experience as this. Surveys of criminals have shown how thoroughly they identify with the attitudes of the police toward law and order, and in his grim view of a not too distant future, Anthony Burgess, (b. 1917) in his novel *A Clockwork Orange* (1962), presents a similar picture as a number of his sadistic juvenile gang members mature into equally sadistic policemen. Godwin wrote several endings to his novel. In one, Caleb is left to more desperation after he tries to tell the truth to a magistrate who refuses to believe in him: in the other, Falkland gives in to Caleb's presentation of the truth. The latter end is more satisfying, but even in this seeming justification of himself and his actions, Caleb comes to doubt whether using the corrupt law to fight corruption is morally proper. Godwin seems to be saying that justice can only be achieved by a change in the entire system.

Caleb Williams succeeds because ideology is blended with some vividly realistic scenes of London and the countryside and with a psychological insight into the relation between Caleb and Falkland that foreshadows similar renderings in Dostoevski. Although Godwin drew on the odd conflict between Defoe's Roxana and her daughter for his psychology, he also relied on contemporary theories of sympathy to create an almost mystical attraction between the pursuer and his victim. After *Caleb Williams,* Godwin went on to write in other fictional modes, but almost all continued to suggest the destructiveness of a system of honour that set up artificial distinctions between men and urged them to seek power of one kind or another. Within our period he also wrote *St. Leon* (1799), in an historical and gothic manner.

The two other novelists who worked in the mode of the Jacobin novel with some success were Mrs Elizabeth Inchbald (1753–1821) and Thomas Holcroft (1745–1809). Mary Wollstonecraft (1759–97) who married William Godwin, might also be included for her very powerful novel about the mistreatment of women, *Mary* (1788), but her real influence came with the publication of her *Vindication of the Rights of Woman* in 1792. Her willingness to put her attacks on the brutality of a society dominated by men into fictional form suggests the directness of the connection between fiction and ideology within this group. Both Inchbald and Holcroft, on the other hand, came to the novel with an interest in the theatre as well. Holcroft's *Anna St. Ives* (1792) appeared in the same year that his very successful play, *The Road to Ruin* was first acted, and Inchbald was already an established dramatist when she wrote *A Simple Story* (1791) and *Nature and Art* (1796). Holcroft was the more conventional novelist of the two. His *Anna St. Ives* handles the epistolary novel skilfully in a work attacking the ruinous expenditures on 'improving' gardens and homes and making the usual Jacobin plea for greater equality. *Hugh Trevor* (1794–1797) is a picaresque narrative about a young man whose pursuit of a proper career in late eighteenth-century Britain allows Holcroft ample room for satire on the corruptions in society. Holcroft was a disciple of the French *philosophe*, the Marquis de Condorcet, and like that writer tended to see the clergy, lawyers, the educational establishment and the class system as corrupt and obsolete institutions, to be replaced by those founded on reason and science as mankind progresses. Hugh's experiences support such an ideology.

The style of Mrs Inchbald was less fluid than Holcroft's, and while often presented with the ideas plainly visible behind a style and plot possessing the clarity of a fairy tale, her novels are less philosophical. The complications of *A Simple Story* are mainly in the character relationships and the psychologies of characters who share some of the almost compulsive traits of

Caleb Williams and Falkland. Here Inchbald's appeal is mainly to greater love and sympathy, and she takes some of the best aspects of the novel of sensibility to fashion a work that is more charming than didactic. But in *Nature and Art* the fairy tale motif dominates from the start as we are given the tale of two brothers, William and Henry, who set out in the world to earn their fortunes. William and his family represent the 'Art' of the title. They follow the path of social manners, rank and forms, and the 'Art' of their life is the artifice of society. 'Nature' is embodied in Henry, who is a musician and a person possessed of a warm heart and a sense of love for his fellow men. He marries a simple girl whom his brother and his aristocratic wife refuse to see, and after her death goes off to live among savages. He sends his son back from this mythical island as a kind of innocent natural man. William recalls enough of his love for his brother to take Young Henry into the family and to educate him, but Young Henry continually questions the values of English society. He cannot understand why some men must be rich and some poor, and with apparent naiveté demolishes the premises of a book produced by his uncle which celebrates the happiness of England. In the end, the family of William is unhappy. Young William seduces an innocent girl and causes her death as well as the death of his child. His father dies a bishop but is unmourned by the people of the area. His mother dies after ruining herself by gambling, and his wife has left him. All he has is his pride. Young Henry, on the other hand, has returned to the island to find his father and returned to England to discover his beloved Rebecca still waiting for him. They settle down to a life of happy labour and family affection, and Young Henry draws a clear moral, 'Let the poor, then . . . no more be their own persecutors – no longer pay homage to wealth – instantaneously the whole idolatrous worship will cease – the idol will be broken'.

Not only is the message of Mrs Inchbald's work apparent but the prose is without moral ambiguity. The ideals are to be found in the key words: innocence, simplicity, benevolence and love. The world of Young William, in which the seduction of an innocent young girl is merely a conquest, an addition to vanity and pride, is shown in its brutality as Agnes almost strangles her child and eventually is sentenced to death by Young William, the very man who seduced her, now a successful judge. The reader is directed to see the proper moral road by satire against the vanity of the rich and complete admiration for the unsophisticated life of gardening. It is Voltaire and Rousseau made into one package.

More crucial for the future development of fiction than the Jacobin novel but somewhat simpler in concept was the Gothic novel. Its origins are clear enough. Horace Walpole (1717–97), whose interest in British history led him to build his house, Strawberry Hill, in a Gothic style, had a disturbing dream, and when he wrote it down, it grew into *The Castle of Otranto* (1764). Walpole used the device of the old manuscript to set his story in the distant past, but the key to Walpole's novel, as to those that followed, was the juxtaposition of heroes and heroines of sensibility against a figure ruled by his passions and by a will to power. In some sense the ancient setting functioned as a psychological rather than a physical reality. The Gothic novel took place in *that* time – a time when men did commit murder, did torture their victims, did rape the innocent young girls they were supposed to protect. And in a world in which the beauty of nature was supposed to reveal an order in the universe and within mankind, the Gothic hero-villain appeared as an example of the grotesque and sense of evil that lay at the heart of Gothic architecture – the grotesque that the Palladian villas of the Georgian period tried to deny.

Walpole accompanied his story with a landscape filled with secret passageways and grottoes. The castle of Otranto seemed to be undermined by these subterranean structures as the pleasant world of the eighteenth century was undermined by the complexities of the unconscious human drives that brought so many of its writers close to madness. Walpole used the supernatural in a manner that made many imitators uncomfortable. When Clara Reeve (1729–1807) published her novel, *The English Baron* (1777), Walpole complained that the attempt to explain away all the strange noises and apparitions was destructive to the form. But such explanations have little to do with the experience of the reader, who encounters all the mysteries he or she could desire. Explaining away a ghostly appearance does not remove the effect of terror for that is incorporated in the continual threat of psychological and physical violation.

Ann Radcliffe (1764–1823) was the first of the Gothic

novelists to link her work directly to effects of landscape description, playing on the contrasts between the beautiful, the sublime, the picturesque and the grotesque. Her two early novels, *Castles of Athlin and Dunbayne* (1789) and *A Sicilian Romance* (1790) were essentially romances, but with *The Romance of The Forest* (1791), she combined the adventures of a young girl in danger of her life with landscapes that varied from the terrors of dark forests and castles to the sublime mountains of Switzerland. She mingled poetry with her prose, moving her work closer to romance structure and away from the social aspects of the novel of manners. In *The Mysteries of Udolpho* (1794), she played in a leisurely fashion with the landscapes of southern France, both its beautiful valleys and its terrifying mountains, and the mountainous areas of Italy. Her grotesque villain, Montoni, presents a continual threat to the heroine, and when she asks why he keeps her prisoner, he replies, 'because it is my will'. Montoni is a real murderer, and even if some of the bleeding bodies the heroine sees are merely wax figures, the implied lesson is even more terrifying than the presence of a ghost – it is that evil exists in spite of the triumphant improvements in the arts of living during the century. In *The Italian* (1797), evil is brought closer to modern times with the discovery that the Inquisition continues to function in the Enlightenment Italy of the eighteenth century. The hero, Vivaldi, is imprisoned and subjected to a terrifying ritual. His demands for the rights and freedoms expected by men at the end of the century are ignored by the mysterious members of the Inquisition. The novel ends with a sunny view of the Bay of Naples. The hero and heroine are united; and the villain, Schedoni, has been removed from the scene. But nothing will restore the social, civilised Italy with which the book begins.

Even before Mrs Radcliffe used landscape as a means of communicating a vision of her time, the more disturbing elements of the unconscious began finding their way into imaginative forms similar to the Gothic. In his oriental tale, *Vathek* (1786), William Beckford (1759–1844) created a figure who sacrifices everyone around him in his quest for the secrets and riches of the Pre-Adamite Sultans, only to find his heart seized by an agonizing pain as, at the conclusion, he must suffer torture until the end of time. The Sultan's quest for a

new experience suggests a warping of the ideals of sensibility.
In a French novel of this period, *Liaisons Dangereuses* (1782),
Choderlos Laclos created a pair of sophisticated lovers who
pursue sensation at all cost. At one point, to impress a lady he
wishes to make his victim, the man, Valmont, gives money to
the poor and finds it a delightful sensation. He notes, however,
that the pleasure in the experience diminished considerably the
second time. We are now very much in the period of the
Marquis de Sade, whose notion of sensibility included
torturing others for one's pleasure. And in the writings of the
homosexual Beckford, as well as in those of Matthew Lewis
(1775–1818), there is an ingredient of sadistic fantasy. Like
Walpole, Lewis wrote *The Monk* (1796) after a dream. Too
much has been made of an essential difference between Lewis
and Mrs Radcliffe. Lewis returns to the supernatural, and his
fantasies of incest and change of sexual identity are more
extreme than in the fantasies of rape in Mrs Radcliffe; but the
difference is mainly between the suggested and the overt. Even
in modern versions of the Gothic such degrees of difference
exist; there is no need to create different categories for each.

The Gothic achieved its height of popularity in the thirty
years between 1790 and 1820, but it has continued to attract
good writers because it has a permanent psychological appeal.
Almost every novelist of the 1790s was influenced by the form,
and some, like Charlotte Smith (1749–1806) produced Gothic
novels that were better than mere popular entertainment.
Although in this history the Jacobin strain has been separated
from the Gothic, it should be noted that most Gothic villains
are tyrants who violate the freedom of their victims, while the
picturesque bandits of the Gothic novel occasionally wander
into the lives of characters in the Jacobin novel. On the whole,
however, the hopeful nature of the one contrasts rather
strongly with the vision of evil in the other.

II   Poetry

Aside from William Cowper, who has already been discussed,
the three major poets of the end of the century were George
Crabbe (1754–1832), Robert Burns (1759–96) and William
Blake (1757–1827). Of this group, Crabbe was probably the

least affected by the intellectual and aesthetic currents of the time. In 'The Village' (1783), Crabbe retained the rhymed couplet of his age and adapted the strain of realism that ran through the period from Defoe onward in depicting the lives of villagers and country people. Crabbe's originality appeared most fully in the following century with 'The Borough' (1810), with its grim story of the murderous fisherman, Peter Grimes, which Benjamin Britten (1913–76) made into one of the most successful of modern operas. But Crabbe had already developed his realistic approach to country life and rejection of the idealising pastoral tradition by the time he wrote 'The Village':

> No longer truth, though shown in verse disdain,
> But own the Village Life a life of Pain.

In his effort at creating an honest sketch of rural existence, Crabbe avoided the emotional view of nature to be found in Cowper, but in his early poetry, he was deeply indebted to the rhetoric of Pope, Gray and Goldsmith. Although he was later to abandon that rhetoric for his creation of short poetic fictions illustrating village life, he was often to purchase his realism by achieving the tediousness of the scenes he was attempting to sketch.

Robert Burns was almost never tedious. He presented himself in *Poems Chiefly in the Scottish Dialect* (1786), his first volume of poetry, as everything the age had been looking for in the way of a poet. He dedicated the volume to Mackenzie and portrayed himself as a man of sensibility. He also filled the role of the natural poet that the age was seeking, since he did not have much formal education and had worked as a farmer. And he fitted the image of the 'minstrel' – in Bishop Percy's classification the man who sang old ballads and wrote new ones. On the title page, he quoted an anonymous poem:

> The simple Bard, unbroke by rules of Art
> He pours the wild effusions of the heart:
> And if inspir'd tis Nature's pow'rs inspire;
> He's all the melting thrill, and her's the kindling fire.

To some extent Burns was everything he claimed. He was not however the first to introduce Scottish words into poetry.

Although it has become customary for critics to find in Burns's use of Scottish words the introduction of new vigour into English poetry, some doubt might be expressed over the formulation of such a comment. Before the Union of England and Scotland, ratified in 1707 the poetic traditions of the two nations were related but separate. After the Union, poets like James Thomson travelled to London and adapted their talents to the larger English audience, avoiding Scottish words and syntax. Although they attempted to assimilate as writers, they kept certain elements of their native land in their choice of subjects. They were less inhibited in their love of nature and their willingness to appeal to the sublime. Perhaps none exemplifies these tendencies more than David Mallet (c. 1705–65), who changed his name from Malloch in 1724 on the grounds that no Englishman could pronounce his real name. Mallet was an admirer of Thomson, and his early blank verse poem 'The Excursion' (1728) outdoes Thomson in its picture of sublime and threatening events. Mallet addresses his poem to 'Fancy' and it was to a similar topic that a much better poet, James Beattie (1735–1803), addressed himself in 'The Minstrel' (1771–74). Beattie has some superb descriptions in his poem, but the subject is not so much nature itself as the growth of the poet's imagination in the presence of nature. Beattie's hero, Edwin, is born in Scotland during 'Gothic days' and grows to maturity as a being sensitive to the sublimity of the landscape and easily roused by Scottish songs with their evocation of the past. Under the instruction of a hermit, he succeeds in deepening his understanding of life through the study of history, science and philosophy, and the poem concludes at the point where Edwin is ready to write good poetry.

Beattie often interupts his narrative to express his own love of the ballads of his native land, but he writes in what might be considered standard English and in the verse form associated with the English poet Edmund Spenser (c. 1552–99). A few poets continued to write in a Scottish dialect, however. For Allan Ramsay (1686–1758), such a decision had distinct political overtones. Not only did he write his poems, songs and dramatic work in his native dialect, in *The Evergreen* (1724–27) he gathered together an anthology of Scottish poetry from earlier centuries. In his *Tea-Table Miscellany* (1724–27) he printed both his own work and that of his contemporaries, and in *The Gentle Shepherd* (1725), he adapted pastoral drama to a Scottish setting and language. One critic writing in 1825 remarked, 'In Allan Ramsay I see the great successor to the royal race of bards, who laid the foundation of the rustic or national poetry of Scotland'. Although Robert Fergusson (1750–74) cannot be given the credit for leading a return to a poetry in his native language, he was a talented poet, and in his picture of various events and the crowd in 'Leith Races', a writer with an excellent eye for realistic and vivid detail.

Like Ramsay, Fergusson wrote in the dialect of Scotland as a deliberate act. In his poem, 'Elegy on the Death of Scots Music', he laments the influence of foreign models:

> Now foreign sonnets bear the gree,
> And crabbit queer variety
> Of sound fresh sprung frae Italy,
>   A bastard breed!
> Unlike that saft-tongu'd melody
>   Which now lies dead.

Yet Fergusson begins this poem with a quotation from Shakespeare and has a substantial body of verse in the standard English of the time. Eighteenth-century readers were impatient with obscure and archaic words, and until Burns directed the attention of the English audience to the richness of the Scottish dialect, the reputation of poets like Ramsay and Fergusson did not extend beyond the Tweed, except for their poems in the standard English of the time or in 'translation'. In one of several attempts to render Ramsay's *The Gentle Shepherd* into English, an adapter quoted the well-known Scottish critic and rhetorician, Hugh Blair (1718–1800) to justify her effort. Blair praised the work and remarked that it was 'a great disadvantage to this beautiful Poem, that it is written in the old rustic dialect of Scotland, which, in a short time, will probably be entirely obsolete, and not intelligible'.

Burns was to do much to demonstrate that Blair was wrong – that at a time when English poetry was burdened by overworked imagery and formal diction, Scottish ballads and the Scottish language could provide a rich and new source of inspiration. Yet Burns also breathed new life into the Scottish tradition of poetry and in some sense, changed the 'union' between the two national literary traditions from one that, in the manner of the political Union ratified in 1707, had left Scottish literature weak and dependent even at the high point of its contribution to philosophy and learning to one that brought from England a new respect for Scottish civilisation. He acknowledged his debt to Fergusson and expressed an admiration for his poetry. But in addition to being a greater poet, Burns had a sense of the way Scottish idioms might transform the English language and give it a fresh sound and appearance. Not that Burns was merely looking into his Scottish heart and writing. He knew eighteenth-century English poetry well, and poems like 'The Cotter's Saturday Night' (1786) were written in the sentimental manner of contemporary English poetry. And well-known poems using Scottish words, like 'Flow Gently Sweet Afton' (1789) were adapted from poems in English, in this case, a poem on the Avon by David Garrick.

In addition to enlivening what might have been a piece of society verse, like his poem 'To a Mouse' (1786), by the novelty and force of Scottish idiom, Burns had the ability to transform a poem from its seeming direction to something very different. Thus the gentle mockery of the speaker of that poem turns to a sense of real terror as the speaker realises the instability of his own life in the face of nature and events more inexorable than the blade of the plough that destroyed the home of the mouse. The poem's statement is ultimately personal and social. Burns was a writer with Jacobin sympathies. He praised 'honest poverty' as superior to wealth, and in his marvellous poetic cantata, 'Love and Liberty', usually known as 'The Jolly Beggars' (1799), the chorus sings out:

> A fig for those by law protected,
>   Liberty's a glorious feast!
> Courts for cowards were erected,
>   Churches built to please the priest.

Oddly enough, Burns's poem draws upon earlier songs of beggars and thieves which tended to be libertine in outlook, and Burns can be regarded as one of the late eighteenth-century flowerings of philosophic libertinism as it merged with revolutionary thought at the time. A portion of his poems are sentimentalised versions of bawdy songs, and some of the originals exalt the joys of love in a manner that is far from Platonic.

In the spirit of libertinism, Burns turned much of his satire against religious and moral hypocrisy – against those in society who set themselves up as the 'unco guid' and believed they had the right to sit in judgement on the young and passionate. Burns himself was forced by the elders of the church to do penance for some of his escapades. But it was the very spirit of song that such figures were enemies to, and Burns would hardly have been the poet he was if the inspiration of songs and ballads was not part of his very being. He admired the richness of ballad topoi, those segments of poetry that may travel from ballad to ballad unchanged and are often irrelevant to the ballad in which they function. Burns managed to improve the ballads and songs by changing the commonplaces into complex metaphors. A good example of this is 'My Love is Like a Red Red Rose' (1794):

> As fair art thou, my bonnie lass,
>   So deep in luve am I;
> And I will luve thee still, my dear,
>   Till a' the seas gang dry.
> Till a' the seas gang dry, my dear,
>   And the rocks melt wi' the sun:
> I will luve thee still, my dear,
>   While the sands o' life shall run.

W. H. Auden (1907–73) was later to take similar material and give his poetry a bitter-sweet and ironic turn, but it was Burns who first showed how such material could be transformed into art.

If Burns was the minstrel of Percy's formulation, William Blake was surely its Bard. Although many critics read Blake's poetry as part of a single vision from beginning to end, his early writings fit perfectly into the complex of eighteenth-century ideas discussed in this chapter. He was essentially a religious poet and has to be viewed, at least partly, in a continuing tradition of religious verse. And since his religious views have some affinity to those Christian groups influenced by mystical and cabalistic thought, his work may appear occasionally somewhat different from that of Isaac Watts or

Christopher Smart. But his poetry owes much to the interest in the poetry of the Bible, particularly the Old Testament books of the prophets. In some senses Blake may have thought of himself as continuing the tradition of prophetic poetry.

Blake was early taken up by an interest in the Gothic. As an artist, he spent much time drawing aspects of Westminster Abbey, and his early verse, written between 1769 and 1778 and published in 1783, *Poetical Sketches,* has a good deal of Gothic material, with Collins and Gray as notable models. And true to the spirit of the age, Blake wrote a considerable amount of satire – satire that has a distinct Jacobin flavour. His 'Island in the Moon', written around 1787, satirised social corruption and the complacent attitudes of intellectuals, while other poems saw the revolutions in America and France as signalising a new era in which old laws of the *ancien régime* would be wiped away. 'America' etched around 1793, and 'Europe' completed around 1794, are both essentially political works. If Blake cast them in terms of prophetic poems in free verse, he was hardly alone in searching for new forms to describe the violent political upheavals abroad.

The most accessible of the poems written during this period are: *Songs of Innocence* (1789), *Songs of Experience* (1794), and *The Marriage of Heaven and Hell* (1793). The *Songs of Innocence* owe much to the many hymns for children written during the period, of which Christopher Smart's *Hymns for the Amusement of Children* published in 1775, is a good example. The effect aimed at in such works was religious instruction through delightful poetry. Blake does much more. He superimposes his image of innocence over a world of corrupt laws and social inequality. Although the spirit of love and innocence appears to triumph over the evils of the short lives of the chimney sweeper, the racial hatred that lay behind slavery, and the excessive ordering of the lives of children, that triumph exists entirely in the realm of spirit. It is hard to see where innocence actually seems to win many victories on earth.

This is apparent in the very earthly vision of the *Songs of Experience.* In these poems, innocence is gone, replaced by a bitter view of a world in which human beings are exploited and the entire world corrupted by something that looks like order but which is actually based on the disorders of human life – on wars and inequality. The magnificent poem, 'London', in its final stanza suggests the way corruption is present from the cradle to the grave:

> But most thro' midnight streets I hear
> How the youthful Harlot's curse
> Blasts the new born Infant's tear,
> And blights with plagues the Marriage hearse.

Blake's ability to use a kind of shorthand to make his imagery powerful and compact owes much to Jacobin thought. Just as Mrs Inchbald was able to show a cycle of corruption in her *Nature and Art,* so Blake is able to show the cry of the soldier running like blood 'down palace walls'. Even the Jacobin's attack on self-consciousness as an aspect of vanity is a kind of socio-political equivalent to Blake's mystical view of the spirit of man having fallen into disunity.

The Marriage of Heaven and Hell is, perhaps, the most accessible of the prophetic books as approached from the eighteenth century, because it does not depend on plunging into the imaginative system of religion, life and art that Blake was to develop. And it breathes the spirit of the age in being essentially a satire on various systems of Christian thought, particularly that of Emanuel Swedenborg (1688–1772). For all his own style of mysticism, Swedenborg retained something of the dualism of traditional Christian thought. Blake stands such thought on its head as the image of hell put forth by the angel who is the spokesman for the religious establishment turns out to be nothing but an illusion. With its satiric play with the printing house of hell, Blake's work resembles a poetic and prophetic version of Swift's *Tale of a Tub.* The 'Proverbs of Hell', which are a parody of the Old Testament Book of Proverbs, preach the importance of energy over prudence, of action over inertia, and of physicality over a moribund spirituality. Within Blake's total system, *The Marriage of Heaven and Hell* represents only one aspect of vision, but as a young man, Blake clearly found aspects of energy and action attractive, particularly where they work hand in hand with imagination.

As an artist, Blake was part of and a leader of tendencies to adapt the rendering of the human figure into a larger intellectual design. He might have discovered from his study of Romanesque and Gothic sculpture that figures were elongated to fit the columns of which they were a part and size made a matter of spiritual and intellectual position rather than a reflection of the physical laws of the real world. In designing his pages to blend the text with the illustration, he sublimated mimetic ideals to the ideas he wished to convey. Even in his own time, the artist, John Fuseli (1742–1821) remarked that Blake was a good person to steal from, and Blake's treatment of form had a major impact on the art of the Pre-Raphaelites as well as on that of poet-craftsmen like William Morris.

III   Drama

While it would be unfair to say that the drama stood in ruins at the end of the century, there was much to discourage the writing of good drama. The theatres had grown to accommodate the growing audience, and this meant large stages that discouraged subtlety in acting. The demands for variety meant that shortened versions of standard plays would be accompanied by various 'acts' that included musicians, magicians, singers and animal tricks. If the late eighteenth-century critics and the Romantic critics who followed them came to believe that drama of any value was better read in the closet than seen on the stage, it was, at least partly, because of the physical conditions of the theatres. German drama, like that of August Kotzebue (1761–1819), with clear, sentimental lines, seemed better suited to this stage than the plays of British writers. Holcroft and Mrs Inchbald were successful dramatists, but compared to their novels, their plays seem thin indeed. Richard Cumberland (1732–1811) was among the more successful dramatists of the time, but while he was a good dramatic craftsman, he contented himself with appealing to contemporary taste. His sentimental comedy, *The West Indian* (1771), was chiefly significant in streamlining the form, making the sentimentality clear and unambiguous. His was the kind of drama that left a great deal to the performers. While it would be unfair to say that an elaborate text occasionally seems like an incumbrance to an ambitious actor, it is true enough that the plays of Cumberland presented more opportunity for interpretation than, say, *The Way of the World.*

But the theatre experienced a brief flowering in the second half of the century. Goldsmith's comedies have already been mentioned. John Home wrote a good tragedy in *Douglas* (1757), and while it was probably overrated in its time, it has some effective scenes. Even pantomime, the favourite of the theatre mob, found in Samuel Foote (1720–77), an actor of considerable merit. His brief satiric plays, such as *Taste* (1752) and *The Nabob* (1772) read more like the outline for a play than the finished product, but some of the scenes are clever even without the actors there to give life to the words. And David Garrick, George Colman the Elder (1732–94) and Arthur Murphy (1727–1805) showed genuine gifts for the little farces or afterpieces that accompanied the main drama of the evening.

The only true master of the drama during this part of the century was Richard Brinsley Sheridan (1751–1816), whose membership of the Literary Club, according to Boswell, was proposed by Johnson with the remark that Sheridan had 'written the two best comedies of his age'. Everything he wrote was popular, including adaptations like his comic opera, the *Duenna* (1775) his tragedy, *Pizarro* (1799), and his pantomime of *Robinson Crusoe* (1781). Sheridan, with Goldsmith, belonged to the school of 'laughing comedy', and more than Goldsmith, he went back to the comedies of the Restoration for some of his ideas. His farce, *The Critic* (perf. 1779; pub. 1781) has some of the same qualities as *The Rehearsal* (1671) of the Duke of Buckingham, and his two comedies, *The Rivals* (1775) and *The School for Scandal,* acted in 1777 though not published in an official edition until 1783, may be regarded as attacks on sentimentality. That attack in *The Rivals* is more oblique, but the play does dwell comically on the doubts and jealousies of lovers. And Sheridan gives the real laughter over to his minor characters like the magnificent Mrs Malaprop. In *The School for Scandal* the criticism of sensibility and sentimentality is sketched out in the characters of the brothers, Charles and Joseph Surface. Charles seems to be a wastrel and a rake from all outward appearances, but he is generous to a fault. Like his name, recalling England's merriest monarch, the appearance of insensitivity is purely a surface manifestation. Joseph's surface appearance also suits his name. He seems to be pious, full of sententious statements about morality, and a man of honour. Behind this mask he is a hypocrite, completely uncharitable and, despite his instantly available moral sentiments, a nearly successful seducer of his friend's wife. For Sheridan, true sensibility is found in the heart, and its outward manifestation is likely to be a lack of worldly prudence. Only by Charles's refusal to sell his uncle's portrait to the man who turns out to be his uncle in disguise is his true character clarified.

This concern with appearance and reality is present elsewhere in the period. In 1777, Maurice Morgann (1726–1802) published his 'Essay on the Character of Falstaff' in which he argued that Falstaff could not really be a coward, since we found him so appealing. If he were a coward, we would have to find him detestable, therefore, Morgann concluded, the critic must look beyond the appearances to the true meaning of the text. Although Johnson may have objected to such an approach, the method of writing in such a way as to present a surface that concealed numerous sub-textual meanings was part of the method of writers as different as Pope, Defoe, and Gray. In the hands of Sheridan, it becomes a complex dramatic metaphor that serves some of the same purpose (by other means) of the complex wit of Restoration comedy.

IV   History, travel and philosophy

Almost every major figure of the period either wrote history or toyed with the idea, and when they thought of history, they considered it one of the arts, rather than some questionable social science. Goldsmith, in a famous essay, allows Hume into his 'Celestial Chariot', not for his philosophic writings but for his *History of Great Britain* (1754–57). That particular history was continued by Tobias Smollett to bring it up to date, and with various additions, it remained one of the standard histories well into the nineteenth century. Hume tried to counter the 'Whig Historians' who tended to see the history of Great Britain in terms of a progress toward greater liberty. Humes's prevailing scepticism served him well in this task, though, for the most part, the Whig view tended to suit the ends of nineteenth-century historians well enough to

continue relatively unchallenged for another century. Another
Scot, William Robertson (1721–93) wrote a series of histories,
the most famous of which was the *History of Charles V* (1769),
but Robertson was one of those accurate historians who
refused to force any very decided view on history. The result of
this was a loss of reputation over the years, for we still read
Hume's history to find out what Hume has to say, while
Robertson seems the kind of historian whom additional
information can make obsolete or even quaint.

The great historian of the times was Gibbon, and his *Decline
and Fall of the Roman Empire* (1776–88) is imprinted with
Gibbon's personal judgements, wit and irony. Gibbon appears
in Boswell's accounts as 'I' – 'I' for infidel, and the reason for
this reputation was not only the suggestion that Christianity
might have been one cause for the fall of Rome, but also the
commentary on the story of Christ. Gibbon pointed out that
Rome was at the height of her power at the time that Christ
was supposed to have lived. The events of his life and death
involved earthshaking experiences – miracles, vast crowds,
darkness, yet no Roman writer seemed aware that such things
were taking place. It was possible to read this famous section as
a commentary on the blindness of Pagan Rome, but most
contemporaries thought that Gibbon was suggesting just the
opposite – that if such events actually happened, they would
have been the subject of much speculation in a time of such
notable intellectual sophistication.

The Decline and Fall was the product of an inspired historical
vision. Gibbon, who had been contemplating a number of
possible subjects for a history, was on a visit to Rome when he
saw the spectacle of some Catholic monks in the ruins of the
Roman Forum. The juxtaposition of the ancient past and what
he regarded as a medieval institution in the midst of
enlightened Europe stirred his imagination. Such a reaction is
hardly surprising. Artists such as Giovanni Battista Piranesi
(1720–78) had been engraving 'caprices' on the ruins of Rome
with notable success during the entire eighteenth century, and
in the paintings of Salvator Rosa (1615–73) and Nicolas
Poussin (1594–1665) of the seventeenth century, the Roman
ruin was almost a necessary ingredient of every landscape.
Rosa, a member of the Neapolitan school, was very popular
among admirers of the picturesque and he is often mentioned

by writers of Gothic novels, but Poussin was considered the true master of landscape painting that had allegorical or historical significance. Gibbon's vision was not very different from that of Constantin, Comte de Volney, (1757–1820) who, in *Les ruines* (1791) indulged in a sombre, visionary brooding over the course of nations and empires, but Gibbon, who passed a large part of his life in Switzerland, was more than most British writers the child of the European Enlightenment, and he approached his subject with a detached irony and wit. He saw human failure and weakness everywhere he looked, and when he praised anyone for various virtues or abilities, it was almost always in a context which showed how such qualities were thwarted by ignorance, malice or sheer power.

If Gibbon invested the history of the Roman Empire with a new kind of fascination, another brand of writers were raising the interest in place and scenery to new levels of excitement. Within the British Isles, William Gilpin (1724–1804), especially in his *Observations on the Wye and South Wales* (1782), tried to show how picturesque the landscape of that area was, and during the wars on the continent, English travellers turned away from Europe and journeyed westward to view the ruins of Tintern Abbey and the wonderful castles of Wales and Herefordshire. And those who preferred to travel through the pages of books could turn to one of the great voyages of Captain James Cook (1728–79) to the South Seas. The relation of the voyage of 1768–71 appeared in Dr James Hawkesworth's collection, *Voyages in the Southern Hemisphere* (1773), but accounts of subsequent voyages appeared independently in 1777 and, after Cook's death at the hands of the natives of Hawaii, in 1784. Johnson may have considered these volumes tedious and argued that all savages were pretty much the same and accounts of them necessarily repetitious and, ultimately, boring, but for many late eighteenth-century readers, 'Cook's Voyages' opened a new and exotic universe.

In some ways, the accounts of distant places appealed to the sense of sight as experienced through the evocations of language, and this was also a major concern of contemporary philosophy. At the end of the century, the dominant force in British philosophy was that of the Scottish 'Common Sense' school led by Thomas Reid (1710–96) and Dugald Stewart (1753–1828). They insisted that Locke had misled philosophers by calling every sensation an 'idea'. Having confused thought with perception, Locke, in their view, had prepared for an excessively introspective view of the world. They argued that our grasp of an external world was immediate and intuitive and that there was no necessity for raising doubts about our grasp of reality. While these writers refined upon the theories of sympathy and the moral sense that we have already encountered in Adam Smith, another moralist was positing a system based on utility. Although Jeremy Bentham (1748–1832) lived a large part of his life in the nineteenth century, his *Introduction to Principles of Morals and Legislation* (1780), with its utilitarian formula of 'the greatest good for the greatest number' was a direct outgrowth of eighteenth-century speculation on happiness within society. Joseph Priestley (1733–1804) and even Francis Hutcheson (1694–1746) had argued much the same formula. Even such a work as Bentham's *Panopitcon* (1791) was part of a theory of prison reform that was little different from that of other proponents at the time, and as Foucault has shown, fits very well into the way in which convicts were seen at the end of the century.

V   Toward Romanticism

In 1798, Wordsworth and Coleridge's *Lyrical Ballads* was published, and in 1800 a second edition with Wordsworth's preface appeared. In England, at least, these two events, particularly the very conscious proclamation of a new movement in English poetry, herald the Romantic Movement. To distinguish the elements in that movement that are significantly different, it is necessary to distinguish what was genuinely new in the approach to art and life. Merely to argue that everything that came before the publication of *Lyrical Ballads* that was imaginative or vivid was 'Pre-Romantic' is no explanation at all. Wordsworth and Coleridge, after a flirtation with the French Revolution, rejected radical politics and turned to a poetry that reflected an imaginative turn inward toward the experience of the poet as he tries to grasp for the meaning of his world.

Although Wordsworth and Coleridge did not go to

Germany until after the publication of *Lyrical Ballads,* they were already in tune with the new idealism of Immanuel Kant (1724–1804) and followers such as Friedrich Schelling (1775–1854). Kant formulated his philosophy as an answer to the questions about experience raised by Locke, Berkeley and Hume. But if the question was a typical one for the period, the answer was not. Kant solved the dualism of Locke by suggesting that we only can know our inner world, that questions about an external world are, to some extent, nonsensical. Our mind is the creative force that imposes its pattern on our existence; space and time are *a priori* configurations within the mind. Although Kant proceeded to develop a complete system of morality based on categorical imperatives that force us to act in certain ways, the impact of his philosophy led directly to the idea of the artist as the defiant creator of his own world and to a kind of philosophic egotism that was the very reverse of the eighteenth-century's insistence that the artist should treat the world around him and put his inner world into a comprehensible context.

The dialectic with which we began was not solved by Romanticism; it simply dissolved before an entirely different system. The debates about reason and imagination, benevolence and prudence, sense and sensibility and the questions about the relationship between environment and heredity as a cause of crime or what conditions are conducive to human happiness, continued to be meaningful, but if such subjects remained the concern of art (and certainly they continued to be the material of novels), they were more often than not treated in a manner that was cloaked by metaphor. Small wonder then that during periods seeking literary ideals that include the treatment of a social world with wit and compassion, the art of the eighteenth century is rediscovered.

Chronological table

Abbreviations: (D.) = drama,   (P.) = prose,   (V.) = verse

DATE	AUTHOR AND TITLE	EVENT
1700	Congreve, William: *Way of the World* (D.) Dryden, John: *Fables* (V.)	James Thomson *b.* John Dryden *d.* Population of London *c.* 550,000
1701	Defoe, Daniel: 'True-born Englishman' (V.) Steele, Richard: *The Funeral* (D.)	War of the Spanish Succession begins Act of Settlement prepares for heirs of House of Hanover to succeed to English throne
1702	Brown, Thomas: *Letters from the Dead to the Living* (P.) Defoe, Daniel: *Shortest Way with the Dissenters* (P.)	William III *d.* Accession of Queen Anne
1703	Rowe, Nicholas: *The Fair Penitent* (D.) Defoe, Daniel: Hymn to the Pillory' (V.)	John Wesley *b.* Samuel Pepys *d.*
1704	Swift, Jonathan: *Tale of a Tub, Battle of the Books* (P.)	John Locke *d.* Battle of Blenheim
1705	Addison, Joseph: 'The Campaign' (V.)	Thomas Newcomen invents steam engine John Vanbrugh begins Blenheim Palace
1706	Farquhar, George: *The Recruiting Officer* (D.)	Victory at Ramilles over French
1707	Farquhar, George: *Beaux' Stratagem* (D.) Prior, Matthew: *Poems on Several Occasions* (P.)	Henry Fielding *b.* George Farquhar *d.* Union of England and Scotland
1708	Shaftesbury, Third Earl of: *Letter concerning Enthusiasm* (P.)	Johann Sebastian Bach becomes court organist at Weimar

DATE	AUTHOR AND TITLE	EVENT
1709	Berkeley, George: *New Theory of Vision* (P.) Defoe, Daniel: *History of the Union of Great Britain* (P.) Steele, Richard : 'The Tatler' (P.)	Samuel Johnson *b.* First Copyright Act Sweden's Charles XII is defeated by Peter the Great at Poltava
1710	Berkeley, George: *Principles of Human Knowledge* (P.)	Tory Party wins majority in the Commons and takes over power from the Whigs
1711	Addison, Joseph: 'The Spectator' (P.) Pope, Alexander: 'Essay on Criticism' (V.)	David Hume *b.* Nicholas Boileau *d.*
1712	Arbuthnot, John: 'History of John Bull' (P.) Pope, Alexander: 'The Rape of the Lock' (V.)	Jean-Jacques Rousseau *b.*
1713	Addison, Joseph: *Cato* (D.) Pope, Alexander: 'Windsor Forest' (V.) Finch, Anne, Countess of Winchilsea: *Miscellany Poems* (V.)	Laurence Sterne *b.* Treaty of Utrecht ends War of Spanish Succession
1714	Mandeville, Bernard: 'Fable of the Bees' (V., P.) Pope, Alexander: 'The Rape of the Lock' (expanded version) (V.) Rowe, Nicholas: *Jane Shore* (D.)	Queen Anne *d.* George I succeeds to throne Whigs take over government
1715	Defoe, Daniel: 'Appeal to Honour and Justice' (P.) Pope, Alexander: *Iliad* (V.) Watts, Isaac: 'Divine Song for Children' (V.)	Louis XIV *d.* Jacobite rebellion in Scotland
1716	Gay, John: 'Trivia' (V.)	Thomas Gray *b.* William Wycherley *d.*
1717	Hoadly, Benjamin: *Nature of the Kingdom of Christ* (P.) Pope, Alexander: *Collected Works* (V.)	Bangorian Controversy Prince Eugene takes Belgrade from the Turks
1718	Centlivre, Susannah: *Bold Stroke for a Wife* (D.) Cibber, Colley: *The Non-juror* (D.) Prior, Matthew: *Poems* (V.)	Nicholas Rowe *d.* Charles XII *d.*

DATE	AUTHOR AND TITLE	EVENT
1719	Defoe, Daniel: *Robinson Crusoe* (P.)	Joseph Addison *d.* Samuel Garth *d.*
1720	Defoe, Daniel: *Memoirs of a Cavalier* (P.): *Captain Singleton* (P.)	South Sea Bubble collapses
1721	Young, Edmund: *The Revenge* (D.)	William Collins *b.* Matthew Prior *d.* Sir Robert Walpole assumes control of government
1722	Defoe, Daniel: *Journal of the Plague Year* (P.); *Moll Flanders* (P.); *Colonel Jack* (P.) Parnell, Thomas: *Poems* (V.) Steele, Richard: *The Conscious Lovers* (D.)	Christopher Smart *b.* John Toland *d.* Peter the Great consolidates power in Russia
1723	Burnet, Gilbert: *History of My Own Times* (P.) Mandeville, Bernard: 'Essay on Charity; and Search into the Nature of Society' [in expanded 'Fable of the Bees']	Adam Smith *b.* Sir Joshua Reynolds *b.* Christopher Wren *d.* Bolingbroke allowed to return to Britain
1724	Collins, Anthony: 'Grounds of Christian Réligion' (P.) Defoe, Daniel: *Roxana* (P.); *Tour thro' Great Britain* (P.) Ramsay, Allan: *Tea-table Miscellany* (V.) Swift, Jonathan: *Drapier's Letters* (P.)	Immanuel Kant *b.*
1725	Hutcheson, Francis: *Original of Beauty and Virtue* (P.) Pope, Alexander: *Odyssey* (V.) Young, Edmund: 'Universal Passion' (V.)	Peter the Great *d.* Vico's *New Science* published
1726	Swift, Jonathan: *Gulliver's Travels* (P.) Thomson, James: 'Winter' (V.)	Sir John Vanbrugh *d.* Sir Isaac Newton *d.* 'The Craftsman' 1726–36
1727	Dyer, John: 'Grongar Hill' (V.) Gay, John: 'Fables' (V) [Second series in 1738]	Death of George I Accession of George II
1728	Gay. John: *Beggar's Opera* (D.) Pope, Alexander: *Dunciad* (V.)	Britain declares war on Spain

DATE	AUTHOR AND TITLE	EVENT
1729	Gay, John: *Polly* (D.) Swift, Jonathan: 'Modest Proposal' (P.)	Edmund Burke *b*. Richard Steele *d*. William Congreve *d*. Treaty of Seville, peace with Spain
1730	Fielding, Henry: *Tom Thumb* (D.) Thomson, James: *The Seasons* (V.)	Oliver Goldsmith *b*.
1731	Lillo, George: *The London Merchant* (D.) Pope, Alexander: 'Epistle to Burlington' (V.)	William Cowper *b*. Daniel Defoe *d*. Cave starts *Gentleman's Magazine*
1732	Fielding, Henry. *Covent Garden Tragedy* (D.); *Modern Husband* (D.) Pope, Alexander: 'Epistle to Bathurst' (V.)	John Gay *d*.
1733	Pope, Alexander: 'Essay on Man' (V.); 'Epistle to Colham' (V.); 'First Satire of Book ii of Horace Imitated' (V.) Swift, Jonathan: 'On Poetry: A Rapsody' (V.)	Molasses Act forbids American Colonies to trade with Spanish Colonies John Kay invents flying shuttle and revolutionises weaving in Britain
1734	Pope, Alexander: 'Second Satire of Book ii of Horace' (V.)	John Dennis *d*. Voltaire publishes *Lettres sur Anglaises*
1735	Pope Alexander: 'Epistle to a Lady' (V.); 'Epistle to Arbuthnot' (V.) Thomson, James: 'Liberty' (V.) [last part published 1736]	John Arbuthnot *d*. War of Polish Succession ends Hogarth's 'Rake's Progress'
1736	Butler, Joseph: *Analogy of Religion* (P.) Fielding, Henry: *Pasquin* (D.); *Historical Register for 1736* (D.)	Porteous riot in Edinburgh John Harrison perfects the ship's chronometer, allowing the determination of longitude Statues against witchcraft repealed
1737	Lillo, George: *Fatal Curiosity* (D.) Pope, Alexander: 'Epistle VI, book i of Horace Imitated' (V.); 'Epistle I, i of Horace Imitated' (V.); 'Epistles I and II Book ii of Horace Imitated' (V.)	Edward Gibbon *b*. Thomas Paine *b*. Queen Caroline *d*. Licencing Act puts drama under government censorship Carolus Linnaeus publishes system of classifying plants in Geneva

DATE	AUTHOR AND TITLE	EVENT
1738	Johnson, Samuel: 'London' (V.) Pope, Alexander: 'One Thousand Seven Hundred and Thirty Eight' (V.)	Treaty of Vienna ratified Excavation of Herculaneum, buried under ash from Vesuvius 79 A.D.
1739	Hume, David: *Treatise on Human Nature* (concl. 1740) (P.) Swift, Jonathan: 'Verses on the Death of Dr Swift' [written 1731]	George Lillo *d.* Henry Fielding and James Ralph start *The Champion*
1740	Cibber, Colley: *Apology* (P.) Richardson, Samuel: *Pamela or Virtue Rewarded* (P.)	James Boswell *b.* Vernon's victory against the Spanish at Port Bello used to attack Walpole
1741	Fielding, Henry: *Shamela* (P.) Richardson, Samuel: *Familiar Letters* (P.)	Frederick II of Prussia wins great victory at Mollvitz taking Silesia as the War of the Austrian Succession begins in earnest
1742	Collins, William: 'Persian Ecclogues' (V.) Pope, Alexander: *New Dunciad* (V.) Young, Edmund: *Night Thoughts* (V.)	Walpole resigns all offices and becomes Earl of Orford Handel's 'Messiah' first performed
1743	Blair, Robert: 'The Grave' (V.) Fielding, Henry: *Jonathan Wild* (P.) Pope, Alexander: *Dunciad* (V.) [final version]	Anne Barbauld *b.* Hogarth's 'Marriage a la Mode'
1744	Akenside, Mark: 'Pleasures of the Imagination' (rev. edn. 1771) (V.) Johnson, Samuel: *Life of Savage* (P.) Warton, Joseph: 'The Enthusiast' (V.)	Alexander Pope *d.* King George's War breaks out in America
1745	Johnson, Samuel: *Observations on Macbeth* (P.)	Jonathan Swift *d.* Bonnie Prince Charlie leads Jacobite revolt in Scotland
1746	Collins, William: 'Ode to Evening' (V.) Warton, Joseph: 'Odes' (V.)	Jacobite rebellion crushed at Culloden Moor and hereditary jurisdictions of Highland Chiefs abolished William Pitt included in the cabinet Benjamin Franklin begins experiments with electricity

DATE	AUTHOR AND TITLE	EVENT
1747	Garrick, David: *Miss in her Teens* (D.) Gray, Thomas: 'Ode on Prospect of Eton' (V.) Johnson, Samuel: *Plan of the Dictionary* (P.) Warton, Thomas: 'Pleasures of Melancholy' (V.)	Victories over French in West Indies Handel's 'Judas Macabeus' performed Citrus fruits established as cure for scurvy
1748	Collins, William: 'Odes' (P.) Richardson, Samuel: *Clarissa* (P.) Smollett, Tobias: *Roderick Random* (P.)	Jeremy Bentham *b.* James Thomson *d.* Treaty of Aix-la-Chapelle ends War of Austrian Succession
1749	Bolingbroke, First Viscount: *On the Spirit of Patriotism; Idea of a Patriot King* (P.) Fielding, Henry: *Tom Jones* (P.) Hartley, David: *Observations on Man* (P.) Johnson, Samuel: 'Vanity of Human Wishes' (V.)	Johann Wolfgang von Goethe *b.* *The Monthly Review* commences publication continuing until 1845
1750	Cleland, John: *Fanny Hill* (P.) [reworking of earlier version, published 1748–9] Johnson, Samuel: *The Rambler* (P.)	Johann Sebastian Bach *d.* Voltaire moves to Berlin until 1753
1751	Fielding, Henry: *Amelia* (P.) Gray, Thomas: 'Elegy Written in a Country Churchyard' (V.) Hume, David: *Enquiry Concerning the Principles of Morals* (P.) Smollett, Tobias: *Peregrine Pickle* (P.)	Frederic Louis, Prince of Wales, *d.* George Grenville head of Cabinet Benjamin Franklin demonstrates the electrical nature of lightning Hogarth's 'Gin Lane' Vol. I of the French *Encyclopedia* published by Diderot and d'Alembert
1752	Lennox, Charlotte: *The Female Quixote* (P.) Smart, Christopher: 'Poems' (V.)	Thomas Chatterton *b.* Frances Burney *b.* Britain changes to Gregorian Calendar
1753	Shiels, Robert: *Lives of the Poets* (P.) [usually ascribed to Theophilus Cibber] Richardson, Samuel: *Sir Charles Grandison* (P.) Smollett, Tobias: *Ferdinand Count Fathom* (P.)	Elizabeth Inchbald *b.* George Berkeley *d.* France bankrupt British Museum chartered

DATE	AUTHOR AND TITLE	EVENT
1754	Hume, David: *History of England* (P.) [various sections finished by 1762] Warton, Thomas: *Observations on the Faerie Queen* (P.)	George Crabbe *b*. Henry Fielding *d*. Duke of Newcastle becomes Prime Minister
1755	Johnson, Samuel: *English Dictionary* (P.) [rev. 1773]	Jean-Jacques Rousseau's 'Discourse on Inequality' Grenville, Legge and Pitt dismissed from the Cabinet
1756	Burke, Edmund: *Origin of Ideas of the Sublime and Beautiful* (P.) Warton, Joseph: *Genius and Writings of Pope* [vol. II 1782] (P.)	William Godwin *b*. Wolfgang Amadeus Mozart *b*. William Pitt becomes Prime Minister
1757	Gray, Thomas: 'Progress of Poesy' (V.); 'The Bard' (V.) Home, John: *Douglas* (D.)	William Blake *b*. Colley Cibber *d*.
1758	Dodsley, Robert: 'Collection of Poems', v–vi (V.) [last vols. of series begun in 1748] Johnson, Samuel: *The Idler* (P.)	John Dyer *d*. Allan Ramsay *d*. Britain allies with Prussia against France
1759	Johnson, Samuel: *Rasselas* (P.) Smith, Adam: *Theory of Moral Sentiments* (P.) Young, Edmund: *Conjectures on Original Composition* (P.)	Robert Burns *b*. Mary Wollstonecraft *b*. William Collins *d*. George Friedrich Handel *d*.
1760	Goldsmith, Oliver: *Citizen of the World* (P.) Sterne, Laurence: *Tristram Shandy* (P.) [final vol. 1767]	Accession of George III France's navy in ruins after British victories
1761	Churchill, Charles: 'Rosciad' (V.) Colman, George, Sr. [with David Garrick] *Jealous Wife* (D.)	Samuel Richardson *d*. Pitt resigns after unsuccessful negotiations with France
1762	Hurd, Richard: *Letters on Chivalry and Romance* (P.) Macpherson, James: 'Fingal' (V.) Smollett, Tobias: *Sir Launcelot Greaves* (P.)	Lady Mary Wortley Montagu *d*. Earl of Bute Prime Minister

DATE	AUTHOR AND TITLE	EVENT
1763	Churchill, Charles: Collected Poems (V.) [vol. II 1766] Lady Mary Wortley Montagu: *Letters* (P.) Smart, Christopher: 'Song to David' (V.)	William Shenstone *d.* Peace of Paris Wilkes Riots
1764	Churchill, Charles: 'The Candidate' (V.); 'The Times' (V.) Goldsmith, Oliver: 'The Traveller' (V.) Shenstone, William: Works (P., V.)	Ann Radcliffe *b.* Charles Churchill *d.* John Wilkes expelled from Commons
1765	Johnson, Samuel: Edn of Shakespeare [rev. with Stevens 1773] Percy, Thomas: *Reliques of Ancient English Poetry* (V.) Walpole, Horace: *Castle of Otranto* (P.)	Edward Young *d.* Stamp Act passed
1766	Anstey, Christopher: 'New Bath Guide' (V.) Goldsmith, Oliver: *Vicar of Wakefield* (P.)	Stamp Act repealed Pitt returns to power, but George III asserts his influence
1767	Farmer, Richard: 'Essay on the Learning of Shakespeare' (P.)	Maria Edgworth *b.* Duke of Grafton Prime Minister
1768	Boswell, James: 'Account of Corsica' (P.) Kelly, Hugh: *False Delicacy* (D.) [with David Garrick] Sterne, Laurence: *Sentimental Journey* (P.)	Laurence Sterne *d.* Wilkes wins Middlesex election and the cry of 'Wilkes and Liberty' is raised as he is imprisoned
1769	Reynolds, Sir Joshua: *Discourses on Art* (P.) [series completed in 1790]	Garrick orchestrates the Shakespeare Jubilee at Stratford 'Letters of Junius' attack Duke of Grafton's ministry
1770	Goldsmith, Oliver: 'Deserted Village' (V.)	William Wordsworth *b.* Thomas Chatterton *d.* Lord North replaces Grafton as Prime Minister
1771	Cumberland, Richard: *West Indian* (D.) MacKenzie, Henry: *Man of Feeling* (P.) Smollett, Tobias: *Humphrey Clinker* (P.)	Walter Scott *b.* Thomas Gray *d.* Tobias Smollett *d.* Christopher Smart *d.*

DATE	AUTHOR AND TITLE	EVENT
1772	Graves, Richard: *Spiritual Quixote* (P.)	Samuel Taylor Coleridge *b.* Under threat of succession issued by Boston Assembly, Lord North withdraws duties on everything but tea
1773	Cook, James: *Voyage round the world* (P.) [additional voyages in 1777, 1784] Goldsmith, Oliver: *She Stoops to Conquer* (D.)	The Boston Tea Party
1774	Chesterfield, fourth Earl of *Letters to his Son* (P.) Warton, Thomas: *History of English Poetry,* vol. I [II 1778, III 1781] (P.)	Oliver Goldsmith *d.* First Continental Congress meets in Philadelphia
1775	Burke, Edmund: 'Speech on Conciliation with America' (P.) Johnson, Samuel: *Journey to the Western Islands* (P.) Sheridan, Richard: *The Rivals* (D.)	Jane Austen *b.* Charles Lamb *b.* American War of Independence begins
1776	Gibbon, Edward: *Decline and Fall of the Roman Empire* (P.) [Vols. II–III 1781, IV–VI 1788] Smith, Adam: *Wealth of Nations* (P.)	David Hume *d.* Declaration of American Independence
1777	Chatterton, Thomas: 'Poems' (V.) Morgann, Maurice: *Essay on the Character of Falstaff* (P.)	Samuel Foote *d.* British forces defeat Washington at Germantown, but Gen. Burgoyne defeated at Saratoga
1778	Burney, Frances: *Evelina* (P.) Foote, Samuel: *The Nabob* (D.)	François Maire Voltaire *d.* Jean-Jacques Rousseau *d.*
1779	Cowper, William: 'Olney Hymns' [with John Newton] Hume, David: *Dialogues Concerning Natural Religion* (P.) Johnson, Samuel: *Lives of the Poets* (P.) [series concluded in 1781]	David Garrick *d.* Spain joins America in war with Britain
1780	Crabbe, George: 'The Candidate' (V.)	The Gordon Riots, eventually suppressed by John Wilkes
1781	Sheridan, Richard: *The Critic* (D.)	Cornwallis loses Battle of Yorktown against American Colonies

DATE	AUTHOR AND TITLE	EVENT
1782	Burney, Frances: *Cecilia* (P.) Cowper, William: 'Poems' (V.)	Lord North resigns as Prime Minister. His successor, Marquess of Rockingham dies and is succeeded by the Earl of Shelburne
1783	Blake, William: 'Poetical Sketches' (V.) Crabbe, George: 'The Village' (V.)	Treaty of Versailles: Britain recognises American independence Coalition under Duke of Portland succeeds Shelburne's ministry, and is replaced by William Pitt the younger.
1784	Bage, Robert: *Barham Downs* (P.)	Samuel Johnson *d,*
1785	Boswell, James: *Tour to the Hebrides* (P.) Cowper, William: 'The Task' (V.); 'John Gilpin' (V.)	First cotton mill and Cartwright's power loom
1786	Beckford, William: *Vathek* (P.) Burns, Robert: *Poems Chiefly in the Scottish Dialect* (V.)	Pitt reforms government finances
1787	Hawkins, Sir John: *Life of Johnson* (P.)	The anti-slavery movement gains ground with the establishment of the Association for Abolition of Slavery
1788	Smith, Charlotte: *Emmeline* (P.)	George Gordon, Lord Byron *b.* Charles Wesley *d.* George III shows symptoms of insanity
1789	Bentham, Jeremy: *Principles of Morals and Legislation* (P.) Blake, William: *Songs of Innocence* (V.)	The French Revolution begins
1790	Burke, Edmund: *Reflections on The French Revolution* (P.)	Adam Smith *d.* French National Assembly abolishes all titles Tories win the election
1791	Boswell, James: *Life of Johnson* (P.) Inchbald, Elizabeth: *A Simple Story* (P.) Paine, Thomas: *Rights of Man* (P.) Radcliffe, Ann: *Romance of the Forest* (P.)	John Wesley *d.* Louis XVI arrested as he flees Paris Most Catholic disabilities removed in Ireland

DATE	AUTHOR AND TITLE	EVENT
1792	Bage, Robert: *Man as He Is* (P.) Gilpin, William: *Essays on Picturesque Beauty* (P.) Wollstonecraft, Mary: *Vindication of the Rights of Women* (P.)	Percy Bysshe Shelly *b.* Sir Joshua Reynolds *d.* Thomas Hardy founds the London Corresponding Society which demands parliamentary reform
1793	Godwin, William: *Political Justice* (P.)	Louis XVI executed
1794	Blake, William: *Songs of Experience* (V.) Godwin, William: *Caleb Williams* (P.) Radcliffe, Ann: *Mysteries of Udolpho* (P.)	Edward Gibbon *d.* Britain, Holland and Prussia sign Treaty of the Hague against France
1795	Blake, William: 'Book of Los' (V.)	John Keats *b.* Thomas Carlyle *b.* James Boswell *d.*
1796	Colman, George: *The Iron Chest* (D.) Inchbald, Elizabeth: *Nature and Art* (P.) Lewis, Matthew: *The Monk* (P.)	Robert Burns *d.* French plan to invade Ireland thwarted by a storm Edward Jenner perfects smallpox vaccine
1797	Radcliffe, Ann: *The Italian* (P.)	Mary Wollstonecraft *d.* Napoleon wins Battle of Rivoli
1798	Baillie, Joanna: *Plays on the Passions,* vol. I (D.) Lewis, Matthew: *Castle Spectre* (D.) Wordsworth, William and Samuel Taylor Coleridge *Lyrical Ballads* (V.)	Thomas Malthus publishes his *Principle of Population*, suggesting inevitability of over-population
1799	Sheridan, Richard: *Pizarro* (D.)	Pitt forms the second coalition with Austria, Russia, Portugal, Naples and Turkey Napoleon made First Consul of France

Further Reading

The following key denotes the author's classification of the suggested books for further reading:

B = Biography
Ba = Background
CS = Critical survey of a group of authors or genre
IA = Study of an individual author
S = Survey of eighteenth-century literature

WALTER J. BATE, *From Classic to Romantic* (Cambridge, Mass.: Harvard University Press, 1946). [CS]

MARTIN BATTESTIN, *The Moral Basis of Fielding's Art* (Middletown, Conn.: Wesleyan University Press, 1959). [IA]

ALEXANDRE BELJAME, *Men of Letters and the English Public,* ed. Bonamy Dobrée, trans. E. O. Lorimer (London: K. Paul, 1948). [Ba]

MORRIS BROWNELL, *Alexander Pope and the Arts of Georgian England* (Oxford: Clarendon, 1978). [Ba]

JOHN BUTT AND GEOFFREY CARNALL, *The Mid-Eighteenth Century,* the Oxford History of English Literature (Oxford: Clarendon, 1979). [S]

ERNST CASSIRER, *The Philosophy of the Enlightenment,* trans. Fritz Koellin and James Pettegrove (Boston: Beacon, 1955). [Ba]

JAMES CLIFFORD, *Young Samuel Johnson* (New York: McGraw Hill, 1955). [B]

——, *Dictionary Johnson* (New York: McGraw Hill, 1979). [B]

RALPH COHEN, *The Art of Discrimination* (Berkeley: University of California Press, 1964). [IA: Thomson]

BONAMY DOBRÉE, *English Literature in the Early Eighteenth Century,* the Oxford History of English Literature (Oxford: Clarendon, 1959). [S]

MARGARET DOODY, *A Natural Passion: A Study of the Novels of Samuel Richardson* (Oxford: Clarendon, 1974). [IA]

IRVIN EHRENPREIS, *Swift: The Man and His Age,* 2 vols completed (Cambridge, Mass.: Harvard University Press, 1962). [B]

ROBERT ELLIOTT, *The Power of Satire* (Princeton: Princeton University Press, 1960). [Ba]

NORTHROP FRYE, *Fearful Symmetry* (Princeton: Princeton University Press, 1947). [IA: Blake]

PAUL FUSSELL, *The Rhetorical World of Augustan Humanism* (London: Oxford University Press, 1965). [CS]

DONALD GREEN, *The Politics of Samuel Johnson,* (New Haven: Yale University Press, 1960). [IA]

J. PAUL HUNTER, *The Reluctant Pilgrim* (Baltimore: Johns Hopkins Press, 1966). [IA: Defoe]

IAN JACK, *Augustan Satire* (Oxford: Clarendon, 1952). [CS]

GARY KELLY, *The Jacobin Novel* (Oxford: Clarendon, 1977). [CS]

ISAAC KRAMNICK, *Bolingbroke and His Circle* (Cambridge, Mass.: Harvard University Press, 1968). [Ba]

ARTHUR LOVEJOY, *Essays in the History of Ideas* (Baltimore: Johns Hopkins Press, 1948). [Ba]

MAYNARD MACK, *The Garden and the City* (Toronto: Toronto University Press, 1969). [IA: Pope]

ALAN MCKILLOP, *The Early Masters of English Fiction* (Lawrence: University of Kansas Press, 1956). [CS]

SAMUEL MONK, *The Sublime* (New York: Modern Language Association, 1935). [CS]

MAXIMILLIAN NOVAK, *Defoe and the Nature of Man* (Oxford: Clarendon, 1963). [IA]

RONALD PAULSON, *The Fictions of Satire* (Baltimore: Johns Hopkins Press, 1967). [CS]

MARTIN PRICE, *To the Palace of Wisdom* (Garden City, N.Y.: Doubleday, 1964). [S]

C. J. RAWSON, *Gulliver and the Gentle Reader* (London: Routledge & Kegan Paul, 1973). [IA: Swift]

JOHN RICHETTI, *Popular Fiction before Richardson* (Oxford: Clarendon, 1969). [CS]

PAT ROGERS, *Grub Street* (London: Methuen, 1972. [CS]

ROBERT ROSENBLUM, *Transformations in Late Eighteenth-Century Art* (Princeton: Princeton University Press, 1967). [Ba]

EDWARD ROSENHEIM, *Swift and the Satirist's Art* (Chicago: University of Chicago Press, 1963). [IA]

PATRICIA SPACKS, *Imagining a Self* (Cambridge, Mass.: Harvard University Press, 1976). [CS]

——, *The Poetry of Vision* (Cambridge, Mass.: Harvard University Press, 1967). [CS]

G. A. STARR, *Defoe and Spiritual Autobiography* (Princeton: Princeton University Press, 1965). [IA]

LESLIE STEPHEN, *English Thought in the Eighteenth Century* (London: Smith & Elder, 1881). [Ba]

GEORGE W. STONE, *David Garrick* (Carbondale: Southern Illinois University Press, 1979). [B]

JAMES SUTHERLAND, *A Preface to Eighteenth-Century Poetry* (Oxford: Clarendon, 1948). [CS]

E. P. THOMPSON, *Whigs and Hunters* (Harmondsworth: Penguin, 1975). [Ba]

J. M. S. TOMPKINS, *The Popular Novel in England 1770–1800* (London: Constable, 1932). [CS]

JOHN TRAUGOTT, *Tristram Shandy's World* (Berkeley: University of California Press, 1954). [IA]

ARTHUR TURBERVILLE, *Johnson's England,* 2 vols. (Oxford: Clarendon, 1932). [Ba]

IAN WATT, *The Rise of the Novel* (Berkeley: University of California Press, 1957). [CS]

HOWARD WEINBROT, *Augustus Caesar in 'Augustan' England* (Princeton: Princeton University Press, 1978). [CS]

BASIL WILLEY, *The Eighteenth-Century Background* (London: Chatto & Windus, 1940). [Ba]

AUBREY WILLIAMS, *Pope's Dunciad* (London: Methuen, 1955). [IA]

ANDREW WRIGHT, *Henry Fielding* (Berkeley: University of California Press, 1965). [IA]

Index